BIG G AND ME

IN PILLNESS AND IN HEALTH 2: A MEMOIR

HENRIETTE IVANANS

ALSO BY HENRIETTE IVANANS

In Pillness and in Health: A Memoir

For Mummy and Nicky

TABLE OF CONTENTS

PART IV

GOD IS

PART V

GOD IS EVERYTHING

There is no love of life without despair of life.

— Albert Camus

Pigs think it's a joy, life in a pigsty, but I'd stay out!"

— Henriette Ivanans, age 8

PROLOGUE

I used to think the worst thing to happen to me was my father dying. Then I thought the worst thing to happen was my kidney transplant and a life of immunosuppression. Then I thought the worst thing was living sober without narcotics. But then I met Pain. Six years of Pain. And I was certain it was the worst thing to ever happen to me.

Turns out it was the best.

PART I

WHAT IS GOD?

1

PAIN

April 8th, 2017: Day 758.

Pain.

I had lived with It for two years. Pain was an electrical current running through my body at all times. My unburned skin flared with red patches that came and went. My ears screeched with tinnitus. Fabric chafed my body, catching on the thorns that sprouted from my skin.

Of course, there were no thorns. There was no electrical wiring running through my body. I knew that. I had looked for the off switch for two years. Everyone had. But no one had found a thing. I didn't want to look anymore.

Each morning, I got a two-second reprieve. A gasp of time when I felt nothing. I forgot about Pain. But It always returned. *TwitchSizzle-Burn.* By the third second of any given morning, I ached with nostalgia for that two-second stay.

I gently placed my legs on the side of the bed, trying to ignore the heat under my thighs, trying to ignore the dread that claimed me every day. Pain controlled every second, and We were only a few hundred seconds in.

I wore an old T-shirt of Kevin's, threadbare from two years of daily use. It had taken so long to find something tolerable to sleep in, and even then I pushed the short sleeves up when skin contact was unbearable. I wore an old pair of Kevin's underwear around the house, like an over-washed hospital gown draped as far from my body as possible. When the waistband snapped from overuse, I used a clothespin to hold it together. I didn't know how to repair elastic and drew the line at asking a tailor to repair my husband's tighty whities. Because then I would have to explain why. And I didn't know why Pain had come for me?

When I found a piece of clothing I could tolerate, it became holy. Just looking at it brought me comfort. I'd shiver in a kind of ecstasy when stepping out of the prison of my jeans and into his briefs. I was grateful for the Los Angeles heat that let me wear muumuu-type sundresses for most of the year.

I shuffled into our living area, folding myself onto the hardwood floor. The front door was cracked open, as it usually was in our cabin in the foothills. Just wide enough for Wahlter, our 13-year-old basset hound, to waddle in and out of. Today, he lay waiting for me, by the patch of wood I had rubbed bare with naked knees.

I'd been showing up here for two years, trying to find a way out of Pain through prayer and meditation. And I *had* found something — moments of relief and connection. I called it (G)od, with a small g.

But this morning, I felt nothing. I was only my body, and my body was only Pain. I shifted on the floor, my breath coming in shallow puffs. *I don't know what to do anymore.* They say pain is inevitable, but suffering is optional.

I say fuck you.

It was all I thought about. It dictated what clothes I wore. It determined my mood. I rated Pain for all my doctors and, quite frankly, anyone who would listen. If Pain was moderately difficult (5/10) I could muster a smile. If Pain was intensely cruel (9/10), I would sob until I ran dry.

When I stood in conversation, Appropriate Me would shift hips and nod, head cocked to the side with interest, while Desperate Me would float up over the person's head.

I want to pay attention to what you are saying, but I can barely hear you over the ringing in my ears. It's like someone screaming inside my head. My legs burn. My arms feel like they are blistering. I want to support you, but really, I just want this conversation to be over. Not because I don't care, but because I can't. How can I care? I am in Hell. I am in a hurry. I have to get away from Pain. But of course, joke's on me. There is no getting away. I am Pain.

I set my forehead on the floor, listening to hummingbirds tick along with the feedback between my ears. For two years, I'd searched. I had been willing to do anything to take It away. I was unafraid of the truth. I'd always been the kind of patient who wanted to know what was going on with my body, unlike those people on TV. *I had a 200-lb. tumor growing inside my stomach and had no idea!* Wasn't it getting harder to button up your pants? To walk? Poop? Didn't you want to know why?

More than anything, I wanted to know why. And how. How could I live through this?

From age 13, I had lived with kidney disease. By 19, my kidneys had deteriorated to single-digit function and I could barely sit up. The options? Dialysis, transplantation, or death. I was lucky. My mother was a match and donated her kidney.

When I had transplant rejection at age 42, I experienced hypertension, bleeding gums, facial rash, nose bleeding, constipation, canker sores, confusion, insomnia, nail fungus, vomiting, loss of appetite and depression. To name a dozen. I'd been down this renal road as a teen and understood it all: The medications prescribed to tackle my symptoms, the side effects that resulted from those medications, and the additional medications prescribed to address said side effects. And yes, I understood how rare it was that Kevin had been a match for my second kidney transplant.

Symptoms. Diagnosis. Treatment. Devastating, but understandable. Medical Science had connected the dots and fixed me. But Pain? No one in my East -West posse of docs understood what was happening to me. And what can't be understood, cannot be solved.

It was their Nothing. It was my Everything.

I wrapped my arms around myself, flinching as my hands brushed my shoulders. I often hugged myself in prayer, trying to love a body I no longer wanted. How many times had I put my arm to Kevin's face and asked, "Does my arm feel hot?" only to have him respond with a slow, sad head shake? And then the occasional and confusing, "Yes. That feels hot."

I swiped at furious tears. *I got sober for this?*

A year ago, Pain brought me to my knees. Desperate to stay sober, I abandoned myself to something I had always believed in but never knew how to access until I got sober. One night, I found something, and it filled me with strength every time I asked. Never killing Pain, but killing my fear, if only for a few moments at a time.

But today, I couldn't find a thing.

Wahlter rested his head on his paws. We locked eyes.

"Here we are again, Bubba," I said. Wahlter blinked. "I don't think I can do this anymore..."

Wahlter shifted towards me as my head fell to my chest. My insides were breaking. Was this real? Was I really thinking of ending my life?

I thought of Kevin on his way to his downtown photography studio. My sensitive and hardworking man, camera in hand, steadfast of heart. For five years we'd lived a nightmare. Our marriage had hung by the finest of threads. I'm not sure how the weight of our Hell didn't rip it clean away: The rejection of my first kidney transplant. My addiction to pharmaceuticals. The Great Recession. Our transplant. Its rejection. Overdose. Rehab. Relapse. Separation. And then two years of relative peace (2013 to 2015). I found sobriety and we found joy again — Laughing at his mustache. In thrift stores. With Wahlter. Was that all we got?

Now I cringed when Kevin pulled me close, his skin sandpapering mine. It was Her all over again — the barbiturate Fiorinal, the drug I'd been obsessed with. I loved the medicinal smell of Her, the feel of Her inside me. She dominated us in a marriage of three, and nearly killed me. I learned my obsessions become a compass that guide my thoughts and choices. *I'll be happy when I get thejob/theman/theweightloss/themoney/thedrugs.*

Now it was Pain's turn. Pain was my new obsession, and (G)od was nowhere to be found.

I'll be happy when Pain stops.

I sat back on my heels. The tears flowed, unstoppable. I raised my hands to the sky. It felt good. Is that why evangelicals did this? I looked down at myself from above.

You look ridiculous, Henriette.

I know. I don't care.

(G)od. Where are you? Take Pain away.

I lay face down, limbs spread in full offering. I'd had dark moments in my addiction. Moments when my brain, altered by Her narcotic seduction, would whisper. *The pills. Just take all of them.* And I would not understand why. I loved Her. Why would She want me to die? Or the night I went under the bathroom sink for the rubbing alcohol. *It's clear. It's alcohol. It's just a higher proof.*

Yes, I had walked the line of insanity. I had hovered over the abyss. But to be clean and sober and standing at the edge was terrifying. No one knew how to help me. Where was my solution? My perfect pill for every ill? For the first time in my life, Medical Science was failing me.

And (G)od? I couldn't feel (H)im anymore. Pain was a punishment I surely deserved. (H)is finger-pointing, heart-breaking agenda was clear. (H)e didn't want to be with me anymore.

And neither did I.

2

JAGUAR

January 1971: Age 3 1/4

Before I had God, I had my father.

I stood tiptoe, peering through the railing where the flower boxes hung, my eyes scanning our Toronto neighborhood for that first glimpse. There it was! Zipping between the brick buildings and huge maples on Bloor St. W. was our navy-blue Jaguar — The Jag. I watched it turn right onto High Park Ave. When he'd almost passed our building, Daddy blasted the neighborhood with our secret honk. *Parp-parp-parp-parp-parp...parp-parp!*

Hands clapping, I tore through the living room. Bye, orange drapes! See ya, shag carpet! Later leather couch (that Nicky and I make into forts)! Daddy was home! Squealing, I scampered down the long hall, three-year-old arms pumping with all their might. I only had a few seconds to spare. I zoomed past one bedroom, the bathroom, the master bedroom. *Hurry!* Giggling, I stormed through the last bedroom's door, throwing myself against the window, hands pressed flat, smushing my heart to the glass. Except, the huge driveway leading into the underground garage was empty. The Jag wasn't there! Had I missed him? HAD I MISSED HIM?

A blue flash! The Jag turned right, angling down the ramp and paused.

Look up, Daddy!

He rolled down the window and reached out to insert a key. With a loud clang the garage door shuddered its way to the top. I spotted his brown hair, and then his face appeared in the windshield. My heart flipped. I watched him count upwards to my window and find me. He waved like mad, his grin spreading wide, and I waved back, my eyes crinkling with glee. Then his head vanished, as the Jag tilted down and disappeared into the darkness below.

NOVEMBER 1974: Age 6

"One in, all in!"

Nicky, my baby brother and I piled into the Jag and clicked our seat belts. We'd alternate school routes daily, screaming out changes at the last second. "Take Davenport! No Dupont!" Like Mario Andretti, Daddy swerved and threw us against the car doors, and we'd shriek, tumbling on top of each other with glee.

School was 25 minutes away. He always smoked not one, but two cigarettes along the way. I heard the car lighter punch in and click. The one that turned scary red when it was ready. With a practiced turn of his hand, he raised it to the cigarette bouncing between his lips.

"No, Daddy! NO!" I cried at the hissing paper meeting fire. But every time he said the same thing.

"Two minutes!" He'd cackle, taking a long drag.

Quickly, I rolled down the window. A freezing breeze pricked my cheeks before I dove face-first into my scarf, burrowing my nose into the material wrapped tight around my neck. Mum tight. *You don't want to catch cold!*

"Open your window, Daddy!" I yelled into my neck.

He laughed, blowing smoke towards the crack. Smoke still filled the car. I scowled. He wasn't trying very hard. What was so great about a stupid burning stick that stunk up the car? It didn't bother Nicky, but then Mum and Nicky liked the smell of gas whenever we filled up at a gas station. If I inhaled any of it, for even half a second, I felt sick. Like I would die. I glared at it, willing it to wrinkle away its short life.

Finally, Daddy jabbed the butt into the overflowing ashtray, until the last flicker of red was gone.

"Can we hear some music?"

We always had the radio on. Usually, CFRB 1010 (Ten-Ten On Your Dial!) for news and sports reports, like the rugby scores from England. But I didn't care about sports. I loved to sing, and when The Beatles came over the airwaves, we'd explode.

In the town where I was born /

Lived a man who sailed to sea /

"Yellow Submarine!" he cried, reaching for the knob to turn it up. Daddy belted out the words, lusty, a little off-key and we chimed in as best we could.

"WE ALL LIVE IN A YELLOW SUBMARINE! YELLOW SUBMARINE! YELLOW SUBMARINE!" Daddy's arms swung high. Nicky and I followed along, our arms tangling together, no mum to shush us. And that was how we got to school.

This was the father I adored — a thrilling companion. Driver, singer and snack master. He was our doctor, too. Mum had explained that Daddy wasn't supposed to treat us because doctors couldn't separate their emotions from their work when family members were sick. But he'd treated us just fine. Gave us polio shots, burned a wart off my foot, and gave Nicky stitches at home when he fell out of bed and bonked his head on the sharp edge of a table. (I ran to the bathroom and buried my head between two towels so I didn't have to hear Nicky cry.)

Daddy popped the swelling in my middle finger after it got smashed between two bowling balls on the rack at a birthday party. The pricking had hurt, but he'd told me it would be quick. He told me I was strong. That I could do it. Bear the pain.

After school we'd run outside, sailor shirts untucked, bags dragging on the ground, and look for where he'd parked. The Jag had leather seats and wood paneling and a jaguar statuette leaping from the hood. He'd have chocolate milk and a banana laid out on tables that folded out like airplane tables. Sometimes he brought regular milk with an apple, which I didn't like as much, but there was always an afterschool adventure.

WE TURNED off Davenport onto Osler St. Over the railroad tracks we went. *Bumpity-bump-bump* as Nicky and I squealed. "Go slower! Make it like a ride!"

Daddy laughed and slowed to park, pebbles crunching beneath the tires. We tumbled out of the car and began to march along the tracks. We were going trainspotting!

It was called The Junction. A rail yard with four intersecting railways in a west end Toronto neighborhood not far from our High Park home. Our goal: To spot CN (Canadian National) or CP (Canadian Pacific) railway engine numbers to cross off our list. Nicky wore his sweet smirk as we trudged, kicking the dust-covered rocks with our Oxfords.

We stopped at our usual spot — a tin shed a few feet back from the tracks. Nicky peered east into the far-off Toronto skyline.

"All red," he announced with the wisdom of a seasoned, four-year old trainspotter.

"Awww! Red is boring!" I pouted, twirling my skirt around. Red meant no trains were coming. I loved putting a penny on the track so when the train zoomed through it would flatten the coin like a pancake! I sighed. Even the train cars parked at the rail yard were still. Some days we'd watch those cars lifted onto a turntable and relocated to a different part of the depot.

I lifted my face to the sun and closed my eyes. Maybe if I stood very, very still I'd hear the promising rumble. But there was only a rhythmic cheeping from the trees, and the occasional honk from way over on Dundas St. Everything was quiet in our secret pocket of Old Toronto. Everything still in our world.

I kicked the gravel, overturning granite and shale. Maybe if I found something to add to my collection, the afternoon wouldn't be a bust.

Suddenly, Daddy howled, "YELLOOOW!"

Nicky and I squealed and ran to meet him at the edge of the railroad ties. We squinted long down the tracks. There it was! A sunshine-bright yellow light, way off in the distance. And then, with a whisperous click another light turned from red to yellow.

"DADDY!" I screamed, "ANOTHER YELLOW!" And then they began to flip. Red-to-yellow-to-green, red-to-yellow-to-green. In a brilliant instant, all of the two-headed light fixtures glowed green. Then out of a faraway shimmer, it emerged. A tiny white light far, far away, moving towards us at full speed.

"TRAIN!!!" we screamed together. I grabbed Daddy's hand and looked up into his face. He was a thin man. His olive Latvian skin held the slightest yellow tinge. His good brown eyes caught mine and I grinned. The ground trembled with the drama of the train's arrival.

"GET BACK!" Daddy yelled, and we obeyed, each clutching a hand as the headlight grew wider, whiter, brighter. Blinding. Crossing arms dropped down to the tremendous clanging of warning bells. I covered an ear with my free hand as the other held tight to my dad. *Clickity-clack. Clickity-clack. CLICKITY-CLACK.*

"TRAINNNNNN!"

It clattered along the crossing. Nicky and I jumped around, our arms flapping like flags in a bitter wind. Our goal? To get the driver to wave back. "CP 8027!" We screamed out the first engine number with sugar-fueled adrenaline. The driver hung out the window and languidly waved back.

"HI DRIVER!" we screeched, returning his tip-of-the-hat-hello with more waving. Daddy called out the second engine's number. "CP 8955!" He cross-checked it in our trainspotting bible — two sets of index cards (one for each railway line) kept inside a hardcover three-ringed binder — just like he did growing up in England.

The caboose hurtled through the crossing. I watched it disappear into a distant labyrinth of rails until it became a speck. The clanging settled into the city silence. Nicky danced around repeating the numbers. "CP 8027! CP 8955! CP 8027! CP 8955!"

"That was so fun!" I cried out.

Daddy's hand moved to touch my face. I smiled up at him, my heart soaring on wings. Trainspotting was our world and ours alone — a place that filled me with an electric calm.

A CLINK RANG BACK from the front seat. I looked up to see Daddy taking a long sip from one of the brown bottles that went with us everywhere. He placed it between his legs as he turned onto Osler. An empty rolled around the passenger seat floor. Sometimes he'd take the empty and pee into it while driving. Why didn't he just pull over at a gas station? One time, we drove outside the city and pulled over on the highway, even though Mum said you weren't supposed to do that unless it was an emergency. I watched him walk deep into a field, the tall grasses covering him to his waist. He never looked back. Just brought his hands in front for a while, and then returned to the Jag smiling.

One in. All in.

And once again we'd be on our way.

I felt funny seeing his penis when he peed into a bottle. It was confusing, because we weren't taught to do that, but I did know that being naked was natural. He was a doctor, and Mum had been pre-med. We walked around naked at home and called body parts by their anatomical names. It was not a belly button, but an umbilicus. Not a dinky, but a vagina. Not a boob, but a breast. But when he did that, I felt sorry for him. I could see Daddy was different, and couldn't figure out why.

THE JAG ROLLED down the driveway into the darkness. The huge garage door clanged shut behind us as we stopped. A big sign read "DO NOT EXCEED 5 MPH."

"Okay. Out you go!" The motor idled as Nicky and I scampered out the side doors and ran to the front of the car. We climbed onto the hood, one sibling on each side, the dent over each headlight like a ready-made seat for our squiggling bums. Then we screamed, "READY!"

The Jag crept forward, our little legs dangling over the headlights. The purr of the engine beneath me felt exciting! Nicky wore his mischievous little grin. We were like Jeremy and Jemima, and Daddy was Caractacus Potts driving *Chitty Chitty Bang Bang* on a magical adventure through our underground garage.

I raised my arms as if I was on a ride! With nothing to hold on to, it felt cheeky. We were cheeky monkeys, as Daddy would say. I could feel his grin boring through my back, anchoring me in place. I never doubted he would stop in time if one of us slipped off. But we never did.

He pulled into our spot and we slid off the hood. As we collected schoolbags and banana peels, Daddy reminded us,

"Don't tell your mother I let you sit on the car!"

Asking us not to tell Mum about the car was easy. *Cross my heart and hope to die.* We didn't see her much, and I wouldn't have told anyway. Daddy was everything to me. He drove us, fed us, sang with us, and healed us. Daddy was home, and I didn't want to leave his world. A place where he reigned as my superhero even as the edges of his cape were yellowing before their time.

3

RASH

March 9th, 2015: Ground Zero

The bathtub was my sanctuary. A place where I learned lines, read books and dreamed big. I loved the ritual. From the waterfall of the fill to the shuddering relief of that first toe dipped into steam and salts and silence. How could it have all begun here?

My arms itched in the cracks of my elbow joints. I reached for the pumice stone that languished behind the Secret Santa bubble bath I never used.

I took the crumbly rectangle and angled the corner deep into my skin, ploughed the plump section until the skin burned with satisfying hotness. First one elbow crook and then the other, tearing away old skin to reveal the new beneath.

It hurt so good. This addict was always down for a bit of instant gratification. I thought nothing more of it. Why would I have reflected upon a barely conscious action in the tub? *Have itch – must scratch.* I had scratched an itch. And now it was gone.

~

MARCH 12TH, 2015: Day 1

I woke to surging heat in my arm. I rubbed my face, eyeing a curious blotch on my left forearm. It was bright red. As if an iron had been placed down to brand. Why did I have a sunburn right there? Even with a 19-year, rosy-brown California base, this burn was strange.

I stood in the bathroom light inspecting it, my coffee steaming on the sink. The blotch was in the curious shape of a boomerang. I frowned. Ah, the pumice stone. I had scrubbed a little too hard. It had taken three nights to present, but there it was. I had never had such an intense reaction to exfoliation. It felt as if a layer of skin had been peeled right off — which I guess it had. *If it looks like a burn and feels like a burn.*

I grabbed aloe vera from under the bathroom sink, and slathered some on, gummy and green. Upon contact, my skin cooled. Looking at the redness smothered in goop, I thought *this will help* But after an hour, nothing changed. It was still hot and hurt. Strike one.

Maybe it was a rash? I ran the bathwater and rinsed the goop off. I slathered the offensive area with the solution *du jour* —coconut oil — flinching just a little at my tenderized skin. Half an hour later, there was no change. The patch was still a violent red. Strike two.

I walked to my laptop and Googled *What are good options to put on a burn?* The top hit was a cool compress followed by petroleum jelly. I re-ran the bath and kept my arm under the tap for several cold minutes, wiping the oil off with a washcloth. Then I smeared a chewy layer of petroleum jelly onto the blotch with gentle fingers. After another hour, it was the same. Strike three.

I didn't panic. Why would I panic? It was inflamed skin that would heal. That's all. When Kevin got home, he cocked his head at it and said,

"Weird. I'm sure it will go away soon, Sweetheart."

Yes, of course it would. Why would it stay? Who had even heard of such a thing? Rashes or burns — whatever it was — healed and went away. It was like a bruise. It would look dramatic for a few days and then disappear from my skin and my life forever.

March 13th, 2015: Day 2

The morning sun streamed in, cocooning my body in peace. I stretched my arms up and jerked backwards. A splotch of red was now on my right forearm. Tentatively, I pressed at the red dots grouping in the corner of my elbow. I shivered. The configuration was a creepy mirror image of my left arm. I rolled onto my back and twisted my arms in the light, this way and that. *What the Hell was going on?* It was time to call my doctor.

As a kidney transplant patient, I run every medication or supplement, or procedure beyond The Land of the Kidney by my nephrologist (kidney specialist) or transplant team. Immunosuppression is a balance of risk versus benefit. Too much immunosuppression leaves me without a working immune system to fight off viruses and infections; too little immunosuppression, and my immune system identifies Kevin's kidney as a foreign object and works to reject it. Standardly prescribed medications like antibiotics or over-the-counter NSAIDs (sodium naproxen, aspirin) are metabolized renally and toxic to the kidney, especially a transplanted one. Everything needs to be declared at medical customs. And the customs officer was my nephrologist, Dr. D.

When we arrived in Los Angeles in 1996, I had a fungus growing beneath my right thumb nail. A general practitioner took one look and deferred.

"I wouldn't know what to prescribe with your immunosuppression."

Instead, he gave me a book of specialists. At the time, there were only three transplant centers in the greater LA area: Loma Linda, UCLA, and Cedars-Sinai. I chose Cedars because it was the closest, and honestly, because it was "the hospital to the stars," where they would be admitted for "dehydration and exhaustion" (read: drug and/or alcohol abuse). It's ironic, as I would also be admitted to Cedars for "dehydration and exhaustion" (read: two drug overdoses).

But in 1996, it was thrilling to run into Quentin Tarantino in an elevator.

By 2015, Dr. D. was more than my nephrologist. He had shown up to every dialysis appointment, visiting with me and Kevin separately, understanding my husband was hurting, too. Dr. D. was there to clasp my hand in triumph as I was wheeled out of the operating room, doing the same with Kevin, my living donor. Our transplant was his transplant. We three birthed "The Kid." Dr. D. would know what was going on with me. Dr. D. would fix this.

I would see him Monday at 11:15 am. (It was the latest morning appointment this night owl could get.) All I had to do to secure a last-minute appointment was lube the situation with a titch of panic in my voice, masterfully anchored by the facts.

"I have a painful rash on my left arm that's spread to my right arm. I've never seen anything like it before. I'm worried this might hurt my kidney."

I didn't feel guilty about gliding my way into an appointment. Five-star medical treatment only happens when you demand it for yourself. Plus, I wasn't lying.

I was worried.

March 15th, 2015: Day 4

I examined my arms in the light. Nothing had worked — aloe vera, coconut oil, petroleum jelly, or time. Over four days, redness swirled across my skin like a drop of food coloring in water. I flipped my left arm over, inspecting the underside. From the crook of my elbow to an inch below my wrist were tiny red spots, hundreds of them swarming towards my hand. Goosebumps sheeted my back as I watched them emerge, one by one, as if breeding beneath my skin. I grazed my finger over my arm, feeling their tactile realness against my translucent fingertip. A creepy fascination came over me. Their spread reminded me of footage of cancer cells suctioning their claw-like tentacles into healthy cells with a pernicious mission to metastasize. Tumorize. Kill. But this wasn't cancer. Was it?

I sighed and perched on our bed, running my fingers through my hair. I was packed and ready to attend my first writers' conference. I was working on my first book, *In Pillness and in Health,* taking classes through UCLA Writers' Extension. I had developed a mentor relationship with an instructor who nominated me for the award I would later win, and she'd gifted me a pass. The conference was in Torrance, 80 minutes from Shadow Hills in good traffic, double that in bad. As I stared at my arm, my mind clicked with questions. Was it responsible that I go? Was this infectious? Was this Happening beneath my skin critical?

The truth? I didn't want to go to the conference. I was a year and a half sober, which, let me tell you, when you are new in recovery, is like a fucking minute. The "firsts" suck. The first time you attend a wedding, everyone is drinking and the smell of tequila shots and wafts of puke from behind the bushes make you feel sad and punished and as overlooked as the proverbial wallflower at a high school dance. *Everyone is having fun but me.* The first time you have sex, everything is right up there in your face. I mean everything. Smells and grunts, and coarse curlies stuck between your teeth. The first time you travel on an airplane and the flight attendant asks what you'd like to drink, you get to say *orange juice, light ice,* when what you really want to say is "With two shots of vodka. And make it snappy."

Today would be a first for my burgeoning writing career which wasn't so much a career as a cliched idea to write the best addiction memoir ever! Who was I? A 44-year-old literary virgin popping her conference cherry with a bunch of writing experts I could have birthed. I had no experience aside from a few unlucid years of blogging. Nothing published. No degree. No connections. As jazzed as I was to tell my story, my fear of new experiences often rationalized away any attempt to try. *Who are you to believe you can write a book? You know nothing about writing.* It was true. I knew nothing about writing.

My fear was such a meanie. And cunning. A cunning meanie constantly devising a plan to see me fail.

Although sometimes plans need multiple architects.

I popped into Kevin's office.

"Mus. I don't know what to do. My arm." I extended a spotted limb. He scrunched his face.

"Oh, boy, Sweetheart. That doesn't look good."

"I don't think I should go to the conference."

"Okay."

"But I don't think I need to go to the ER. They'll just tell me to see Dr. D. which I'm doing tomorrow."

"Then you can go to the conference."

My chest squeezed in frustration. "But this might be contagious?"

"I can drive you to the ER." I paused, then clicked my tongue.

"But remember how long we waited last time?" My husband looked at me with a loaded stare. "It's Sunday. They only have a skeletal staff, no testing until Monday..."

Yes, I knew what I was doing. More importantly, Kevin knew what I was doing. I needed him to find the loophole I couldn't — a way to get out of the ER and the conference that wouldn't make me feel bad.

This had been my thing. Lawyering people to the ground and manipulating folks into my line of thinking. It was an old look, one I didn't wear well in recovery. These threadbare ideas on how to behave hung poorly now that I was sober. I could feel the wrongness of my pursuit.

"It's up to you, Sweetheart." I hated a diplomatic answer more than any other. He didn't agree with me. Kevin knew I wouldn't go anywhere if I didn't want to, and he was tired of fighting when he knew he was right and I was wrong. Not only was he tired of fighting, he wouldn't fight at all.

Kevin's life had changed with my sobriety, too. My recovery from pills had become his recovery from me. He was done. He was polite and never unkind but resolved to let me to wander around Crazyland alone. He wouldn't even meet me at the border of Crazyland: Republic of Rationalization and Justification. And without booze or barbiturates to coat my foul motives, my manipulation was all I could feel, and it made me sick.

"Why don't you call Lori?" he offered.

Brilliant! Lori was a friend who had sustained four kidney transplants and 13 years of dialysis from age two. She was also the CEO of the Renal Support Network, which provides resources to kidney disease and transplant patients. I had volunteered for their proms for teenagers on dialysis, fundraiser casino nights with Jack Black, and submitted to essay contests. She was only 4' something, but I looked up to this giantess of altruism.

Lori picked up her cell. Dang. It was always easier to leave a voicemail and congratulate myself with *I tried!* Lori suggested I go to urgent care. Yes. That was good. It should be quick, I could get assessed, and if that doctor thought I should go to the ER, I would. I could get out of the writing conference, too.

But when I hung up the phone, I didn't do any of it: urgent care, the ER, or the conference. I emailed my writing instructor, telling her an odd medical issue had presented itself, and I wouldn't be able to attend. I closed my computer with a head-hanging thud. My conference ticket was unusable now. She wouldn't be able to find anyone at such late notice. And the truth of it hit my sober heart hard.

My judgmental finger that used to strike down others was now pointed at myself. The truth was jabbing at my soul. I should have acted better. There had been plenty of times in my life when I'd had to break a commitment because I was sick, but this wasn't one of them. I knew I had avoided the writers' conference because I was uncomfortable. I had wanted to go. I had acted out of fear and it felt awful.

Leaning against the kitchen counter, I sucked back giant tablespoonfuls of peanut butter drizzled with honey, filling up on sugar and fat.

I was sick of it. Sick of being sick. Of hospital and doctors. Of pills and procedures. Of the Cedars-Sinai-Shadow Hills slog. The longer I could stay away from Cedars-Sinai, the better. The big Beverly Hills hospital with its glittering guests had run its course. I was done with struggling with my health.

And who could blame me?

Turning towards the golden afternoon light, I closed my eyes and relaxed in the glow. When I opened them, the red dots continued to swarm.

4

BEER

January 1974: Age 6 1/4

We would go on Saturdays. Or after school instead of trainspotting. Or after trainspotting. But it was always just the three of us — another Daddy adventure where Mum never came along.

We pulled up to the Brewers' Retail on Dundas St. W. and parked as close to the door as possible. I didn't know what "brewers" or "retail" meant, but I knew why we were here. The empty beer bottles that sat between Daddy's legs or rolled around on the passenger seat floor had to be returned. We got money for them, which was good because Daddy would always buy more.

We met at the back of the Jag, the trunk wide open and crammed with jangling boxes of empties. Daddy unfolded the trolley (my friends at school called it a bundle buggy) and stacked the cases on top. If there was a smaller case of six or 12, he plopped that inside the trolley, but mostly he bought 2-4s. (A 2-4 is Canadian slang for a case of 24 beers.)

"Can I slam the trunk?" I grinned, my fingers twitching.

"Yesss..." Daddy drawled, focused on his incredible balancing act, one hand steadying the cases as the other hauled the trolley through the gray slush and onto the curb. *Clink, clink, clink.* He was balancing three cases of 24 bottles. I only knew my three times table up to the twelves, so I didn't know exactly how many bottles we had, just that it was a lot! I ran ahead to activate the automatic door opener. Like magic it swished open like a butler welcoming us inside with a flourish of his hand. The nutty smell fluttered in warm waves and filled me with a cozy feeling, like when I hugged Daddy in his bathrobe.

He parked the trolley at the end of the "track," hair flopping into his eyes as he hoisted the boxes up high. Next, he lined them up in a neat row like cars of a different kind of train. The "track" was a conveyor belt about 20 feet long, studded with silver wheels that sometimes spun long after a case had rocketed towards its destination. At the end of the track was a plastic curtain the cases would hurtle through into a mysterious room I could smell but had never seen.

Daddy said the backroom was where bottles were sorted before being taken away to be recycled. Sometimes I'd glimpse it through the gate that looked like a hula skirt. I'd hear clanking, or the occasional bottle crash, and smell the amber droplets dribbling across the floor.

"Now can we push?!" Nicky and I hung off the sides of the belt like monkeys, waiting for Daddy to give us the green light. He smiled and nodded. We placed our tiny hands against the cardboard sides, its corners damp from runaway droplets, and assumed the position.

"Ready?" Nicky and I looked at each other and giggled. "Steady?" Daddy raised his arm. I bit down on my lip. "GO!" he cried, dropping his arm like a flag.

"Weee!" we cried, the box catching momentum from the wheels below. It roared through the gate and into the room that smelled like the roasted caramel potatoes Mum fried on Christmas Eve.

Daddy stepped up to the cashier to place his order. I stood back and took in the wall of beers for sale. Empty bottles with prices were displayed on shelves like a fine jeweler showcasing his wares. There were regular, premium and imported. The bottles were elegantly shaped and came in startling shades of green, amber, and gold. There were different kinds of beer, too. Pale ale, lager, sour beer, stout, pilsner, porter —so many! If I drank beer, I would want to try them all! Like when Nicky and I would walk to the tuck shop, I wished I could try *all* the chocolate bars instead of having to choose just one. But beer wasn't for children, even though the whole family knew the story of Daddy giving Nicky a sip when he was three.

Daddy always got the same beer. Molson Golden. Bor-ing. Even the bottle was dull. Short, brown, and stubby. He would always get a 2-4, sometimes two. It wasn't the most expensive, like the premiums and imports, but it wasn't quite the cheapest. I thought Daddy was smart to get a cheaper beer, since he bought so much.

The cashier spoke into a thin bendy microphone. "One 2-4 of Molson Golden." I would have to wait a long time before I could order my own beer. I was only six and you had to be 19 to buy alcohol.

Sometimes a bottle on the shelf would catch the light when the door soldiered open, and another veteran of the drink entered. The bottle glowed from within, deflecting the truth: that this beguiling glass shell would be the source of our future pain. But I had no idea. All I knew was that beer was a drink my father loved. All I saw was colored glass that shimmered in the sun, lighting up the shadowy corners of a curious place that always left me with a funny feeling.

What was the big deal? What was so great about beer? It was foamy. It stayed foamy a lot longer than pop did. But it tasted awful — bitter and sharp. He had let me sip it once, although Mum didn't like that very much. There had to be something about it because he had it everywhere. On the floor next to the sofa, on his desk when he worked on his stamps, in the car, on the car, in the fridge. Maybe I would understand when I grew up and acquired a taste for it, the way I was trying to acquire a taste for olives.

Beer seemed to be his anchor, the way Mummy and Daddy were my anchors. They were there in the morning with a cup of baby tea

— Red Rose with milk and sugar. They were there to tuck me in, close the door just right, and find the sliver of light I needed to fall asleep. *Not that much. That's too much. That's just right*. Like Goldilocks searching for the perfect something to fill her up. A strange darkness was creeping into my world, and I needed to know the light would never disappear.

Nicky raced over to the other side of the store, his head flopping from side to side. Daddy often called him accident-prone. For a long time I thought that meant my brother had some kind of medical condition when it just meant he was clumsy. I joined him at the end of the track, waiting for the 2-4 to arrive. This was a different kind of trainspotting. There'd be no white light in the distance, just a whoosh of surprise to make us laugh. Nicky ran to the gate, and peered through the plastic.

"Nicky! Your noggin!"

Our parents used the funniest words sometimes, like flannel for washcloth or plait for braid. Daddy had grown up in England and Danish-born Mum learned English when she met him there. Sometimes I would use their words at school and get a confused look from a classmate, which made me feel like I was from a different world. Which I guess I was. We lived in an apartment, not a three-story house. We played in the rock garden around the base of the building, not "up at the cottage" or "down in Florida." And I didn't know anyone else who went to the beer store with their dad.

Nicky loped back to meet me at the end of the track. *Thwomp!* We felt the case thrown down and a rumble build in our toes. It roared through the gate and raced down the track, winding to a stop just before it looked like it would fall off the track. *YAY!* We cheered as if Daddy had won a prize.

He cradled it in his arms, placing it on the trolley. They had sent the right one. I knew because I could spell *Molson Golden Ale* on the side of the box. I ran forward to activate the door, our electronic doorman bidding us adieu. The sign on the window said, "Please come back soon!" *We will! We definitely will!*

I ran back to escort him to the car. I loved being able to help him.

It was as vital to me as breathing. But with my devotion came confusion. Daddy drove us to school, cooked our meals, and worked as a doctor. He was the parent. Yet, I carried a restlessness knowing that he needed something. I just didn't know what.

DADDY WAS deaf in his left ear from an infection at age 13. I often forgot because it didn't require much besides leaning into people and asking them to repeat themselves. It was just a fact about him like, he was a doctor, married or liked beer. He also had something called Type 1 diabetes, which he got at age 30 when Nicky was born. That required a lot.

He opened his doctor's bag with the silver lock where he kept his stethoscope and blood pressure cuff and pulled out a glass jar of blood sugar tests. The bag also held needles and jars of something called insulin. That was medicine for when he felt funny. Feeling funny could mean shaky or dizzy, which meant his blood sugar was dropping. That was called low blood sugar. If he peed a lot or had tingling in his hands and feet, it was called high blood sugar.

We were in his bathroom, the one he shared with Mum inside their bedroom. I perched on a bench watching him pee into a cup over the toilet. He placed the cup on the side of the sink, opened the glass container and pulled out a paper stick. It was thin and delicate, decorated with raised boxes of yellow, gold, and green. He dipped the stick into the pee, held it there for a few seconds, then took it out.

"Now we wait 30 seconds." Daddy looked at his watch.

I scrunched my face at the stick. Yellow meant his blood sugar was normal, but if it went into the greens, he would have to give himself a shot of medicine.

"Do you feel funny, Daddy?" I watched the stick change color, morphing like one of those mood rings I got in a goody bag at a birthday party in one of those three-story homes.

"Only a little, Darling," He called me darling like a fact of his life like the sun is hot.

"A little elevated," he said, tossing the stick into the wastebasket.

"Do you need your chocolate bar?" I chirped.

Daddy carried a Mars bar in his doctor's bag, too. I was a little jealous he got to have a chocolate bar more often than I did. I felt bad for thinking this because I knew it was a kind of medicine for him, and that I should never ask him for a bite. Mum was very strict with our sugar. I couldn't wait to be an adult so I could have a Mars bar whenever I wanted. Nicky and I were allowed to have candy once a week on Friday nights when we'd watch *The Donny and Marie Show*. On Candy Night, we'd each get a salad bowl full of goodies — gumdrops, chocolate-covered raisins and Licorice Allsorts. But never a Mars bar.

"No," he tugged on one of my pigtails, "but I do need to give myself an insulin shot." He pulled out a packaged syringe and insulin vial. He peeled the paper back from the needle, jabbed it into the top of the bottle and pulled up the plunger.

"Can I watch?" I asked.

He nodded as he unbelted his pants and twisted around to pinch a section of his bum. I knew the medicine was supposed to go into a layer of fat. But Daddy was so thin even his bum was skinny.

"Does it hurt?" He shook his head.

"No. It's just a little prick like when you got your polio shot."

Oh! That hurt! I'd been so scared to be "inoculated" that Daddy had promised me a quarter for every second I counted during the shot. But I was so distracted by how sharp the pain was that I forgot to start counting. After I recovered, I got to five scoring a lousy $1.25 (when I'd been hoping to impress Daddy and get to 10). Needles were mean! Daddy was brave to do it as often as he did. It seemed like a lot of work having diabetes.

He was starting to look different. Maybe that's what diabetes did. It made you unfat, slowed your gait, and darkened your skin. I watched him as he cleaned up, heaviness like a rock in my tummy. I could see his hands shake — just a little — as he locked his bag, a place I was never to explore.

I didn't disobey, but I wanted to learn more about him. To find the thing that could explain the flip-flop of my heart. Everything was changing. The way he and Mum spoke to each other. The quiet between them that seemed unquiet. He was standing right in front of me, but I was seized by an urge to grab his hand, and follow him wherever he went.

5

SHOES

March 16th, 2015: Day 5

Dr. D. looked closely at the blotches on my arms and whipped out his prescription pad.

"Dermatitis. We'll do blood, too," he mumbled into his beard.

My ears perked up. Once upon a time, the sound of a pen scratching on a prescription pad was the Pavlovian bell that got me salivating. But my doctor shopping days were over and I wasn't browsing anymore. I was desperately seeking sobriety, and Dr. D. was privy.

"Are you in pain?" he asked.

"Yes. It burns and...sizzles." I twisted my hands together.

He handed over the prescription. "This should take care of it." My heart danced as I looked down at the script. A six-day, 4 mg Methyl-prednisolone pack. Ha.

A methylprednisolone pack is a more powerful version of the corticosteroid Prednisone, my daily bud since age 13. Its skunky ejaculate still coats my throat every morning after 40 years. Bearer of anxiety, insomnia, and increased appetite that triggered a teenage eating disorder. My first frenemy — the friend I hated to need. Smiling, I slipped the script into my purse. This was exactly what

I'd wanted — pharmaceutical explosives to blow up this stupid rash.

The phlebotomist wrapped the tourniquet around my upper arm and tap-tap-tapped for a vein. *Ironic that I'm excited about taking more of this asshole.* (I wrote a whole chapter about Prednisone's jerkassedness in my first book, *Pillness.*) But I was. In high doses, it's brilliant at reducing inflammation. Like any good frenemy, it has its moments.

Because in six days this nightmare of a rash would be vaporized.

APRIL 9TH, 2015: Day 28

Over the six days of steroids, I watched fascinated, as the rash scaled and flaked off. Less than three weeks later, I watched stunned as it returned, as red and hot as a wildfire sun, with an extra layer of dots smeared across my arms.

This time, Dr. D. mumbled a referral into his beard.

Dr. M., a Cedars' dermatologist, was nice enough, a little on the slick side, which didn't surprise me after clocking the ad in his waiting room for age-defying skin care featuring a circa 1998 Jennifer Lopez.

It was a long appointment. I was a new patient with a 30-year medical history to plough through before we could get to my ailment *du jour*. Transplantation — *Your husband was a match? Incredible!* Addiction — *Two years sober? Bravo!* Migraines — *Triptans are very effective.* (I know.)

He had an awfully pretty physician's assistant shadowing him which took up extra time. However, I was always willing to be a Guinea pig for Medical Science, in honor of the animals that had been Guinea pigs for me, although those were probably monkeys or rats. But you catch my drift.

Dr. M. wasn't in network which I didn't understand. I mean, I understood this meant I would pay $135 out of pocket every time I saw him. I was already paying $900 a month just to carry health insurance. But what could I do? Go to a physician who wasn't recommended? Deflated by pain and confused by the American healthcare system, I chose to believe Dr. M. would be the one to destroy the rash.

I sat on the exam table, explaining last month's events with a Post-it of bullet points in my hand. Dr. Slick and Ms. Shadow (as I preferred to call them), took turns peering at my arms under one huge magnifying glass bubble, all slight movements and breathy mumbles, like they were playing the board game Operation.

Dr. Slick looked up. "It's a virus."

"In my skin?"

I had never heard of a virus in the skin. He explained it wasn't from a viral infection. Nothing systemic that would cause rash-like symptoms like mononucleosis or shingles. It was like catching a cold in my skin.

"I'll give you a script for Steroid Cream #1." Which weren't his exact words, but you will see where I'm going with this.

As I took the prescription (Clobetasol Propionate Cream, USP 0.05%) he offered, "Do you want a steroid shot?"

I hesitated, thinking of The Kid. Was this okay for my kidney? I knew steroid shots were a temporary solution. Kevin had been maxed out after a handful of ineffective epidural injections for his back. Steroid shots could accelerate bone loss, and I already had osteopenia (pre-osteoporosis).

He saw my hesitation and raised me a "It'll make you feel better."

Well, that was an offer this addict couldn't refuse. As I offered my butt to Ms. Shadow I thought, *It may not be morphine, but I'll hop on any bus that gets me out of Paintown.* If only it hadn't been such a short ride.

FOR 18 DAYS the rash retreated, then returned, raging over my body making up for lost time. Red dots now ravaged my thighs.

Over the next month I finished Steroid Cream #1, started Steroid Cream # 2 (Fluocinolone Acetonide 0.01% with peanut oil), dropped my pants for Steroid Shot #2 and offered up a chunk of my forearm for a biopsy. When I called the office to report the flare-up, Ms. Shadow suggested I buy Sarna lotion — the strongest anti-itch lotion you can buy without a prescription! I rolled my eyes, pretty sure the condition morphing under my skin and dodging the whack-a-mole of steroids coming at it was laughing at any relief found on the shelves of Target.

At my next appointment, Dr. Slick proudly presented a theory.

"Graft vs. Host disease."

It was odd the way his chest puffed out. His delivery suggested a *Ta-da!* with an arm flourish. He paused. I waited. Did he need a parade for doing his homework?

Graft vs. Host disease (GvHD) is a systemic disorder where immune cells from Kevin's kidney (my transplanted kidney) recognize my body as foreign and attack it. In transplantation, the primary concern is that my immune system does not attack Kevin's kidney. Not the other way around. Kevin attacking me? I could barely process this possibility. Google assured me that GvHD is extremely rare in kidney transplants. Like five cases in the recorded history of transplantation. Still.

May 15th, 2015: Day 59

I sat waiting for my biopsy results. The rash had spread to my calves.

Suddenly, I was 13 and scared. My Glomerulonephritis (chronic inflammation of the kidneys' filters) had developed from a virus that nailed me with multiple high fevers over a year. That virus had never been identified. After my first kidney transplant at 19, I'd had a thought:

"Is there a chance the virus that took my kidneys will come back?"

My Canadian nephrologist didn't blink. "Yes." This guy. Dr. C. was as serious as they came, oddly wearing unserious ties, like a pop of shiny purple against his slick suit and white coat. But I wanted the truth. I could handle the truth. Was today's virus the one that had snatched my tween kidneys? Had it come back for more?

Dr. Slick walked in. “Good news. It’s a virus, but not one that will attack the kidney.”

Doctors, man. They can be so weird. Intellectually, I understood this news was preferable to lupus or any other autoimmune illness. But dude, viruses are never good news — especially when you’re immunosuppressed.

“It’s non-specific perivascular dermatitis. Inflammation around the blood vessels.” He went on to say it could be from allergies or an infection or be genetic. I frowned. None of these possibilities applied. Was he even listening to me?

My skin *burned*. It was white hot rage. Irritated blood vessels? A virus? No. This wasn’t the right diagnosis. I knew it. I knew it as deeply as I knew any fact about my life: Kevin is my husband. I live in Los Angeles. I love opiates. Something was wrong.

“That pumice stone I used on my forearms. It must have been filthy. Maybe it had a fungus?”

Dr. Slick crossed his arms. “No. When you used it, your skin became susceptible to catching a virus.” Doubt swelled inside. “The bad news is we can’t prescribe any anti-viral meds because it’s non-specific. The good news is it will run its course.”

“How long?”

“Seven to ten months.” That was the good news? “One more shot for the road?”

I bent over and we fucked that virus into a four-month remission.

By March of 2015, I had known my sponsor Liz, for three and a half years. In Alcoholics Anonymous, a sponsor is someone who guides you through The Twelve Steps to help you find a Higher Power. Not necessarily God, capital G, but something bigger than you.

Finding a Higher Power had me confused. It’s not like you can walk into the Higher Power store and spend an afternoon digging through the clearance rack for one that fits.

"Henriette, do you believe in God?" Liz asked when we spoke over the phone in rehab. My answer had been quick and surprising.

"Yes!" The sky filled my mind. Bright and colorless. "I was raised Catholic, but I'm not practicing..."

She told me AA was spiritual, not religious, and suggested I write about my old God — Catholic, formal, and distant — and then envision a new God I would like to know — kind, listening, something to hold my hand. A Friend.

And she suggested I pray. The 11th Step is: *Sought through prayer and meditation to improve our conscious contact with God, as we understood Him, praying only for knowledge of His will for us and the power to carry that out.* The capitalizations were a little Creepy, but the "as we understood Him" part relaxed me. Liz encouraged me to try.

I got on my knees and clasped my hands on my bed. The position felt comfortable. For the first while, I pictured Bedstemor, my Danish grandmother who died four years earlier. In my prayers, we'd talk and have tea, and I'd hear her laugh, wide and free, suggesting joy was always possible.

Bedstemor had not been religious, but she was a giver and a doer. I once asked her how she swam five days a week well into her 80's. She looked at me like, *Isn't it obvious?* "You just do it!" Bedstemor was not a woman who lived in her head mulling over how to get out of a writing conference. She would have gone. I was humbled by that. I wanted that.

Was that what a Higher Power would give me?

Liz told me her Higher Power was something she carried with her (which could mean a purse or herpes or an EpiPen), but I kinda knew what she meant. Something inside. Some Source. Something people meant when they said, "Bless you." or "Peace be with you." or "God is good." Something I didn't understand.

Maybe there was a God. Maybe there wasn't. But I suspected there was something, mostly because mankind talked about God all the time. He was the protagonist in the big religions *(God, my God)*, essential to meaningful cursing (*For God's sake!*), could dictate a trend (*Oh. Mah. Gawd!*) and was the punctuator of transcendent orgasms (*OH GOD!*). God was everywhere. We just hadn't met yet.

God was still a faraway place, but Liz felt like home. She was a tiny woman who wore cardigans and pearls befitting a nurse administrator. She loved generously, slipping off her flip flops or ballerina flats before curling up on the couch with me and our Big Books.

She dropped spiritual gems that helped me change my relationships. I collected and admired them, and tried to wear them as my own. "Your friend is a dry well of support. You keep going back to her expecting sparkling water. Call her. Tell her you love her. But accept her the way she is. The dynamic will change if you bring a different attitude. Come to me. Come to us. We will fill you up, Henriette."

She was right. Liz did fill me up. When we were together, there was peace in my world, and I wanted to stay there forever.

~

May 8th, 2015: Day 57

My phone rang. It was Liz. It had been weeks since we'd connected beyond voicemails. Caught up in my pursuit of a diagnosis, I had been distracted from seeing this.

"Hi, Liz!"

"Honey..." She was crying. Dread sheeted down my back. She cried so hard I couldn't make out the words.

"I...I have to change my date."

What did that mean? I slipped to the floor. We had hardwood floors throughout the cabin. Sections of them were gorgeous and rich, unscuffed after eighty years. But other sections were warped. We woke on our first morning to find water pooling on the floor. There had been a slow leak all night. We couldn't save it. The damage was irreparable.

"Your what?" I whispered. Then it hit me. She had to change her sobriety date. Liz had relapsed.

I heard it. The slurring, the rubbery jaw unable to form words. I pictured her in a tiny ball on her couch, clothes sopping from tears and opiate sweat. My heart cracked. My bones felt the weight of her shame, unable to meet my eyes even over the phone.

She said she was going to rehab. I said I loved her. She said she loved me. And she was sorry. So, so sorry. Tears rained down my face.

I had more time than my sponsor.

I no longer had a sponsor.

Fear pounded down on me, a violent rainstorm like the one she'd been in the first time we spoke.

"Hi, Henriette. I'm Liz! I'm in Atlanta, and it's raining! I'm holding an umbrella and getting into a cab, but I really want to talk with you."

It was so messed up. The person I wanted to talk to about Liz was Liz. But she was no longer mine. Just like that.

That's the thing about addicts. We're two-faced. Spiritually fickle. Jekyll and Hyde. Jekyll will give you the shirt off his back. Hyde will steal it. When we use, you lose us. We lose us. We become Vodka. Vicodin. Her. Lost inside a roar of rationalizations so loud we can't find the truth. Take one pain med three times a day. Take three pain meds three times a day. Take three pain meds an hour. Take as needed for pain. Always needed for pain, no?

Where are you going, Liz?

I hung up and all I could hear was the sound of Liz's flats padding out of my life.

June 18th, 2015: Day 98

A few days later, I received the Allegra Johnson Award for Memoir Writing through UCLA Writers' Extension. A month later, I drove home from the awards dinner, my stomach gurgling. Overwhelmed, I'd only grazed my gourmet Italian meal.

It was about 11 pm when I pulled off the freeway. We lived in a rural pocket of Los Angeles. Not a lot of options. Ranches. Coyotes. And your friendly neighborhood 7-11.

I saw her tearing through the garbage can, digging for her version of gold — plastic bottles for cash or a half-eaten sub from Giamela's next door. She was emaciated with matted gray hair, or was it just a dirty blond? Eyes like black marbles. Wrinkles scribbled across her face. She wore a T-shirt and shorts stained with dirt and desperation.

I turned off the car and watched her. My personal policy is never to give money. Does giving money enable or help? On this matter, the jury of my heart remains hung. I have never known if my choice is wrong. I plopped the $5000 check from UCLA into my purse and zipped it tight.

I emerged from the car in a fancy creation from Bloomingdale's. My dress held a unique fondant-like form, tiffany-blue with an angular red and black design. I had never spent this much on a piece of clothing, with the exception of my wedding dress.

My shoes? Kevin had spotted them through the window of a Steve Madden store in Las Vegas. They were not particularly expensive, but they were particularly green — an eye-popping blend of 80's neon and Midori Sour. I was no shoe gal, defaulting to the Danish shoe of choice — the clog. But, oh, when I slid my foot into this pump, I'd twisted and preened with delight. *So, this is what all the fuss is about!*

I clicked the short distance from the car to the door and braced for the question I knew would land like a missile.

"Hey! Can you help me with...OH, I LOVE YOUR SHOES!"

"Sorry," I muttered, striding through the door.

I grabbed an iced tea and a bag of baked pea crisps, auto-smiling at the cashier. I tapped my finger on the counter, watching her. *I love your shoes!* With those four little words, we were equalized. No longer the Have and Have Nots, but two gals doing fashion.

I glanced over my shoulder at the fridges. Within seconds, I could pound a bottle of white wine. How quickly I could topple from this cloud-brushing, fairy-tale evening to plucking pills from my tomato juice vomit. How surely my $5000 award would be liquidated into wine. Vodka. Rubbing alcohol. Less than two years ago, I pilfered through a friend's medicine cabinet instead of a garbage can. How were we different? She was me, and I was her.

So many people had helped me get sober. Kevin locked up his

pain meds to curb my obsession. My in-laws paid for my first month in rehab, and a girlfriend paid for the second. And Liz, who had loved me for nearly four years. Did this woman have anyone to love her? I took $5 out of my purse and rolled it up. I walked up to the garbage can where she was still scrounging and stuck out my arm.

"Here you go."

She looked at the bill. "OH MY GOD!" she screamed. "Thank you! You have NO IDEA! You just SAVED MY LIFE!" And then she ran.

I sat for a few minutes watching her, the car's A/C caressing my arms. Roadrunner-style, she'd beelined for Sunland Park across the street, toward the small government building. It was a daycare center that held AA meetings at night. In the park's shadows, exchanges of the less spiritual kind took place. Sex, drugs, and demoralization. *She probably went to score.* But suddenly, she headed back towards the store. She was talking to the cashier when I lowered my foot on the pedal and pulled away. *Maybe she bought some water, or a sandwich.*

Did I help her?

I passed the Rite Aid, where I'd picked up 120 Fiorinal that led to my first overdose. I pictured the scrawny woman-child hobbling through triple-digit heat for her fix. *But for the grace of God go I.* Some headshaking, eye-contact-avoiding folks might have said that about me. But I couldn't say that about Shoe Gal. I couldn't believe in a God that would choose. You get disease. You don't. You get sober. You don't. You die. You don't. A God like that couldn't live in my heart.

But I had been warned. *You have to find a Higher Power.*

I arrived home to a dark cabin. In 2015, I often found myself alone. Kevin had been away most of the year working. *CLIPCLIPCLIP.* Wahlter tap-danced in from the bedroom as I flipped on some lights.

"BUBBA!" My senior hound wiggled his bum. Peeling off the heels with a sweaty pop, I landed with a thud on those beautiful floors.

"You're lucky you don't have to wear heels, Bud." Wahlter's tail thwacked against my leg.

I slipped on my clogs, the chosen ones, the grounding reminders of my childhood and culture. Opening the back door, I followed

Wahlter outside to a small patch of sand and succulents that bumped against our patio and Hollywood view. Our stoic cabin-that-could, with no central air or heat and a tarped roof with sandbags, was upstaged every night by a moving picture show. Helicopters fluttering, freeways buzzing, and a shimmering spectacle of lights.

I exhaled into the warm night. Staring across the canyon, I thought about Liz. What happened? Why hadn't she been able to ask for help? Where was her God? The one she said she carried with her.

I rolled back on my heels arching my neck to the sky. There were no stars, just patches of muddled light staining the urban dark. It was not the sky I pictured when Liz asked me in rehab if I believed in God. That sky had been bright and colorless, illuminating a new world where I felt lost and scared. Where Liz had been my guiding force — the hand I held and the voice I followed.

And then it was clear. There had been no room for me to find a Higher Power because Liz had been standing in the way. I had made Liz my Higher Power. *That probably no human power could have relieved our alcoholism. (pg. 60)*

I clomped back into the house and pulled out the check. The thrilling show of faith in my talent. The award that would never have happened had I still been living like Shoe Gal.

Shoe Gal hadn't known if I would help. She had just asked. And she would have kept asking all night. She had been that desperate. Going forward without Liz, I would have to be that desperate.

There was no more walking in someone else's shoes.

6

CATHOLICISM

Easter 1974: Age 6 ½

It was Good Friday. I sat with Daddy in a pew in my white dress with a light blue sash in the St. Joan of Arc Catholic Church. Nicky was too young to sit still for an entire service, so he was at home with Mum. The priest wore a long white dress with pretty gold accents, almost like it was Bedazzled. Mum wouldn't buy me a BeDazzler kit because she said she could do the same thing for a lot less money than K-Tel charged, but her Bedazzling never quite looked the same as the commercials.

I looked at the cross behind the altar and the swirl of a sign behind Jesus' head.

"Daddy, what does INRI mean?" I whispered.

He leaned into me, his soft hair falling across his forehead. "Jesus of Nazareth, King of the Jews."

"But we're Catholic. Why is he King of the Jews?"

He smiled and brought a finger to his lips. The giant crucifix was covered in a purple cloth. I pictured Jesus gazing heavenward, a crown of thorns on his head, his sad eyes glazed with pain. I couldn't look at the nails through his hands. It made my stomach hurt. I was glad Jesus was covered up today.

"Daddy," I loud-whispered. "Why are the crucifixes covered up?"

His lips curled. "On Good Friday, it reminds us that Jesus died for our sins."

"Why?"

"That we might receive forgiveness. That Man might be saved."

"From Hell?"

"Yes." I knew God had ordained it. He had sacrificed his own son. Joseph wasn't really his dad.

"But why would God do that to his own son?"

"Henriette. Not now." I pouted and crossed my arms. It was all so confusing. Why would God want his own son to suffer? Daddy would never want Nicky to suffer.

A younger man in a less Bedazzled dress entered swinging the smoking box. Daddy called it a thurible. The man swung it up and down the aisles and it coughed out the stinkiest incense. It smelled like skunk and hurt my throat! Daddy said it purified our prayers. I slouched down and pulled my dress over my nose.

Behind the priest, a young boy used a cup-on-a-stick to snuff out the candles. I knew he was an altar boy because I had seen a picture of Daddy as an altar boy in England. He'd held a cross-on-a-stick and wore what looked like a costume — a red dress with lace or a doily sewed to the bottom. Doily was so much fun to say. *Doily. Doily. Doily.*

I sank into Daddy as he read from a prayer book. Some of the words were capitalized. I guess the important ones. Thy. Thou. Lord. Father. Heaven. Hell. It made them seem creepy. I turned my face into his sleeve. Church kinda gave me the squirmies. I never felt this uncomfortable in Chapel at school.

EVERY WEDNESDAY MORNING, all the junior school students Grades Two through Six attended Chapel. We had to wear a stupid white veil, not a delicate and gauzy thing, more like a pillowcase with straps on the bottom. They shielded our baby faces, making a perfect cover for whispered conversation. I hated wearing them. The straps were too tight, and they messed up my hair. (Mum was the best at putting my hair in braids or pigtails and color coordinating ribbons with my uniform. She always made me feel pretty despite the gigantic sheet on my head.)

We sang hymns and prayed together. I loved to sing. I wasn't the best in the class, but I wasn't tone deaf like Helen A. I could recite The Lord's Prayer perfectly. It didn't mean much to me, although I did wonder what a temptation was. Something to do with being an adult? Maybe it was thinking about the bags of candy with elastic bands on the top shelf of the kitchen? Sometimes I wished Candy Night wasn't just on Fridays.

I felt safe in Chapel. My friends were there. My teachers who we gossiped about behind our white curtains were there. Were those veils worn to remind us of something higher than ourselves? Did I know God in Chapel? No. I knew of gossip and giggles and the glory of song.

THE ORGAN CLUNKED out some chords and Daddy rose. I jumped up. I knew this one!

Joyful / Joyful / We adore Thee /

God of Glory / Lord of Love

Daddy smiled over the hymn book as I proudly sang every word.

Hearts unfold like flowers before Thee /

Opening to the sun above

"Daddy. What's it called again?"

"Crucifixion." Daddy had once told me it was the worst thing a human being could do to another.

"But they don't crucify people anymore?!" Daddy shushed me again. I couldn't imagine that. Those nails. I bit my lip. *Leaving. I thought leaving was the worst thing a person could do.*

"Let us pray," said the Bedazzled man.

Daddy lowered the kneeler, and we knelt. A call and response rumbled through the sanctuary, but I said my own prayers. I never prayed for toys or clothes or even candy. I always asked for the same thing.

Dear God, please make Daddy well.

I glanced at him. His hands were clasped on top of the pew in prayer. There were strange pockets under his eyes. My heart squeezed. A new and strange sadness clung to me like a mist whenever I was with him.

With God all things are possible. These words were on the wall as you walked into church. If God could bring Jesus back from the dead, surely, he could make Daddy well? Maybe I just had to pray harder. More often? Maybe write him a letter the way I wrote one to Santa every year.

If you'd asked, I would have told you God was an old white man in the sky. He had a beard, a staff, and a rod. *Thy rod and thy staff they comfort me.* I didn't understand how those things were supposed to comfort me. All I knew was that God lived in heaven, which is where we went when we died, and I should send my prayers there. To a backlit face emerging from the clouds.

I liked the Old Testament stories. Adam and Eve. David and Goliath. Noah's Ark. They were as dramatic as the TV shows we weren't allowed to watch. I didn't like that God got so angry with mankind that he drowned everything. Scarier than being trapped on a huge boat in a flood with two spiders was thinking about how angry God had to have been to do that. Sometimes I wanted to be angry with Him, but that didn't seem right. I wouldn't yell at my teacher or a policeman or a librarian.

One night at the dinner table I said, "Oh, for God's sake!" instead of "For Pete's sake!" Shocked, Mummy and Daddy both exclaimed "Henriette!" One surprised parent could be ignored. Two meant I had done something really wrong. You did not speak to God that way.

Maybe I wanted a takedown with God. I was getting sadder. Impatient. A confused daughter tired of unanswered prayers. Desperate for Him to answer the question that orbited my heart every day.

OH, FOR GOD'S SAKE! Why won't you fix him?

Understanding God was like the time Daddy tried to explain space to me.

What's beyond the solar system?

Galaxies.

And what's beyond galaxies?

The Universe.

And what's beyond the Universe?

Infinity.

What's beyond that?

Infinity is infinite. It has no end.

But it has to end.

No.

There has to be a wall.

No.

A border?

No.

Something!

No. Space is infinite. It goes on forever.

And my head exploded.

I had so many questions about God. And Daddy answered all of them.

"Daddy. Does God love us?" The parishioners gathered their coats.

"Yes, my Darling. God loves all of us." I grabbed his hand and leaned against his leg. "As much as I love you." His voice softened as he stroked my hair, claiming me as his.

God was lines in a big book with creepy lettering. He began my prayers, hung from my neck, lived in the sky. I knew of God but did not know Him. And when you don't know God, anything or anyone can take up that space in your heart.

"I love you, too, Daddy."

I swung my father's hand as we started down the aisle, walking towards the light on Catholicism's darkest day of the year.

7

JUMPER

October 23rd, 2015: Day 225

For five blissful months, the rash disappeared. I was grateful to Dr. Slick for pushing the second steroid shot, and I dared to believe the virus was gone. But one night in October the rash returned. *TwitchSizzleBurn.* And so, I returned to Cedars.

"I don't like the look of this." Dr. Slick was up in my face, staring at the butterfly-shaped rash glistening across my cheeks. I squirmed on the table, trying not to think about my jeans scraping my skin. Why had I worn pants?

I knew a little about the butterfly-shaped rash associated with lupus erythematosus. At 18, I was hospitalized for a biopsy as my kidney function plummeted. One afternoon, amid a swirl of whispers, a young girl was admitted to my room. *Lupus. Losing kidney function.* She slept a lot and was usually alone. No flowers, just a worn stuffie at the end of her bed. On the morning of my discharge, I picked up one of my bouquets and walked over to her. I stared at her sleeping face, swollen with steroids, a wing-like rash shimmering across her cheeks. I wondered if her growth would stunt like mine? I placed the chrysanthemums on her table and went home. I still wonder what happened to her.

The idea of having lupus scared me. Medical Science often treats auto immune conditions with immunosuppressives, but I was already maxed out. More immunosuppression? I'd literally need a bubble to live in. Let's dodge that bullet, please.

"We need to check you for lupus."

I'M HERE BECAUSE OF A RASH, NOT LUPUS! I wanted to scream. I didn't want another condition. Lupus upon virus upon transplant upon addiction upon migraines upon eyes-that-don't-see-so-good. Geezus. But I had to concede. In addition to the butterfly rash, my energy levels were plummeting. I was finding myself in bed at 7 pm, 6 pm, 5 pm. Was that a) Lupus? b) The virus? c) Stress? d) All of the above? Dr. Slick couldn't tell me until the specialized blood work came back next week.

I stood on the Third Level Plaza bridge that links Cedars' East and West office towers. It was a ridiculously gorgeous day. October, 78 degrees and sunny with warm winds dancing through the facility. Two huge palms stretched into the painfully blue sky. My heart hurt. Oddly, this perennial patient wasn't quite ready to go home.

I went up two floors and slipped inside the door marked Dialysis. No one staffed the desk behind the glass, so I moved toward the unit's door. My pulse pattered. *I shouldn't be doing this, but I'm like alumni, no?* I peered through the small window at the dialyzers, feeling their ominous clank and hum through the door. I observed patients in parts. Lifeless limbs on gurneys or in chairs. Slacken heads. Glazed eyes. Souls disappeared beneath layers of clothes, blankets, and fear.

I remembered the skull cap and gloves I'd worn inside that freezing room. An outrageous idea on such a sultry fall day, but with renal failure I was always so very, very cold. Twelve machines filtering twelve humans' blood. Clear, serpentine tubing gargling all the shades: bright scarlet, deep ruby, toxic red. Removed. Cleaned. Returned.

Dialysis works like a kidney but it's a fake out. Dialysis filters the toxins from your blood and removes fluid from your tissue. The rub? The second you are taken off the dialyzer, your blood fills right back up with toxins because your kidneys still don't work. I never felt good on or off dialysis: nauseous and zombie-like when on, and detox-like shaking when off. The process of dialysis isn't unlike the Greek myth of Sisyphus: the dialyzer pushes that rock of toxicity up the hill, only to have it roll back down and nearly crush you.

Dialysis is my Room 101. My greatest fear. Kidney transplants last 20-25 years, sometimes more, sometimes less. In 2015, I was 47, and my transplant was four years old. I knew lupus could take people here. Maybe it had taken my young Toronto roommate here. Kidney failure. Dialysis. Transplantation. Death?

I stayed for a very long time, reminding myself of where I was standing today. And that I could stand at all.

Why had I been drawn up here? Fellows in AA might call this moment a godshot — a divine nudge. Maybe. I only knew my (G)od with a small g. One I "served" through rote recitation of 12 Step prayers. *My Creator / I am now willing that you should have all of me, good and bad.* It was a (G)od I didn't feel. But I did feel gratitude, and I had been reminded to stay in the day, to not future trip down a road on which I may never set foot.

My blouse billowed with the Santa Anas as I walked back to the car. The fabric soothed, distracting me from my resurrected pain. Folding into the driver's seat, I called Kevin from the car.

"I have to be tested for lupus." Hot tears fell on hot cheeks. I pictured Kevin at his parents' kitchen table in Winnipeg. He had spent much of 2015 there taking headshots and performing in *The Addams Family*, *Les Misérables* and now *Stars of David*.

Two years into my recovery, we were finding moments of humor as I found my sober footing. He teased me by singing *Hen. On. Pills.* to the tune of Duran Duran's *Girls on Film.* He dubbed this daily crier "The Roller Coaster of Hen." I retaliated by knighting him "My Robot" because I could count on one hand the times he had cried. He determined I should star in my own series titled "The Emotionalist." I felt baptized by our showers of laughter. I gobbled up his teasing, starved for our loving connection that felt shiny and new because I'd never known our love sober. I'd watch him throw his head back in laughter, stomach-clutching howls over a silly TV show, and feel a feathery gratitude swirl around me and hold me in its light. *Thank you.*

"Oh, sweetheart. I am sure you don't have lupus." I squeezed the wheel, frustrated.

It was the comment I loved to love / hate. Kevin offering something I so badly wanted to be true, something he would do anything to facilitate, but ultimately had no control over. A comment rooted not in the fertile soil of fact, but in the fickle terrain of magical thinking.

"Wow. It took me forever to get to La Brea and Franklin." (Sorry, non-Angelenos.)

"Well, it is Friday," Kevin offered, as I endured 10 minutes of merging from the 101 onramp onto the freeway. And then suddenly everything on the freeway stopped.

This does not look good. I took a quick snap and facetiously posted it on social media. *This really really sucks when you have to pee.* Then I got a private message from an acquaintance.

101 is closed at Lankershim both ways. I believe someone is trying to jump off a bridge.

"Matt just texted me. Someone is trying to jump off the bridge at Lankershim."

Just then my dashboard trilled, and not in that *Yay! You have successfully connected your Bluetooth!* way, but with a *D-oh! Something's not right!* clang.

"What was that?" Ah, Kevin. The man whose protectiveness kicks in even 1900 miles away.

"It says the car is overheating." This made no sense. My car was a few months old.

"WHAT? Pull over."

"I can't! It's a parking lot!" My phone buzzed again. "Shit. I have almost no charge." I had 5% remaining and did not have a charger. In 2015, my phone was not yet a limb, and I did not consider my charger an umbilical cord.

Sweat flowered on the back of my neck. We decided to each call Ford Roadside Assistance in case I lost connection. When I spoke to the operator (not based in L.A.), she told me the wait would be five to six hours as there were mudslides in my area. I pointed out I was stopped on a Hollywood freeway with zero mud nor was anything sliding. And then my phone went dead. Now I really had to pee.

A sick feeling grabbed my insides. Should I pull into the median? What if emergency vehicles came racing towards the jumper? I would be smashed from behind. But if I didn't turn the car off, it might overheat and die. I couldn't keep turning it on and off. Cars were inching forward, funneled around the suicidal situation ahead. Swiping my palms, I drifted left and merged into the median. Switching on my hazards, I turned the car off. My world went quiet.

Click-click. Click-click. Click-click.

Nothingness echoed hard. No music. No radio chatter. No engine humming. Just the snappy beat of my hazards marking time. How long would I be here? How would Roadside Assistance find me? How would they get across five lanes of Friday night traffic? I glanced to my left. On the other side of the median cars raced by, freed from the inconvenience of the dreaded freeway stall.

Click-click. Click-click. Click-click.

To my right, cars floated by. Drivers turned their heads and stared. Who was I? Why was I on the median? A stalled Angeleno! Not a rare species, but one you couldn't help gawk at when spotted. I wanted to throw down my practiced *Whatthefuckareyoulookingat* scowl, but figured it wasn't the wisest facial expression without guarantee of a quick getaway.

No one smiled. No one waved. Just selfish drivers in tense cars, poised and ready to bolt. No-one wanted to be anchored to a stranded soul.

Why does the quiet inside a sealed car feel so ominous? I shifted on the seat, my legs crying foul. My heart fist-bumped into my ribs.

OK. What can I do? Talk to anyone? No. Get off the freeway? No. Pee? Short of dropping trow on the 101... No. Switch off my skin? I wish. Eat? No. Drink? No. Do I have lupus? You won't know for a week. OK. So. What can I do?

Breathe. You can breathe.

And so, I did. In and out through my nose, yoga-style. 12-Step phrases drifted by. *Easy does it. Feelings are not facts. Let go and let God.* Ideas that were still more like bumper stickers than a truth I understood. And yet, my double-beat slowed, my shoulders softened, and I felt a small smile land with grace. There was nothing I could do but be. I would get out of here even if it took until midnight with soggy pants and a scrounging under the seat for a wayward mint.

Just then, a woman in a black Prius rolled by and mouthed *Are you OK?* A flush of relief washed over me. *Yes!* I mouthed back *Thank you!* with a big ol' thumbs up. I was okay. I had been seen. I wasn't alone.

The freeway opened, the way it always does, with a noiseless *WHOOSH!* Cars accelerated hesitant, then with I've-got-places-to-be fury. *Zoom! Zoom! Zoom!* I had to move. I tensed my fingers around the ignition. *Pleasepleaseplease.* Turn. Click. ROAR! *OMG! Yesss!* Now to cross five lanes of traffic in half a second to exit Barham. Sometimes the only way to cross an L.A. freeway is to put your blinker on, close your eyes, and pray. *One-two-three-four-please don't hit me!-five!* I missed Barham but zoomed down the offramp at Lankershim. There was no sign of the jumper.

I stopped at the *Coffee Bean* at Lankershim and Riverside and asked to use the phone. I told Kevin that Sunrise Ford was just down the street, but the car was running fine. I peed, then bought a gigantic cookie, adrenalized by my empty bladder and freeway prison break. My breath caught in that half second before the engine turned over, but the car roared to life. If it didn't start in the morning, at least I would be in my own driveway.

FLOPPING ONTO MY BED, I shoved the cookie in my mouth. The mashed sweetness flooded my exhausted bloodstream. I Googled *Lankershim 101 today* and an image appeared. A man stood at the edge of the bridge clutching a chain link fence behind him with claw-like hands. Another man stood on the bridge behind the fence, surrounded by several police cars. A massive Life Net (inflatable pillow) waited on the 101 below, surrounded by 13 firefighters and multiple fire engines. I could feel the tension in the jumper's bent legs, poised to spring into a future he felt would be less painful than today.

I popped the last bit of cookie in my mouth and sighed. I knew darkness. Bare-minimum days. Pour glass of water. Pee. Shuffle back to bed. Some days that would be all I could do.

But in my darkest moments had I ever been suicidal? I had overdosed. Twice. Influenced by Her dark force. *Take all of the pills. Take them all.* I had not wanted to live in pain. Had I wanted to die? No. I had never truly wanted to die.

I wiped my face clean of crumbles and buried it into Wahlter's back, inhaling his nutty scent. A rush of contentment warmed me. Gratitude for Kevin, Wahlter and the woman in the black Prius. Grateful I had never felt like the jumper. A man in so much pain, his only solution was to try and end his life.

I looked out the window, past our magnificent gold medallion tree, to the freeway beyond. I was oddly grateful for that time in my car — that bubble of aloneness. Inside the 12-Step platitudes and yoga breath and strange silence, I had known peace.

Which made me wonder if perhaps I hadn't been alone after all.

8

PELÉ

July 21st, 1975: Age 6 ¾

They screamed at the sight of him. A brown blur in a white uniform. He tore across the field in funny shoes with giant spikes on the bottom. Chunks of dirt and grass sprayed under his feet as he ran.

His name was Pelé. The world had crowned him the greatest soccer player ever. Daddy, Nicky and me were in the stands at Varsity stadium in Toronto, watching the Brazilian soccer star play with the New York Cosmos against Toronto Metros-Croatia. Daddy had seen Pelé win the World Cup in 1970 in Mexico City. He had driven all the way from Canada with his friend, Eric. That's how much of a fan he was!

I was smushed between Nicky and Daddy and thousands of stomping fans, my Holly Hobbie T-shirt stuck to my back.

"PELEEEEEEE...!" Daddy whooped. His dancing eyes followed the athlete's every move. My heart bobbed in my chest. I poked Nicky, my eyes twinkling. He grinned. No one would shush us here.

"PELEEEEEEE!!!!!" we screamed, bouncing in our tiny sneakers on the cement.

I wiped at the sprinkle of sweat on my nose. Daddy pointed to the field, explaining to Nicky why the referee blew the whistle. I didn't care about the rules. I liked watching Pelé run. He wore a huge smile and white socks pulled up to his knees, just like me! His feet twitched beneath him as if he was dancing, gettin' down to the rhythm of the crowd.

Nicky whispered into Daddy's good ear. As Daddy leaned in, his shirt slipped easily from pants that sagged in the back. His clothes were always so baggy. As he reached around to pull them up, he coughed. Then coughed again.

My tummy twisted as he reached under the bench and brought out the paper bag, wrinkled and soft. I tingled all over, weak, like a giant had stuck a straw inside my blood and sucked it all away. Daddy brought the bag up to his mouth and spat.

My face burned. My throat tightened as he retched. I could feel Nicky beside me, quiet, his five-year-old arms hanging at his side. Nothing to cheer about now.

He spat into the bag again. The glob landed with a *thwack!* The yellow stuff I'd seen him spit on the ground was called phlegm or sputum. It was mucus coughed up from the lungs. I'd asked. But Daddy didn't tell me everything, like why was it sometimes green? Why was it happening more often? Why did his body look so different from other dads? And why did his hands shake as he held the bag to his lips?

A sour smell wafted over. Nicky looked at me. His little lips turned down at their corners. I wanted to take his hand and run.

Daddy reached under the bench again and brought a bottle of that pink stuff to his lips. He said it helped his stomach, but I'd almost barfed when he let me try. It coated your tongue with chalk and tasted like medicine. How did that help an upset stomach? His hair fell back as he chugged. Soft. So soft. Why did he look so small? Like a wind could blow him over. Why was his skin turning gray? A yellow-gray. Like mucus.

When he did this, I felt like everything had been scooped out — my heart, my lungs, my stomach. I stood emptied. A hollowed-out girl. Just bleeding scrapes left behind. I wanted to heal him, to fill him up the way Mum filled our air mattresses with a foot pump, making them tight and right for sleepovers. I just had to figure out how.

My back burned. No-one looked at us, but I could feel their red-hot judgment. I scanned the stands from beneath my eyelashed scowl, taking in the boys and men around us. No little girls like me. They were looking towards the field, but I knew they were watching us. I knew what they were thinking. *What is wrong with that man?*

I don't know! No one will tell me!

Daddy sat, shifting to hunch over the bag, sweat spotting his lip. *I love you, Daddy.* My love surged, as total as the roar of respect that swept through the stadium for Pelé. My small hands curled into large fists. If one person had even glanced his way, I would have punched them. I would have screamed "STOP LOOKING AT MY DAD!"

He brought the bag to his lips again, coughing harder. I had to do something. So I did the only thing I could think of. I lied.

"Did you find it?"

It was the finest acting of my life, years before I'd have a professional career. With my six-and-three-quarters-year-old voice I projected to the cheap seats. A little girl distracting her father with a question. It wasn't such a stretch to believe he was looking for something. His head was almost inside the bag. He could have been looking for something. Except he wasn't.

Maybe they couldn't hear him cough. I could believe that. The game was loud, thrumming around our eye of sick. I knew my clever question was dumb. If they'd heard him hack and spit, no one would believe my father wasn't collecting bodily fluids in a bag. He wasn't publicly sick. He wasn't the only person doing this in front of Pelé.

But he was.

So, I lied to myself to not make it true.

"Did you find it?"

Daddy didn't hear me. And if he did, he ignored me, which I doubt. Daddy would never do that. It was just as well. If he had asked *Found what?* what would I have answered? Keys? Lighter? Cigarettes? Or would he have known what I was doing and acknowledged my brilliant performance? *My clever girl.* I like to think so.

The game pounded on. His coughing wound down and he tucked the wet sack under the bench for good. Then he handed us each a can of pop. Nicky got a Crush Cream Soda and I got Crush Grape. *GRAPE SODA! We only get these on special occasions!* The bubbles burned as I gulped the juicy purple sweetness down. Daddy cracked open Nicky's can as a blanket of quiet fell over the crowd. Pelé centered himself, two-stepping in front of the enormous goal. The other players gathered in a wiggling line behind him. The goalie bopped back and forth. Mum would have said he had ants in his pants.

"What's happening, Daddy?" With sport and religion, I knew to loud-whisper when asking a question. He brought a finger to his lips.

"The penalty kick."

Nicky wobbled on tiptoe, tilting his head back to see. Daddy lifted him onto the metal bench. I was still taller than Nicky, though Mum kept sewing us identical outfits, like a kilt for me and kilt shorts for him. Strangers would tell us how cute we were and ask if we were twins which made me so mad. I was nearly two years older!

Pelé loped towards the ball and then seemed to fly backwards, booting it over his head, his kicking leg extended like a rocket straight up into the sky. There was silence. A quiet so intense I forgot to breathe. The goalie dove towards the ground and slapped the ball away with an angry smack.

A noise like radio static swelled inside the stadium. Then an explosion of moans.

"NOOO!!!" Daddy howled. Nicky and I joined in, tiny mouths daring to cheer again. "NOOO!" We wanted Pelé to score a goal.

We all wanted to see him win.

Toronto would win over the Cosmos, but Pelé had been the star of the day. When it was over, he waved his arms to the crowd, running in a giant circle around the field. He beamed a gigantic smile, not caring he had lost. I waved back, eager, my little arms desperate to be seen. *Over here!* He was everything I wished I could give my father. Greek god-like muscles glistening with effort and joy, and a lightness for life that seemed to be missing from ours.

9

UNDIAGNOSIS

I did not have lupus, but had my third steroid shot in November 2015.

That fall, Kevin was home studying Judaism, I was writing *Pillness*, and Wahlter waddled along. For three months, life felt routine and calm. I dared to call it. I was happy.

In February 2016, Pain landed. No longer just a prickly rash on my arms and thighs, but scalding, screaming Pain. As I called Dr. Slick once again, I still believed we would find a solution: A different cream, a pill, IV treatments. My patient history had often taken the long and winding road to solution.

With renal failure at 18, I'd been prescribed an experimental blood pressure medication. (I can't recall its name, but I know it was free.) In 3% of cases, you would lose your sense of taste. Well, you can see where this is going. Within days, the only things I could taste were hard-boiled eggs and French fries with tons of gravy and pepper. It was mind-bending to bite into a piece of rye bread expecting the malted flavor to flood my senses only to taste...nothing. After feeling like I'd been chewing an old piece of gum for two months, I complained.

I'm already losing my kidneys. Can I at least enjoy lunch?

We switched medications.

There was the epic biopsy fail that removed liver tissue instead of kidney. Bloodwork which never corroborated with my symptoms (read: *You shouldn't feel this sick*) and another biopsy with "almost zero chance of a post-bleed" to which my kidney decided to bleed all the live long day. If the odds of something happening were low, it usually happened to me, and so Kevin dubbed me the 3% Girl.

February 26th, 2016: Day 351

I squirmed in the office chair. *Stop wearing pants! Why do I even own pants anymore?* Dr. Slick and Ms. Shadow towered over me, the way a child studies an ant on the ground. They stared slack-jawed and stupefied, inside a silence so long I could have recited the alphabet. I inhaled and puffed out a sigh. Finality was in the air.

"It's not a virus."

Huh?

"It's gone on too long to be a virus."

Come again?

This is the confusing part about being a professional patient. For as much as you never want anything to be wrong with you ever again, when your diagnosis is removed, you want it back. With Undiagnosis, you are hurtled back to the beginning of your medical nightmare.

Inside, I screeched with Stage One Kubler-Ross denial, watching my diagnosis fly out the window. On the horizon I saw more waiting rooms, calls logged, miles driven. And Pain. Because now that they knew nothing, I knew that until someone knew something, there would be more Pain.

My Auntie Teresa, herself a doctor, shared frankly that dermatologists are millionaires because there are few solutions for skin conditions. Notoriously hard to diagnose and treat, patients can find themselves trapped inside a revolving door — shot-relief-flare — that never addresses the root cause. I was beginning to see what she meant.

"So, it's not a virus."

"Right."

"And it's not lupus."

"No."

And it's not a reaction to my meds. Or Graft vs. Host. Or the PUMICE STONE IN THE CORNER OF THE TUB! IS IT?

"We don't know what it is." There it was. My heart dropped with a thud.

"I'm going to send you to an allergist, just to dot our i's and cross our t's.

What? Why? We'd determined this wasn't an allergy right out of the gate. My chest tightened to cry. *And what happens when you've checked off those two letters, Dr. M? What do I do with the rest of the alphabet?* But I knew. With Undiagnosis, you go back to the very beginning whether you want to or not.

MARCH 8TH, 2016: Day 362

The allergist/immunologist (a.k.a. the Next Dr. M.), took one look at my rash, ran what looked like a wooden coffee stirrer across my forearm and tossed it over his shoulder. (He didn't actually do that, but you can picture it, right?)

"You don't have allergies." *Wow. They taught you that in medical school?* But he was kind.

"I can't believe all those medications you're on haven't knocked it out of you." He was right. I hadn't looked at my treatment from such a macro perspective. That my daily cocktail of Cyclosporine (Cell-Cept), Mycophenolate Acid and Prednisone, which suppresses my ENTIRE IMMUNE SYSTEM, was not enough to kill this virus, meant I was dealing with something major and mysterious.

I only saw the Next Dr. M. once. "You need to be a part of some dermatological trial". He made two calls for me. One to a derm who conceded that if a year at Cedars hadn't helped, they couldn't offer me anything, and one to UCLA Dermatology who said I could come in next week.

MARCH 14TH, 2016: ONE YEAR

I looked down at my arms. They were flesh-colored calm. A flutter rose in my throat. They needed to look angry. These were my hard fought 15 minutes. I had learned that when describing Pain, you need Proof.

"Come back to me when you're in a flare up." Dr. H. wasn't playing.

I pursed my lips in frustration. "I am. Right now."

"I just had to hospitalize a patient with hives all over her body." *Did she just compare my pain?* I would have laughed if this wasn't so horrifically unprofessional.

"This is what it usually looks like." With a dry swallow, I swiped images from my year of redness and burn. She barely turned her head, too focused on entering her interpretation of my symptoms into the computer. I heard a door slam. Hope had left the building and was validating its parking ticket. I wanted to tell her my Hell might not be found in the pages of her textbooks, but its flames were still consuming me. My suffering was just as real as her patient's.

If you could just feel what I feel.

She prescribed Tacrolimus ointment, which worried me as I couldn't tolerate this immunosuppressant in oral form, but she said it wouldn't be an issue. I didn't understand anything about chemistry or skin conditions (although apparently neither did the derms). Maybe Tacrolimus would be the miracle treatment. The divine smear. I saw a glimmer of hope in the shimmer of new lubrication. *Maybe this time.*

I believed in Medical Science, indeed revered it. At 19, I had 2% kidney function. If my mother had been in renal failure at age 19 it would have been 1960 when people with kidney failure had little hope of survival. Dialysis was a rare treatment restricted to very few. Transplantation was a new and bumbling science with no long-term survival rates. In 1983, the breakthrough drug Cyclosporine was introduced, the first of many drugs that effectively treat organ rejection by suppressing the human immune system. Just in the pharmaceutical nick of time for my transplant in 1988. Medical Science had saved my life on the daily for 35 years.

I had to believe it would save me again.

LIFE WENT ON. Tacrolimus was smeared. Pain was downgraded from a 6 on the pain scale (severe pain that interferes with concentration) to a 4 (moderate pain that interferes with tasks). I kept writing, often directing a fan to cool my forearms, or switching out icepacks as I wrote. I backed up 500 pages of a first draft of *Pillness.* I started a short-lived support group for women suffering with chronic pain, calling it CHICKSA — Chronic Illness Can Kiss My Sweet Ass! It folded after the first meeting because one of the attendees breezed through our cabin in the hills and snarked, "I wouldn't mind being sick here."

Kevin remained steadfast, my biggest cheerleader, but I was aware that my constant focus on Pain was wearing him down. The winds of another medical storm were forming, but I was determined. I would not lose us inside another tornado. And so, although not my favorite place to visit, I said yes to one of his — Vegas, baby.

Las Vegas is an odd experience the first time you land sober. I had four months clean the first time I hit The Strip with a friend in 2013. I wouldn't say I was tempted to drink, but it was a strange sensation feeling alcohol clinking and flowing around me. Knowing that, for my body, it is a poison that triggers a bottomless thirst, unquenched even by rubbing alcohol. Cessation found only in death. I held a morbid fascination for the booze, like being at the zoo. You know you shouldn't reach for the gorilla, but you kinda wanna stick your arms through the bars and wave 'em around just to see what happens.

In July of 2014, I participated in a Star Trek convention. I played the role of Maggie O'Halloran in one of the least popular episodes of

Star Trek: Voyager. Maggie was a love interest of Ensign Harry Kim (played by Garrett Wang), a flower seller in an Irish village who gets turned into a cow inside a holodeck. (Don't ask because I still don't get it.) Wang convinced me I would make bank selling autographed photos of myself, so I gave it a whirl. It ended up being less bank and more pocket change, but it was a solid adventure in being a C-List celebrity.

At 6 pm, I would pack up my 8 x 10 glossies and walk back from the convention center, dodging California gurls just turned 21 with their smoking test-tubes of margaritas. By the time Kevin and I went for our 20th anniversary in 2015, nothing needed to stay in Vegas because for me, nothing ever happened there.

April 26th, 2016: Day 411

I prayed inside the hotel closet. It was one of those walk-in deals with shelving for ten wardrobes and an ottoman the size of a small car. But my morning spiritual ritual was far from five-star. I'd mumble the Third Step prayer by rote and read a few pages of the Big Book of Alcoholics Anonymous. I found no cosmic connection in or out of a closet that would have made Carrie Bradshaw drool, but getting quiet every day helped me. I was trying. At 2 ½ years sober that went a long way.

"Can I get you a drink?" The pool waiter, all pimples and Polo shirt, offered me a cup of frozen grapes.

"Oooh!" I giggled, reaching for the icy fruit. "I'll have a soda water with extra lime, please. Like three."

"I'll have a rum and coke." I caught the flick of Kevin's eye.

Is it okay if I have a drink?

So, here's the deal. I can't wipe drugs and alcohol off the face of the earth. What I can do is change myself and my reaction to it. Intellectually, Kevin understood that. Sure, I'd rather not have a full bar at home or a bottle of Percocet loitering in our medicine cabinet, but hanging by the pool at The Four Seasons? *Enjoy, Sweetheart, enjoy* I wanted to say to the man who had also been slammed by the Mack truck of addiction, just from a different angle.

When alcoholism is called a family disease, I want to roll my eyes. It's an accurate statement. All are affected. But when I hear it, I picture a group hug and laughter through tears. Fist bump! *We got this!* Inside our family of two, alcoholism was Kevin paying the bills and me stealing his pills. Screaming. Swearing. The pounding of his flesh. Existence inside a spiritual void barren of touch or conversation. Breath so labored inside my barbiturate-soaked sleep that Kevin would set a timer every two hours to make sure I was still breathing. It had taken a long time to get back to a group hug.

"I'm going to the bathroom. Kiss?" I bent over my husband, blocking the hot Nevada sun with my sober shadow. He offered up pursed lips. *Kiss! Kiss! Kiss!* I smashed my lips against his again and again until a funny giggle escaped. Was that sound...joy?

In the bathroom, I held my forearms under the cold tap, cooling the rash that never cooled. My arms burned all the time, in and out of the pool. Chlorine agitated them, yet moving them soothed. *This hurts. That helps.* I twisted them under the stream, studying the flare. Over the past year, my rash had morphed from a bespotted torment to a simple branding of red. Handmaid's red. Concubine red. Appropriate as I was its bitch.

I wiped my hands and leaned into the mirror. Almost four years ago to the day I had been inhabiting this same yellow bikini, studying myself in this same mirror. I was scrawny then. Junkie-thin. My transplant scar was raw, a kindergarten scribble poking out from my bikini's edge. Two months post-surgery, we'd been in Vegas to celebrate, but breaking in a new kidney by guzzling gallons of vodka was not what Kevin had planned.

Four years ago, I had just taken my last prescribed Vicodin. I shivered, remembering the sickening sound of the empty bottle. Nothingness. Dread. I was so tired of feeling that way. Like I had no choice.

I remember thinking, *I have to stop. I will not go to transplant clinic and hit them up for Tramadol. I will not call my gynecologist and refill the*

Vicodin. I will not call the Pain Center and score Roxicodone. No more. No. More.

Then euphoria struck. The Vicodin tablet with my morning vodka soda eased me into a caramel-thick river of peace. My soft bones leaned into the mirror. I smirked at my pinning pupils. *Maybe just one more prescription. I mean, if they're willing, I'm willing. Since the transplant, I've been taking my painkillers as prescribed. Well, almost.* My legs weakened with an orgasmic shudder. I strutted out of the bathroom, resolved. If I could get more pills I would.

I would never stop.

But I did stop. I had stopped for over 1000 days now. Four years ago, I could not look past pupils black as tar and see my beshert* waiting for me by the pool. Today, my eyes were clear. I had a choice. I never wanted to lose sight of him again.

I turned from the mirror deciding. I would not complain to Kevin anymore. He knew I had Pain. It caused him pain that I was hurting. I felt it in the furrow of his brow, the mumbled *I hate this for you*, the Post-its left before every appointment. *Mouse they will fix it.* I would not be the person that spoke only of herself. The one so scared people will forget about their pain they speak of nothing else. I would not flinch when his chest hair scraped my skin. I would hold him in all the ways a person needs to be held. The way he had held me for so long.

KEVIN WAS READING me his spiritual journey. An autobiography documenting his experience with religion and a crisis of faith that led him to Judaism. In a few days, Kevin was "jumping in" — an inside reference to the *mikveh*, a warm pool of water Jews use to purify themselves through cleansing and prayer before holidays or marriage or conversion.

He sat at a sterile desk in our hotel suite. It was a curious space for

* *Hebrew for soulmate, preordained, or inevitable.

a spilling of the soul. I stared at him from a couch that reminded me of living rooms where no one ever sits lest they disrupt the carpet. My breath caught as he recounted his days of Hell when I had been under Her spell: a post-crash economy that crushed his business, a drug-addicted wife he could no longer depend on, and real and total anger towards his God. Kevin's voice cracked as he detailed the erosion of what he'd dreamed his life to be. My body ached to hold him, to make up for the days and months and years he'd existed alone.

"...I was terrified that she would be taken from me..."

I wiped at my wet face, inhaling the eucalyptus scent that permeated every part of the hotel. It was Kevin's favorite scent. The elegant medicinal aroma fluttered everywhere — the lobby, hallways, and rooms. It was invigorating. Cleansing. The smell of healing? Then what do lies smell like? Do they smell foul or delicious, tempting you to believe them? And loneliness? Loneliness must have the sweet smell of someone you love, all the better to twist your nostalgia into unbearable pain.

"Is it okay?" he looked at me with soft eyes.

"It's beautiful." I managed, my heart shredding. I had never known that he prayed. He had never shared that with me. Or maybe I had never asked? *You will never know what he went through.* Tears dropped from my face to my arms. *Plunk. Plunk.* Each salty drop landing with a satisfying sting.

"I'm so, so sorry," the tears streamed.

"Henriette, I have forgiven you."

Kevin never calls me Henriette. It's always "Sweetheart" or "Mus" or "Clumsy" or any one of a thousand terms of endearment we've developed for each other over the years. So when he does call me by my given name it means he wants me to hear him. To know something to be true. And I did. I heard it. We were good.

And then, as if on cue, my arms zapped through to my shoulders.

No. NO. Fuck you, Undiagnosis. I will not talk about you. This is Kevin's moment. You will not be the thing that rips my marriage apart, so loosely held together by stitches that could easily catch on the thorn of Pain.

No.

I got up to kiss my husband on his forehead. Maybe this was having the power of choice. I had Pain. I had no choice over that, but I did have the choice not let it run my life.

Didn't I?

10

DEN

November 1975: Age 7

Saturday night, hanging out in Daddy's den. A mysterious room with shadowy lighting, rugby scores crackling from the radio, and an air-conditioner that roared on even the coldest days of winter. But that can't be right. Maybe that was the quiet roar always rumbling through my heart.

Sometimes there was a bed set up for visits from my Danish and English grandparents. Nicky and I would jump around and chant the infectious theme song to Hockey Night in Canada. *Da-da-da-da-da-DAH!!!* Daddy perched on the edge, beer mug in hand, as we all cheered for the Toronto Maple Leafs to win. After the first period, Nicky always fell asleep. Daddy carried him to our room, tucking him into the bottom bunk. That's when I had to beware! I couldn't let sleep infect me, heavy and warm, snatching my time with my dad.

I didn't understand the rules of hockey, but it was exciting when the puck whipped into the net. The red light flashed and the crowd leaped to their feet. Daddy jumped up, beer sloshing, throat tearing with joy. *GOALLL!* Everything he loved he gobbled up, ravenous for more. Trainspotting. Soccer. Hockey. I loved it when he screamed his joy. It gave us permission to scream, too. To eat life up the way he did.

I could name four players from the Leafs. There was #27 Darryl Sittler who had a huge head of soft-looking curly hair and kind eyes. Daddy explained the giant C on his shirt meant he was the captain. #9 Lanny MacDonald had a bushy mustache and was kinda boring. #21 Borje Salming was a slithery defenseman from Sweden. And #22 Tiger Williams was crazy! He didn't wear a helmet, had no front teeth and was always getting into fights. Daddy and Nicky screamed at the TV when Tiger started punching other players. They loved the fights, but I thought all the flying blood and sweat was disgusting. I loved it when the players circled around each other after a goal, laughing and hugging, boxing at each other with their gloves. The Leafs seemed like a happy family.

But there was no hockey tonight. Daddy sat at his desk and I loitered around, touching the spines of his books, pronouncing the titles out loud. "Catch-22. The Andromeda Strain. The Works of Shakespeare. Agatha Christie." I took in the towers of papers — newspapers, letters, doctor billing — wondering what clues they held about my father. Swinging off the back of his chair, I spotted a pile of postmarked envelopes.

"Are you saving those, Daddy?"

"Yes, Darling." His British accent landed on my ears like a melody.

Daddy was a philatelist — a stamp collector! He'd taught me how to save a stamp. If a stamp from a mailed letter was unmarked by ink it could be saved. I'd cut a wide margin around it in case my hand wobbled. Then I would fill the sink with warm water and submerge it, watching as the glue melted and the stamp floated away to the ceramic shore. Daddy would cheer *YES!* and I'd feel all sunny inside. Once he showed us how to do something, he would never show us again. He expected us to use our noggins.

I loved the simple stamps like Queen Elizabeth II's tiaraed head. The different prices came in a rainbow of colors — pastels, bold, muted. Everything from hot pink to brown to lime green to aqua. So pretty! I had a small book of stamps Daddy didn't consider perfect for his collection, but I didn't care. I just wanted to spend time in his world, and if that meant drying wet stamps on a towel, I was in.

I wondered why my father loved collecting stamps? Was it because he grew up in a time of war? He was born Peter, in Latvia in 1940 and fled in 1944. His family spent four years in German refugee camps and made their way to England where he was raised in Coventry and went to medical school in London. In 1960, he met Mum, Birgitte, at a party. She was there from Denmark, working for a year as an *au pair*. He was in the middle of a poker game when he spotted her across the room — tall, elegant, and blond. He stood up and said, "Deal me out, Boys." Very James Bond. Long-distance phone calls were rare and expensive. While he finished medical school, letters would have been the fuel of their long-distance relationship. If letters were the wings of their love, maybe stamps were what made it soar.

Or maybe he just liked to collect stuff. I collected rocks and didn't really know why. I know my collection never seemed to be big enough, and I always wanted more.

Daddy took a sip from the metal mug with the lid that creaked open. He had glass ones with indents that looked like French doors, and two thick-handled ceramic ones with a fine blue sketching of the København zoo on the side. Most times, he just drank from the bottle.

"How is Henriette's milk?" he clapped. He pronounced my name as if I were royalty, as if I was entering a castle wearing my fanciest princess dress, deserving of every set of eyes upon me. He rolled the "r" and emphasized the "e" in a way no one for the rest of my life could duplicate. Somehow making the "e" sound elegant and strong and not the sloppy "a" everyone thought it was (or should be because they were dumb).

"Perfect!" I said, slurping with my twirly straw. He made the best strawberry milk. I'd watch him dump a rounded spoonful of shimmering pink crystals into a glass of milk, making designs in the condensation as he stirred. Like magic, the stark white milk turned oh-so-pretty in pink! Then I moved in for a sip. Too sweet? Daddy added more milk. Too milky? He'd add more crystals. Then he'd twist the ice cube tray and with a loud crack a cube would pop up and plop into my glass. Sweet alchemy.

I don't remember where Mum was that night. She might have been in the other room studying for school, or out with friends. She was probably out. I wouldn't have been allowed to stay up this late if she'd been home.

Mum was a shadowy figure who wisped through my days. So many times I tried to pin her down, to get her to stay and play with us, or just watch TV, but she was like the prettiest butterfly always fluttering away. Why wouldn't she want to stay? Daddy was so much fun. It hurt my heart that she didn't.

The TV flickered, muted. I realized the end credits for *All in the Family* were rolling up the screen.

"Oh, too bad. I love that show."

Daddy looked up. "No, it's just starting."

My head jerked toward him. Why would he say that? The show was ending! The credits zoomed up the screen as the camera moved down a row of houses. If the show were starting, Edith and Archie would be sitting at the piano singing, all snuggled up, fleshy and tight. Edith always smiled, and Archie had a twinkle in his eye even though he was super loud and grouchy. (I never understood why that black man smiled when Archie was so rude to him.) You could tell they loved each other. I never saw Mum and Daddy sit together like that.

Guys like us we had it made / Those were the days...

"No, Daddy. I'm sure it's the end."

He whirled around to face me. "Wanna bet? I'll bet you $20!"

My heart somersaulted. Betting was such a grown-up thing. And $20! Our allowance was $1 a week. I'm not sure where he thought I was going to get $20 from, even though I was a very good saver. I was in!

I think Daddy liked gambling. He challenged us for money with word scrambles. One time the scramble was: i-e-l-v. I kept answering "veil" because of those stupid white veils we had to wear in Chapel. Daddy kept saying *No, try again* but all I could see was "veil." Daddy had wanted me to see "evil," and he'd seemed a bit annoyed. I argued you could also see "live."

Another time, we were to complete a lap of High Park on our bikes, followed by a second lap to improve our pace. He'd pay us a quarter for every second we knocked off our original time. I was confused by the concept and rode the first lap super slow, barely pedaling — a 15-minute ride taking 27 minutes. Nicky just followed my lead. I remember Daddy's frown when we returned. He snapped *Why did it take you so long? You were supposed to bike normally!* Until then, he'd never been short with us like that.

I knew the show was ending. I knew I would win. So why did I feel funny? Still...$20!

"OK!" I grinned. He stuck out his arm, his Medic Alert bracelet dangling from his wrist. I grabbed his hand and shook it hard. He offered me his sloppy grin that I returned with a loopy smile. It wasn't the money I knew I was going to win; it was how he treated me as his companion. His best pal. As if there was no one else in the world he would rather be with on a Saturday night than his seven-year-old daughter.

We didn't wait long. After a few commercials a car appeared driving down a dusty-looking highway. It was that waitress show. It wasn't that great. Although, her son was kinda cute in a dorky-looking way.

"Ha, HA! I get $20!" I cried, wiggling around the room. He threw his head back and laughed, delighted that his "intelligent girl" was right.

Handing me the cash, I noticed his nails were a little yellow. Looking at the bright green bill with the Queen's face, I exhaled. Wow. I couldn't believe I had $20! ($20 in 1976 is equivalent to $108 in 2024.) I wouldn't tell Nicky. I loved my brother. It wasn't his fault he was nearly two years younger and couldn't stay up as late as me. Secretly, I was glad I had Daddy all to myself.

He tossed his wallet on the bed and offered up his mug. *Skøl!* I clinked my pink drink against his and sipped. My milk was icky now, warm and runny. Daddy's beer smelled sour.

"It's 9:30, Darling. *Arrivederci!*" he smiled, turning back to his desk. Daddy knew words from all kinds of languages: Latvian, Russian, German and even a little Italian. *Arrivederci* meant it was bedtime.

My warm feeling vanished as I took in his back. I knew if I hugged him I would feel his ribs. Daddy was a doctor. He was too smart not to know that *All in the Family* had been ending.

Maybe he had pretended not to know so I could win the bet. But I knew that was a lie forming inside my heart, like a tornado of protection. A whirling, swirling lie on a mission to level a truth I didn't want to see: That sometimes it seemed like I was smarter than my 36-year-old dad.

He lifted his mug from beside the typewriter where I'd hear him write letters to Auntie Teresa in Jerusalem. I titled my head, watching him sip. Daddy made everything so much fun. Teaching and cheering and concocting. Eating life up. But the quiet roar had returned. The one that was always with me.

The feeling that somehow life was actually eating him.

PART II

WHERE ARE YOU, GOD?

11

PRAYER

August 7th, 2016: Day 514

It is 2 am. I am lying in the bathtub. My hands cover my face. I am trying not to move. Pain chatters beneath the water, but it's muted like when someone speaks from another room. I shift and it stirs up a whirlpool of underwater needles. My arm plunges in to grab my thigh. *Sizzle* as my skin meets the water. It doesn't make that sound, of course, because my skin is not literally on fire, but it seems wrong that sparks don't fly. There is no sound but a gentle splash against the side of the tub.

Burn BURN BURN! The turning point has come. I have soaked too long and my skin is revolting. *Get out now!* it demands as I shift one leg over the tub, flinching as the other emerges from my lavender cocoon turned acid bath. I stand, drip drying in the freon breeze.

I lie on the bed, feeling them with every short breath — javelin-like spikes tearing through my skin. Bed used to be a sanctuary. A holy place. Where I read and wrote with a computer tray on my lap and a basset hound suctioned to my thigh. Where I buried myself into Kevin's armpit declaring his personal scent *tobacco leaf!* and erupting into giggles at his bemused expression. Where I'd been loved and cherished in sickness and in health.

Bed is now Hell. A place with specially purchased sheets of smooth and cooling polyester. Where holding my husband feels like punishment. Where I dread Wahlter's flop onto my chest because his fur feels like hundreds of quills stabbing my skin to bleeding. It's strange how I never find any blood on the sheets.

I discontinued Tacrolimus in May (unsafe to use for an extended period of time). I am finished at UCLA. There is nothing more Dr. H. can do.

I drift off for a second, exhausted by the mental games Pain and I play. There is no lasting distraction. When I watch a movie, It sizzles through my limbs. My brain clocks It. *Is that a 6? 7? Should I write this down?* I lose my place and rewind the movie. The lump in my throat reminds me the reason I'm rewinding is because Pain distracted me, defeating the purpose of watching a movie for distraction at all.

It's 2:30 am. I am awake. Maybe because I shift on the bed. Maybe because I don't. I can find no rhyme or reason or pattern or code as to why It blazes up. My panicked breaths chant *no. no. no. no. no.* I'm getting hotter. I'm a flesh bonfire. I'm the gradual sautéing of your feet as you walk across the scorching asphalt by a pool. But there you have a choice. You can plunge into the chlorinated cool, your blistered soles relieved. Here I have no choice. There is nowhere for me to go.

I feel on the verge of hysteria. Cornered. A beast tangled in barbed wire. If I flip out on the mattress Pain will reprimand me with a belt snap warning. Warden to prisoner. *Who do think you are? There is no leaving this place.*

I get up. This is another distraction technique. The flicker of time it takes me to get out of bed provides me with three seconds of relief. Long enough to keep me on this side of the ledge.

I slip on Kevin's t-shirt and shuffle out the front door, Wahlter trailing me. A warm breeze greets us. I perch on the edge of a patio chair, a green and white striped pillow cover sewed by a friend with rash-friendly fabric I'd purchased downtown. Everything revolves around Pain. It is my master.

I watch the moving picture below, follow the snake-like wind of

Sunland Blvd. through the canyon toward the city's chaos. The hum of the 210 freeway rises up like cicadas. My heart bends with melancholy back to Toronto summers choking with humidity, green trees rustling with the real shit-disturbers. The oaks and maples that lined my street swayed with the hot breeze as I sat, mowers whirring, 10-year-old heart stirring, on the porch of the house purchased with my father's life insurance.

Have I ever known peace?

I rub my hands up and down my arms, watching Wahlter sniff a succulent. I stare at the lights below and picture people fighting and eating and fucking and sleeping and driving and stealing and dancing and yelling. The magic and horror of life happening right in front of me. I used to feel like I was standing beside it. Or above it. Disconnected by an ache that consumed me, and I did not know why.

Now I know. I believe that ache it is my alcoholism. I understand this disease as a threefold condition. 1) A physical allergy: When I take a drink or pill, a craving is triggered and I cannot stop. It's like an allergic reaction. I break out into an insatiable need for more. 2) A mental obsession: When I think about pills it's all I can think about. I lie, steal, and doctor shop. Getting pills moves to the top of my list and nothing matters until I do. 3) A spiritual deficiency: Every morning I still wake up with some version of that ache. A restlessness I cannot drown with drink or fill with pills or stuff with 4 to 6 to 8 to 10 Fudgesicles until I go to bed nauseous, wake up with a sugar hangover, and pop Excedrin until there's a raging pain in my abdomen.

Now I know there will never be enough Pills or Likes or Sugar or Weight Loss or Money or...that is the ache. Feeling like I need to fill myself with something when I've just been going in the wrong direction. I've been taking instead of giving. The last of the 12 Steps is giving of self. Listening. Sharing. Guiding. But all I think about is Pain. How can I help anyone if I can barely help myself?

I shift in the chair, marking the strains of a coyote's falsetto cry. Wahlter wags into the distance. My anger flares as I think back to this afternoon.

When I was in renal failure in 2010, my cousin, disappointed she was the wrong blood-type to donate her kidney, offered to help me anyway she could. I believed her promise, as airy and cross-country as it was. This afternoon, I wrote and asked if she would lend me the money for a consultation at the Mayo Clinic. A week of hotel and tests were about $10,000 which I vowed to pay back. It had been humbling, maybe even humiliating, to ask.

Her response was quick, too quick. They didn't have the money. (They do. They have 1000 times $10,000.) She suggested I read a book called *Gut* about diet. I wanted to punch her in the face. My sponsor reminded me it was my cousin's money and nudged me to write a response. *Be kind.* My sponsor also reminded me that things could be worse. I could be on dialysis and know Pain. I then wanted to punch her in the face.

Afterwards, I sat in this same chair, reeling. I stewed in the sun and let my burning body burn. Kevin called from Scotland and was furious I'd asked to borrow money. *I can't do this anymore!* I cried. Kevin insisted. *This is Los Angeles. You still have options!*

After our call, I shook as I circled the house. I wanted to take a bat and smash my foot to experience a secondary pain that might distract me from the fury inside. "What are my options, Kevin?" I screamed into the scorching canyon, pounding on my arms, my betrayers, until my voice cracked and bled. Tears flew off my cheeks. I wanted to smash something. Hurt someone. Make them hurt as much as me.

Wahlter licks my leg, and I pat his funny narrow head. We head inside. I know Kevin's anger is fear over money. We are always behind. Always in medical debt. Always without disposable income. Yet he's in Scotland for the Pipe Band championships. A week of piping and drinking and laughing which the breadwinner deserves. He does.

But tonight, I hate him.

I lie back in bed. Wahlter sleeps inside a tumbleweed of bedding. I stare at the ceiling. Past it. All I see is a giant yellow sign. DEAD END. Where do I go from here? *What are my options, Kevin?*

I want drugs. Drugs work. Everybody is entitled to relief from Pain. If I was burned in a fire, I would get drugs. I feel like I am living inside a fire. I am the fire, but with Undiagnosis I can't prove shit, which gets me nothing. I shift onto my side and look out the window into the blackness. Being a drug addict in legitimate agony is some kind of narcotic karma coming around to bite me in the ass.

Benzodiazepines, barbiturates, opiates. Tremors calmed. Anxieties soothed. Pain crushed. Xanax, Adderall, Fiorinal, Ambien, Roxicodone. The colored shells spin inside my mind like a kaleidoscope. That pharmaceutical rainbow where the pot of gold is a life without Pain.

Am I truly incapable of taking one pill? Have I not proved this? I overdosed on 120 barbiturates, then 130 benzodiazepines. I know that one pill is too many and a thousand is never enough, but this is different. I don't want to get high. I just don't want to feel Pain. I don't want drugs. I need them. I even have a sponsee begging me to take them. *You don't have to be a martyr, Hen.* But I am not a martyr. I am a drug addict. Am I supposed to live like this? Why would I want to? I must have something.

A thought comes.

What about medical marijuana?

It is medicine. Effective medicine, apparently. And it's everywhere, wafting out of cars and stores and backyards. I have tried it, five or six times in my life. I never got anything out of it, it just stunk up my hair. Pot seems so chill. How can you get addicted to it? My heart skips a beat and then it stops.

You know you can't take anything.

Today, drugs are no longer on the invite list. But Pain? I did not invite It here, yet It lives inside me and I live in Pain.

A second thought comes. It is what AA fellows talk about in the rooms. And it is a Step.

(Step 11: Sought through prayer and meditation to improve our conscious contact with God as we understood Him, praying only for knowledge of His will for us and the power to carry that out.)

Why don't you pray on it?

Desperation slides me to the floor and my knees. I look up past the bed. I can't see Wahlter anymore, but I can see the top section of our window, and the blackness pouring over our home. My bones are tired. I am exhausted by the weight of my powerlessness. I bend my neck, sinking below the dark. My back relaxes. I feel safe.

Where do I start? I have read that I shouldn't ask for anything except (H)is strength and guidance. (G)od is not Santa Claus! Ask and you will not receive! Can I ask (H)im how to get rid of Pain? But isn't that asking for a thing?

Tears swim, ready, always ready to run. I clasp my fingers over my head. My forehead surrenders to the floor.

(G)od. I'm so scared. I'm in so much pain. I'm trying to be grateful for what I have. I really, really am, but Pain blinds me. It feels like no-one cares. They care for a second, but then they forget. I understand. They can't think about It all day like I do. I do. I think about It all the time. Every second of every day. Do (Y)ou care? I feel so alone.

But I do not say any of this. Sadness, like a sponge, absorbs my words. My voice peters out and all I can manage is a whisper.

Please, (G)od. Help me.

I hold my heart with shaking hands. My insides shift like sheets of ice cracking. My chest hurts. I am splitting open. Am I falling?

I keep praying. The tears flow as I rock on my knees.

Please help me.

I lift my head, swiping at my puffy face. I look into the night. I do not see a shooting star, or a burning bush. Wahlter does not hang his head over the side of the bed and lick me on my nose. I clock my arms. Still burning. But I feel a lightness. I do. There's a buoyancy inside my chest. An electric calm.

I crawl into bed noting a flinch of resentment from thighs unfolding to straightness. I inhale a few times, long and shaky. How do I feel? Like the blocks of rage I hurled today have crumbled, and inside the dust cloud of my surrender, I feel calm. Cleared out. Empty, yet full.

I lie down to sleep, kissing Wahlter on his head. I don't want to analyze what happened. I have nothing to testify, no waving hands or speaking in tongues, but sleep comes for my brutalized body tonight, and I am grateful.

It is 8 am. I wake up with a gasp. I am Pain-free. And then It lands. *TwitchSizzleBurn.* The Pain groundhog sees its shadow and then my forearms, calves, the tops of my feet. Pain is staying. I am not healed.

Why don't you pray on it?

Why don't you fuck off.

12

TEETH

February 1977: Age 8 1/4

Her name was Joy. She wore big glasses and a smile as bright as the Trinidadian sun she had left behind. She taught me how to make perfect eggs, lightly fried with a yolk of sunshine. Her dark cheeks wobbled when she laughed, which made me laugh, which made her laugh even more. Sometimes she cleaned the apartment, but mostly she took me and Nicky places Mummy and Daddy couldn't. Mum now worked full-time as a secretary in the English department at The University of Toronto. Daddy had been in the hospital for over two months.

Joy took us to see "The Sound of Music." The lights went down and the music swirled around me. I bounced on the patchy velvet cushion, my eyes zig-zagging across the screen. I loved Maria! With her kind eyes and elegant voice, I wanted to jump onto the screen and twirl through the hills together, our skirts flaring wide.

At the fancy party with gold decor and forbidden champagne, Baroness Schrader looked like a real-life Barbie doll in a gold lamé gown with a gigantic gossamer flower brushing her chin. *Will I ever look that glamorous?* I wondered. When Maria danced with the captain her cheeks went all red, just like mine do when I'm feeling extra happy or sad or embarrassed. Was she embarrassed? She brought her hands to her face and started packing her bag with help from the Baroness who had become all still and breathy. Then Maria snuck downstairs and closed the front door behind her.

NO! My eyes widened, my mouth forming an "O." Was that the end? Why is Maria running away from the children? She loves the children! And then a huge word shimmied onto the screen — Intermission! The movie was only half over. I smiled at Nicky who rested his head on his hand. Was he bored? Maybe he was tired. He did have a big head. "Full of brains" Daddy always said with a smile.

"Thank you for taking us, Joy!" I squealed.

"I knew you would like it," She patted my hand.

"I love it!" I cried, wondering which of the captain's five daughters I was most like. Liesl was so pretty, but Brigitta was clever, and her name was very close to Mum's — Birgitte. I didn't know why, but I felt like it might be better to be clever. Or both. Clever and beautiful.

Or maybe I should just be like Maria, and when I was feeling sad, think of my favorite things, and then I wouldn't feel so bad.

SOME NIGHTS JOY sent us to bed, but on the nights Mum tucked us in, I always asked her the same question.

"When is Daddy coming home?" Mum kissed my cheek. I loved the calm breeze of her, her bob swinging like curtains, the curl at the bottom framing her sculpted face.

"Soon. Your father needs to rest." She tucked my comforter up to my chin without meeting my eyes. I knew she was lying. Daddy could rest at home.

Daddy is going to be fine was all she ever said. But fine from what? No one would tell me. Nicky and I hadn't been allowed to visit him because we were six and eight. You had to be 12 years old to visit someone in the hospital, at least that's what Mum said which made me believe there was something scary about hospitals, something too grownup for my eight-year-old heart to bear. I believed Mum because you had to be 14 years old to use the gym at the rec center. Sometimes I slowed down as I walked by the cracked door and tried to sneak a peek inside the room of mysterious machines and clanking noises. I couldn't wait to grow up. So many secrets I would finally understand.

Her fingertips danced across my forehead. My eyelids fluttered shut. When she turned to go, a thin cloud of her old-fashioned perfume settled on the sheets. Drippings of love left behind to comfort me throughout the night. Her perfume was a hard scent like the strong-scented flowers I loved. Lilacs, roses, hyacinths. Those were my favorite. I loved burying my nose inside the blooms, inhaling the nectar, cleansing my nostrils of the stench of medicine or beer or spit.

"Like this?" she asked, leaving the door open two inches so the light could shine in. I nodded.

"Are you going to run the dryer?" She nodded again. I had to have noise and light and hear her moving in the other room. An arsenal to quiet the noise in my head at night.

"Will we see Daddy soon?"

"Yes, Pussepige. Very soon." Her soft hair swayed as she walked down the hall, and my heart dropped wondering if that was a lie.

THE ELEVATOR REEKED. Sour and old, like the pharmacy across the hall from Daddy's office. I scrunched my nose. The antiseptic stink overwhelmed me, as if I was drowning inside a bottle of medicine. I had just learned what to do if you're drowning — you tread water. You move your legs calmly and wave your arms on the surface like a ballerina. You don't splash around and make things worse. I dug my face into my mitts and breathed in and out. Treading water can save your life.

The elevator clunked as it went up, and the fake wood walls were stained, not like Charlie and his Great Glass Elevator where he could see the whole world shiny and clear below. I swallowed. We were finally going to see Daddy. Why did I feel so jumbly inside? I looked at Nicky who had almost disappeared inside his coat, holding Mummy's hand tight.

The doors opened and we stepped out. Everywhere was bright white light. People moving. Nurses on the phone, bending, writing, typing, standing behind a long counter called the nurses' station. A man pushed a silver frame on wheels full of towels and sheets and blankets. He wore the same clothes as everyone else. Mum said they were called scrubs, a kind of medical uniform. They were an awful green. Not leafy and bright, but infected-looking like snot or vomit. The PA system crackled. *Dr. --- please come to the --- floor. Dr. --- to the ---*. She sounded very stern, like he'd better hurry up and get there.

I hated it here.

Mum leaned down and whispered, the hum of her love brushing my ear.

"There he is..."

My eyes darted around taking in white blurs and flashes of green. Noises flew up around me. Electronic beeping. An abrupt scream from down the hall. Then a burst of laughter. Laughter! There was nothing funny here. My body was shaking, electrified. *Where are you, Daddy?*

Then I saw him. He was walking through the chaos, wearing a hospital gown with dark socks and slippers. He held a silver pole with wheels and plastic bags swinging from the top. One bag was filled with clear liquid, the other a pasty yellow. There were tubes dangling from the bags, moving over him like plastic snakes, slithering into his skinny arms that poked out from his gown.

And then he found me. Our eyes connected. *Daddy!* My heart squeezed so hard I couldn't breathe. His face was smeared with joy. As he shuffled towards us, I watched the gown swirl around him, large and gaping, ridiculous, like a circus tent.

And then he went to smile.

Mum had warned me, but with all the chaos I forgot. His smile spread wider to a grin, and my insides stopped. I felt myself turn, just a little, towards Mum, and then looked at my smiling father again. There was nothing there. Just blackness.

They were all gone.

I wanted to cry. His cheeks drooped without the teeth that had been yanked and drilled from his mouth. It was a horror movie, but real. I couldn't change the channel. I couldn't hide like when the Child Catcher appeared in *Chitty Chitty Bang Bang* with his bug eyes and creepy sing-song promise, "Children! Candy! Allll freeee today!" Daddy would always tell me when to hide my eyes. *What do I do, Daddy?* I wanted to look at him, but didn't want to see. He stood waiting for me, his gummy grin so pure and open. It was Daddy. It was actually him. But it wasn't him at all.

They had started to crack off years ago. One night at supper, we watched as he pulled a piece of tooth from his mouth. Mum and her 16-year-old cousin, who was there to nanny laughed as he put it on his plate. I was so mad at them! Why are you laughing at him? He smiled in a way that hurt me, a smile that came from the head and not the heart. He didn't cry, but he must have been sad. He was 36 and a doctor and his teeth were falling out. His adult teeth would never grow back. You couldn't leave those under your pillow and hope that the tooth fairy would come.

My pity felt like a weight that would break me in half. Like when our Guinea pig, Whiskers got sick. Daddy fed him pink antibiotics from a dropper, holding him so still in his hand. We'd all taken turns holding and kissing him, but Whiskers had still died.

I wish I had a memory of hugging my father. Of burying my nose into his chest and breathing him in, his arms locked around me, growing strong and solid, without infection or tubes or medicine, the reek of hospital drifting away. My cheeks flushing like Maria's. But I don't. I have a shadowy recollection of his room, dark but for a light over the bed, the early winter darkness outside, and homemade get-well cards taped to the wall. But I can't be sure. Maybe I'm just remembering every hospital room that came after his.

And those would be mine.

~

MY PHOTO HAD to be retaken. Mrs. Barter didn't say why. When she told me, I wondered how hideous my first picture had been. Did I look like Medusa with snakes for hair that turned whoever looked at her to stone? Things like this made me feel like there was something wrong with me.

The photo was meant to be a gift for someone special. Right away I knew I would give it to Daddy. Mum was fine on her own. She didn't need a special gift. She was always smiling, even if it didn't reach her eyes, and when Daddy came back from the hospital, it was like he had forgotten how.

I gave him the photo at supper. I don't remember a big response. I think he nodded or said *Thank you, my Darling.* Maybe I expected this photo — with its odd close-up of my awkward smile, my uneven pigtails, my uncentered tie that made me crazy to look at, and my messy *To Daddy* scrawled at the top — to switch the light back on in his eyes.

"MUMMY," I whispered. "Scott Padmore hurt my feelings."

"What did he say?"

"He said what's wrong with your dad?"

Mum lips disappeared. She fiddled with the top of my nightgown. It was my favorite. It said *No I Will Not Go To Bed* on it.

"You have a hole here." She fingered a tiny rip at the top. "I'll fix it for you. Won't that be nice?"

"Mum..."

"I don't know why he would say that. Your father is just tired. He needs to go on vacation." She turned off the light by my bed.

That wasn't the first time I'd heard *Daddy just needs to go on vacation*. Why didn't he? I loved summer vacation! Swimming at the rec center, exploring the rock garden beneath our building with Nicky, finding caterpillars under the leaves with their millions of feet and wild circus tent-like stripes. Sometimes I saw my friends, wore dresses, and had candy. Vacation was magic.

Could I convince him to go? I turned towards the light coming through the cracked door. I couldn't drive or cook and barely used the phone, although I had memorized our phone number in case of an emergency. I was such a child. A dumb baby girl. But I was smart enough to know I wasn't being told everything. I could smell the lies. They stunk like skunk, touching everything. Mum couldn't hide her lying beneath her soft distractions and the sweet smell of her perfume. Even Scott Padmore could see the truth. At least, part of it. What was all of it?

I'd be asked to leave the room, then strain to hear through closed doors, my heart pounding, knowing I should "give them their privacy." I curled my legs into my chest. There was a pit in my stomach all the time. And I didn't know what to do.

I turned onto my back and looked at the ceiling for a while. I thought about Joy who was gone now that Daddy was home, and I kinda wished she was still here with her bright smile, and her eggs.

I brought my hands together and closed my eyes.

Dear God. Please keep Daddy alive until I am 20.

Was it okay to make up my own prayer?

I didn't know.

I didn't know anything.

13

MITTELSCHMERTZ

August 11th, 2016: Day 518

And so I began to pray.

What I love about AA is their way to recover from alcoholism is suggestive. *We realize we know only a little.* (pg. 164) In one of our founder's story (Bill's Story), his now sober friend Ebby suggests, "Why don't you choose your own conception of God?" (pg. 12) and Bill's head explodes.

Upon a foundation of complete willingness I might build what I saw in my friend. Would I have it? Of course I would! Bill wanted a relationship with (G)od, and so did I.

I figured if I got to choose my own conception of (G)od, that meant I could talk to (H)im any way I wanted. I chose to pray on my knees because I felt safe there, like something was watching over me. Sometimes I rocked, and as feelings rose, I'd let (H)im have it. *I've been sick my whole life! I don't deserve this!* I'd give (H)im the middle finger yelling *Fuck you!*, flailing around in the throes of a 44-year-old temper tantrum, which looked pretty much the same as a 5-year-old's.

The most curious thing began to happen. By offering Pain

through prayer, something inside me would shift. Every time, I'd be gifted with the same feeling. Electric calm. Empty, but full.

In 2016, I had been alive for 28 years because of kidney transplantation. Every time I went to Cedars for those early morning blood draws, I was reminded that science fiction wasn't a world set in The Future with spacecrafts and armored uniforms, but the complicated simplicity of my daily fistful of pills.

"Good morning!" My extra sunny greeting is known as "fake it 'til you make it" in the recovery community. Be nice even though you feel like garbage, and we promise you'll be glad you did!

"You look wonderful," my phlebotomist offered, organizing the tubes.

"I do?" My eyes narrowed, suspect.

"You do. You are glowing." he added with a snap of the tourniquet.

Surely you jest, Blood Technician Man. Was he blind? (This would not be the best quality in a person who sticks needles into people's arms for a living.) I had taken note of my puffy eyes (Thank you, Pain) and cold sore (Thank you, Kevin). What the heck did he see?

Pulling off my jean jacket felt like fingernails scraping a sunburn. As the needle plunged into my vein, I said a little prayer. *Please, (G)od. Please. Help them find something they can treat.*

Undiagnosis triggers a peculiar longing — wanting something to be wrong with you. A condition that can be highlighted in a textbook. Black print means treatment. I wanted a diagnosis like blood cancer or MS. Forgive me, but I did.

Living in medical limbo meant there was no arc of treatment and healing. No "Beginning, Middle, and End." This saying also gets thrown around the rooms of recovery by well-meaning fellows who believe every problem is fixable, or to be fair, want every problem to be fixable. The idea that Pain ends.

While this saying might apply to coming up with rent or breaking up with someone you've known five months, it was hard for me to believe in an end to Undiagnosis, without a diagnosis. I needed a Future to believe in. Just knowing what I had would help me, even if it was terminal. I believed that.

Even more, the What Ifs were getting loud. *What If I had gone to the ER that night? What If I had gone to urgent care like Lori suggested?* And the If Onlys were even louder. *If Only I hadn't used that pumice stone in the tub.* Yes, The Past was a minefield of regret I had to dodge.

So where did this leave me? In lockstep with The Present, with a band aid on my arm and an undercurrent of fear I couldn't shake. As I pushed the door open onto Beverly Blvd., I remember saying out loud, *Now I am going to cry.* And I did.

All the way home.

~

A FEW HOURS LATER, I screaming was on my floor, clutching my stomach. I knew what this meanness courtesy of the female reproductive system was — a ruptured ovarian cyst.

In January of 2013, I'd been diagnosed with this and sent home with a script for Percocet which sparked a seven-month narcotic run that, by its end, found me nodding off as I drove down Big Bear mountain. I knew that's what Kevin was thinking when I called him in Scotland and told him a sober girlfriend was driving me to Saint Joseph's Medical Center in Burbank.

I hobbled through the sliding doors as Michelle parked. My pain was a 10! 10! 10! In my addiction, I'd been careful never to say 10, playing my cards against the desperate drug addict that I was. *Only an amateur would be obvious and say 10 when seeking drugs!* Now that drugs were off the table, I was owning my 10.

I flinched as the nurse practitioner inserted an IV. The groovy thing about being a transplant patient is you often get a Fast Pass in the ER. Front-of-the-line hospital admission because certain medical issues can take The Kid south pretty fast. Fever. Infection. And yes, a ruptured cyst can interfere with kidney function, which is dicey when you only have one. The not-so-groovy thing about being a transplant patient, well, I don't have time to make that list.

My nurse practitioner was Nicole. Efficiency reined. Intake. Check. Blood and urine. Check. Ultrasound. Check. Then Nicole asked,

"How bad is your pain?"

"It's pretty bad."

"Do you want something for pain?"

Oh, Heck. Did I want something for pain? Please. Does a bird have wings? Nothing turns the crank of this pharmaceutical whore the way those words do. I heard a whisper, not untrue: *You are in pain. You are justified.*

"I'm okay."

"Well, let me know if you change your mind." Yup. I know where the call button is, Honey.

Bedside Wi-Fi was spotty, so I shuffled to the bathroom. Kevin was relieved to know Michelle was with me. I'd had her text him from her phone. It had taken Kevin three years to trust my sobriety enough to attend a meeting and give me a cake celebrating three years clean. 1,095 days may seem like a while when you're waiting for a check to clear, but in our world, the one littered with not-so-little white lies, it was a blip. Inside the tornado of my addiction, I wouldn't have been above texting Kevin that Michelle was with me when she wasn't.

Our marital storm had passed, but the wreckage lingered. Some nights we'd watch TV, relaxed and engaged and a scene with drugs or alcohol would pop up. I'd feel a shift in Kevin's energy, like a storm cloud moving in. He'd turn to me and confess, "I can't go through that again." It hurt, his eyes gone suddenly black, but it was the reminder I needed. Often. I had not been the only one who had suffered.

I flushed the toilet and opened Facebook. Hmmm. A hospital check-in. How lame would that be? How self-serving. How millennial of me.

As I sat on the lid, I typed. *In the ER with abdominal pain. Having an ultrasound to make sure "The Kid" is safe and sound. #Sobergirl* I paused. My finger hovered over "Post." I bit my lip. There's just no coming back from cyber space. I pressed my finger down and *WHOOSH!* The truth was out there. A truth I wanted to live.

Nicole came 'round again. I declined again, which was starting to be a real drag when I heard the patient on my left get Ativan and the patient on my right get morphine. As I squirmed in the bed, my once-upon-a-time twistedly blissful cocoon of illness and euphoria, the voice whispered again. *You can have one pill. The ER is a pharmaceutical Switzerland. Drugs don't count in here.* Nicole handed me some papers.

"You have something called Mittelschmertz."

Mittelschmertz is German for mid-cycle pain caused by ovulation. Why the medical establishment chose to appropriate this bonkers word, I have no idea. Maybe because it's so much fun to say, less to experience. Now that I had my diagnosis, I knew this pain would pass. There would be a Beginning, Middle, and End. For the second time that day, tears flowed.

"I turned down pain meds." Michelle got up and kissed my forehead.

Then I looked at the printout of my labs. My creatinine was 0.89 — the lowest it had ever been, even immediately after transplant. This number means nothing to you, but everything, everything to me. A low creatinine for a transplant patient is the joy of a normal blood sugar for a diabetic or a clean PET scan in a cancer patient. As I placed my hand over my abdomen, where The Kid called home, it was impossible for me not to think about the myriad ways addiction had nearly destroyed everything. Somehow, by seconds and inches, I had not lost my kidney, my marriage or my life. And looking at Michelle, I knew with a shivery certainty that these miracles had not happened because of me alone.

Michelle had a migraine brewing and left just ahead of me. Guess who I bumped into with literally one foot out the door?

"You sure you don't want anything?" Nicole asked. I was this close to throwing my arms around her in surrender. *"Okay! If you insist!"*

Can there be a course burnt into every medical professional's mind that if a patient says they are in recovery NEVER OFFER

THEM PAIN MEDS AGAIN. Because with Michelle halfway home, that voice whispered once more: *You could just ask for four pills. One for tonight and three tomorrow. Or eight. Two for tonight and six tomorrow... Maybe nine. A final one for the morning after...*

But I was #Sobergirl. Did you know the "S" on Superman's chest does not stand for Super but is the Kryptonian symbol for hope? If I could turn down my kryptonite, it must mean somehow, somewhere, I had Hope. I smiled, feeling pretty goddamn heroic.

Which brings me back to Blood Technician Man. That morning, he'd spotted a glow. Something I was not feeling but existed all the same. Dared I name it?

With a small g.

~

AUGUST 22ND, 2016: Day 529

11 days later, we were having sex in Palm Springs, and I wanted it to end. I know what you're thinking. It wasn't that. It was Pain. Consuming our frolic, the way a fire consumes a home. The curtains, carpet, drywall, and then explosive flame as the roof collapses into the inferno. Dramatic? Perhaps. But it was tragic that I found no joy. I never I wanted to be here. Here meant the unbearable friction of Kevin's chest hair against my nakedness. Skin rubbing. Heat flaring. I counted the minutes, my heart breaking with each thrust. Even with my husband inside me, Pain was the only one I thought about.

We were staying at The Ritz in Rancho Mirage courtesy of Kevin's obsessive quest for The Deal. Super fanciness abounded. There were multiple pools, high thread counts and a candy bar every afternoon. (My kind of bar!) I had hoped that midday temps of 118 degrees would somehow counteract the heat of Pain. Two negatives equaling a positive and all, but no. There was no escape. Not even with a cliffside view of Palm Springs and Joshua Tree National Park in the distance.

"I'm going to take a nap," Kevin turned over, hugging a pillow.

"I'm going for a walk." I had no plan as I wandered through the conference area. A ballroom was being set up with flowers and a fake wood dance floor that clicked together. The smell of money wafted from the freesias in crystal and appetizers on warming trays. In a hallway, I sat on the edge of an exquisitely upholstered couch thinking how meaningless wealth was when you couldn't exist comfortably in your own skin. In AA we shared about being comfortable in our skin emotionally. I was neither. I had to get out of this.

Shirley was a fellow alcoholic. A regular attendee of my home group — your most regularly attended meeting where you have a commitment, like making coffee or stacking chairs, and people miss you when you don't show up. The thing I loved about Shirley was the way she wore her heart on her sleeve. I latched onto vulnerables. When she admitted her sponsor said she'd never known a greater mental masturbator than Shirley, well, I dug that kind of honesty. She was as self-obsessed as me!

She was smart but cripplingly insecure, yet secure enough to share about how insecure she was, which might have been deflection, but I was into it. She had a strong message about recovery. In Detroit, she had been able to stay sober for some time through fellowship (hanging out with other recovering alcoholics) but had relapsed. She said she'd needed a Higher Power.

We'd exchanged a few calls. She'd called when Liz relapsed, wanting to be there for me. We'd commented on each other's shares, but I wouldn't classify us as friends. That I felt compelled to call her is the magic of Alcoholics Anonymous.

"Shirley?" my voice felt contained. I swallowed hard. A vacuum cleaner hummed down the hall. The thing about recovering alcoholics is that we don't mess around with the amuse bouche or half-salads. We dive right into the main course. The ache. Our hurt. Where we are bleeding. Show me. Help me cut my meat.

"No one can help me." I told her about the two dermatologists, the allergist/ immunologist, my transplant team and neurologist, Dr. A., who five days ago said my Pain had nothing to do with my nerves and he couldn't help me.

"I can't take it anymore."

Shirley told me about the debilitating headaches she'd suffered with for over a year. How she endured a similar journey without answers. How one day, on a repeat brain MRI, when she teetered at the edge of hope, an extra area of her neck was unintentionally scanned, and bingo. A radiologist discovered the source of her pain had nothing to do with her brain but was an upper vertebrae issue.

"Don't let anyone's else's limitations stop you. Keep going, Henriette."

She was right. My body relaxed with the bonding that happens between two alkies, so quick and permanent, like spiritual crazy glue I didn't mind getting all over my hands. I felt it from Rancho Mirage to Panorama City, through our soup cans and long white string, with nothing getting lost in translation.

"Thank you." I whispered.

She quoted from the Big Book: *"...and I can find no serenity until I accept that person, place, thing, or situation as being exactly the way it is supposed to be at this moment. Nothing, absolutely nothing, happens in God's world by mistake."* (pg. 417)

She continued. "In your world, this pain is bad. You don't know what this pain means in God's world."

I flinched. *How can Pain be anything but bad?*

"Do you believe in a punishing God?"

"No," I breathed.

"I don't think God is punishing you, Henriette. And I don't think he makes mistakes."

I circled the hotel, the desert sun unable to scald me anymore. "Hot stuff!" Kevin would joke when I got back to the room. I felt the lightness of a small smile land on my lips.

Oh, how I craved making sense of this. Of course, I was going to look at Pain as bad. In my world that's all it could be. It hurt. I was having trouble sleeping. It affected Kevin. It affected everything. How could Pain be anything but punishment?

Shirley's words came back to me, and my stomach flipped with possibility. Was there another way to look at it?

You don't know what this pain means in God's world.

So maybe I needed to spend time more time there.

14

DENMARK

Summer 1977: Age 8 3/4

In June, Nicky and I went to Denmark to spend eight weeks with Mum's parents, Bedstemor (grandmother) and Bedstefar (grandfather), which literally means "best mother" and "best father" in Danish. And they were.

They lived in an area south of Copenhagen called Greve Strand. Bedstefar built a two-room structure on this plum-tree filled land in the early 1950's and over the years had further built it into a home. It had a rose garden with blooms of every shade — white, coral, red, pink, and even a few yellow. He trimmed them with ancient iron clippers, while Bedstemor hung the laundry on the line outside. But just as often you would find Bedstefar washing the dishes and Bedstemor organizing paperwork.

Summer moved slow. On rainy days, Bedstefar, tall and strong, would bring down Aunt Elsebeth's Barbie collection from the attic. She had a Barbie and a Skipper with outfits from the 60's and 70's. The clothes were bold and fun, with hats and purses and sunglasses — a snapshot into the era when my parents dated in London and sailed to Canada. Sometimes Bedstefar set up a massive table where Nicky and I created cities with train tracks and Matchbox cars. The rain pattered on the roof as we made up stories of families going to work and school until Bedstemor called us for lunch, and I felt relieved. Sometimes playing family would make me sad.

Denmark was breezy and rarely hot like the stifling Toronto summers that required the air conditioning of Daddy's office. On warm days we went to the beach. Bedstefar biked as if he sat at a desk, his thick glasses fixed to his face. Bedstemor leaned forward on her handlebars, closing her eyes against the sun, her gray-blond hair blowing everywhere. The streets were lush and quiet, just birds chattering and the satisfying crunch of pebbles beneath our tires.

I kicked my legs off the pedals as wings. I could smell the water from here. Fresh and wild, not chlorine-sharp. The air felt lighter. I felt lighter.

Suddenly, I felt a *whoosh!* and Nicky zoomed past me, head down, legs whirling.

"Last one there is a rotten egg!" he smirked.

"No fair!" I called. Nicky was almost seven, but getting stronger than me every day, which I wasn't sure I liked.

We loped down the white sand hills, landscaped by tall, thick grasses whipping in the wind. Bedstemor organized the blankets and open-faced sandwiches as Nicky and I ran to the shore. The water was clean, but the beach had masses of seaweed. It was dark brown and a bit smelly but had neat bulbs that popped when you stepped on them, which I didn't do that often because the seaweed was really slimy and felt super funny to walk on.

Bedstefar waded in, scanning the water. I knew he was looking for jellyfish, transparent blobby things that floated near the top of the bay with four lavender-colored eyes in the center. Those ones were harmless, but we'd always scream *vandmand!* (Danish for jellyfish) if we ever saw one because I sure didn't want to brush up against its creepy-looking self. The ones that were dangerous were called *brandmand!* which literally means fireman, which was funny because Bedstefar was in his last year working as a fireman. Bedstemor said their sting was a hundred times worse than a bee's. Sometimes there were so many bobbing in the water it was dangerous to swim. But

Bedstefar was already in past his knees, so I galloped after him, water splashing under my feet.

He reached for my hand on one side and Nicky's on the other. I giggled with anticipation. My shoulders were so lovely and warm in the summer sun. Did I really want to get wet? The water lapped up on my bathing suit and I screamed.

"Chicken!" Nicky taunted, his eyes crinkling against the bright sun.

"I'm not ready!" I sputtered. The water wasn't freezing, but it definitely wasn't warm like the rec center pool back home.

"Okay, nu begynder vi!" Bedstefar boomed. We squeezed hands and began our countdown of tens.

"Ti! Tyve! Tredive!..." Cold drops sprayed us as we squatted in time. I laughed, leaping away from the water.

"...Fyrre! Halvtreds! Tres! Halvfjerds!...Bedstefar's grip was both tender and firm.

"...Firs! Halvfems! HUNDERE!" SPLASH! Underwater we all went, Nicky holding his nose as he plunged. The shock of the cool electrified me, sending me wiggling back to the top. With a gasp of delight I surfaced, feeling cracked open, shooting my arms high above my head.

"Bedstemor!" I called out, waving. She was always there, game to swim, but usually hanging back with a camera in hand, documenting it all.

I took a huge breath and exhaled. And it was easy.

But that feeling had followed me here. The feeling that Something Is Wrong. It had followed me across the vastness of the Atlantic Ocean. It had not stayed behind at the Air Canada gate in Toronto. It landed in Copenhagen, greeted by Bedstemor and Bedstefar, Elsebeth and my soon-to-be Uncle Willy, all of them waving Danish flags and hands like we were royalty, but we were just Nicky and me.

Velkommen til lille Danmark, søde børn! (Welcome to little Denmark, sweet children!)

It was here. Branded on my heart the way the medicinal stink of Daddy's pharmacy burned my nose and made me frown. It was here, along with the strange language and bag of black licorice in my lap as I removed the *Unaccompanied Minor* lanyards we had to wear around our necks the entire flight. (They were wrong, though. Nicky and I were not unaccompanied. We had each other.)

Maybe Nicky felt the feeling, too.

He got homesick in a way I didn't. He was so sensitive, watching me with big eyes over a freckled nose, often disappearing alone in the garden for a long while. One night, I woke up to crying. He was missing Toronto: our bunk beds, Mummy's soft touch and Daddy's curious games. By the time Bedstemor came in I was crying, too. *I do miss my own bed!* (Crying felt like an infectious disease sport. If I saw someone else cry, I was compelled to participate.)

"If you are so sick for your home, we send you back?" Bedstemor offered in her broken English with her whole heart. My breath caught. "You want that?"

NO! We shook our heads, Nicky wiping his nose with his pajama sleeve. We didn't want that. I loved the sweetness of summer life here. The ease of awkward conversation with Bedstefar — his broken English to our broken Danish. Bedstemor's permanent smile. And the smells that calmed: fresh cut grass that Bedstefar buzzed down with his reel mower, the drizzle of melted vanilla ice cream on my dress, the waft of butter and onions sizzling in the pan, and the drops of paint thinner that Bedstefar wiped off his hands. It all smelled like good.

We got mail from Toronto. Mum's letters written in her contained elegance on thin Aerogramme paper folded and sealed to form a letter. Daddy sent brown-paper packages with his dramatic penmanship on the front. Inside were cassette tapes he created like an audio variety show. They were full of songs from the radio, snippets from rugby games (I didn't care about those!) and segments from radio plays. Sometimes he told us about his patients. *Mrs. Kelley also has asthma troubles in her chest.* I'd picture him in his office, newspaper spread on his desk, the sun coming in the window that overlooked his parking spot for the Pacer. It was a different car from the Jag, but still a fun ride because Nicky and I would squish together in the trunk that was like a giant glass bubble.

We sat by Bedstemor's cassette player, black licorice on the table, heads on hands, chomping on sugar and joy.

"You want to send your love to Henriette and Nicholas?" Daddy held Mr. Brown, our Guinea pig up to the microphone. Brownie's *squeaksqueaksqueak* made my heart flip.

"Brownieee!" I squealed, laying my head on the table closer to the machine. Brownie's fur was a rich chocolate brown like Daddy's.

"Ohhh, you're a darling, aren't you?" Daddy laughed, his voice all gooey. Then I heard his voice lift.

"Oh, here's your mother. Come and say a word." The machine clicked off. When Daddy returned he sounded different. "Ah, as usual she's too busy. Off to see a play at the theatre..."

Why couldn't she just say hello? It made no sense. She'd been right there. My disappointment stung like a paper cut. I glanced over at Nicky, his eyes fluttering in sleep. I was glad he hadn't heard this. He didn't need to know what I already did. They mailed their letters separately, so what were the chances they were ever together? I turned off the cassette player. Sometimes I wondered if I would be homesick for Denmark once I got home.

ONE AFTERNOON, as walked into Bilka (think Target), I spotted the front page of a newspaper.

ELVIS ER DØD.

I shivered. I knew what død meant. Dead. The word looked scary in Danish, especially the creepy ø. Like the capital letters in the Bible. Alarming-looking letters from a foreign world.

Elvis Presley was dead.

I knew Elvis from our records and Saturday afternoon movies full of dancing and fainting women. He seemed so full of life in his Bedazzled clothes and wet black hair. How could he be dead? I stared as we passed the newspaper stand, unable to stop looking at the headline. How could death have landed here, among the teeny daisies that sprinkled Bedstefar's lawn, where Bedstemor's warm hand guided me through the turnstile into the store?

I stayed close to my grandparents as we shopped, unable to explain how icky this news felt. They said his heart had given out, but Elvis was only 42! Bedstemor was 57 and Bedstefar was 59. Why would he die before them?

On his next cassette, Daddy talked about Elvis.

"Today is Tuesday August 16th. Well, the big news of course, Mr. Elvis Presley, the guy with the swivelling hips, the Rock 'n Roll King, he died today. He was very, very popular at the same time as the Beatles..." Then he played one of Elvis' songs.

Oh, well a-bless my soul / But what's wrong with me?

I'm itchin' like a man on a fuzzy tree.

Daddy came back on the cassette energized, his voice higher, as if he'd been filled up like a balloon. "Well, I don't know about you, but that really makes me feel good!" Then he started riffing, loud and silly-sounding.

"...My heart beats so...and I don't know if I'm gonna die...oh my, I'm all shook up!" I sat up with a shock. Die? Why would he say that?

I pictured him wiggling around, a cigarette locked between his fingers, his dentures ("choppers" as he called them) beaming out a smile so straight and new. Alive. He sounded so alive.

"And your father happens to be a mad dad!" He paused and breathed, "And I do love you both so much." Then he laughed, rich with emotion. "I really do, even though I'm all shook up. Yup!" Then he made a funny sound and stopped the cassette.

Tears filled my eyes, and an ache burned in the bottom of my tummy, as deep and wide as the ocean between us.

~

Bedstemor and Bedstefar were very active, swimming and biking every day. Bedstefar would bike the 21 km into Copenhagen for his fireman shifts. Biking was a huge part of Danish culture, so we got hand-me-down bikes to use for the summer. Nicky's was orange, and mine was purple, just like my favorite drink, Crush grape soda.

After supper, in the brightness of a Danish summer night, we biked. Sometimes we'd go to my aunt's new house by the beach, passing small markets that sold IS! (ice cream). I'd mull the choices in my head in case Bedstemor made the rare offer to stop and get one, but usually we'd just pedal on by. Sugar was still a rare treat even way across the ocean.

We'd ride deep into the countryside, passing old farmhouses from the 1700's with yellow walls and thatched roofs. We drifted down flat and silent paths, biking without hands, the wind whispering through huge patches of bright yellow mustard stalks swaying as if locked in a dance.

For non-practicing Lutherans my grandparents sure loved to visit churches. I felt the same way about churches in Denmark as I did at home: I'd go if I had to. The church in Greve was all white inside with accents of gold — gold crucifixes, gold candle holders and a wooden pulpit covered in gold murals of scenes from the Bible.

We leaned our bikes against the crumbling wall bordering the cemetery. Bedstefar opened a gate that complained with a squeak, then started down a pathway of tiny stones. I made a face. I didn't really want to follow him but didn't want to be left behind. *Crunch. Crunch. Crunch.* Some of the headstones were flat to the ground, grasses crawling over their iron façades. I could barely make out some of the names. *Søren. Jens. Annette.* Henriette was a very Danish name. I didn't want to find Henriette on a headstone.

I looked back at Nicky. He shuffled along, quiet. Mum would have told him to pick up his feet. I wasn't sure why Bedstemor and Bedstefar thought this was fun. I looked away from the headstones into the surrounding gardens. There were bushes of strong-smelling wild roses everywhere, blooms of fuchsia, coral and cherry pink. I loved picking them and bringing them home for Bedstemor. She'd put them in a vase with a smile, but said it was a shame because they died soon after.

I turned down another path of headstones. Some dates were hard to imagine. 1878 seemed so long ago. I noticed on one headstone the year of birth and death was the same. A child had been alive for forty days. Then I thought I would make a game of it. I would try to find the youngest baby to die.

A small, moss-covered headstone caught my eye. I gently pushed the greenery away with my hand. A child had been alive for four days. The backs of my knees wobbled. That wasn't even a week. What had happened to that child? It had died in the 1930's before Daddy was even born. Four days. Was that even a life? What had that child done in four days? Opened its eyes? Drank milk? Pooped? I shivered, wondering what had come for that child. Was it like what had come for Elvis?

THE SUN DISAPPEARED, but the night sky was tinted a warm periwinkle. Unsettled, I lay with my eyes open. It was weird going to bed when it was still light out. Nicky lay across the small room from me, not above me in our red bunk bed at home with the drawers that held our Brio trains and Legos. It was so quiet here. No dryer running or vacuum cleaner humming in the background. Bedstemor did all her cleaning in the day when she could see best, and running the dryer was too expensive.

Outside our window birds chirped into the night. Their song made my heart turn inside out like a backwards sweater with the tag showing. It was a beautiful sound that promised an understanding of the confusion in my heart. Things I would one day understand. Like what was the point of a child being here for four days?

One night, Bedstemor told us there was a movie on TV about the Lindberg baby kidnapping. We were excited to give our brains a break from this weird language. We learned Danish mostly through immersion, by looking in stores or at billboards when we drove into Copenhagen or pointing to objects and asking Bedstemor and Bedstefar what they meant. Whenever there was English programming we were allowed to watch it for the subtitles that helped us learn.

The movie was a little boring. A man named Richard Hauptmann was arrested after taking a ransom for kidnapping the Lindberg baby. There were tons of court room scenes that went on and on. I wondered if Bedstemor would let me have an open-faced sandwich with chocolate for night-time tea. Nicky was falling asleep across the room. His head kept slipping off his hand. The better story would have been Charles Lindberg flying across the ocean like we had. In 1927, Lindberg had flown from New York to Paris (3800 miles) which took him over 33 hours. Our flight from Toronto to Copenhagen (3900 miles) only took 7 ½ hours!

Suddenly, Hauptmann was found GUILTY! and sentenced to DEATH!

I felt a sharpness in my chest. Nicky had drifted off on the couch, looking so nice with his long eyelashes closed. Bedstefar sat in the throne-like wooden chair he'd made. It had pillows on the base and back that were tied with thin fabric straps. I didn't like sitting in it because it was a straight up and down chair like in school. His arms were folded and he wore a slight smile. He didn't look scared at all. Clanking sounds came from the kitchen where Bedstemor prepared tea for after the movie. My heart pounded. When was she coming back?

A group of guards and priests lead Hauptmann into a room with a chair like Bedstefar's, but bigger. It had huge arms with straps on them, but the straps hung down and were made of leather. I wanted to tell Bedstefar to turn off the TV, but I couldn't open my mouth. I was frozen with fear. Hauptmann's head had been shaved which made his eyes look huge. Two guards strapped him to the chair and I realized: this was an electric chair. They were going to kill him.

The priest sounded robotic as he read lines from the open Bible in his hands. His voice was distant and unfriendly, not like the warmness I felt when Mum tucked me in for the night. I would not want to hear those voices right before I died. I would want Daddy. And Mummy. And Nicky. And Mr. Brown. And Bedstemor and Bedstefar.

"Bedstemor..." I squeaked. My throat had gone dry. Daddy wasn't here to tell me to look away. I couldn't make myself look away. I couldn't move. I couldn't stop them from killing him.

Then a man lowered what looked like a lamp shade over Hauptmann's head. The camera moved across a row of men holding pens and paper in their hands, watching Hauptmann's final moments on Earth. The camera went close on Hauptmann's face. His eyes were blank. Their light had gone out.

And then the scene ended.

Lying in bed later, I remembered this was a true story. It was called non-fiction. Not Fake. That was the way I remembered it for school. I rolled onto my side so I could watch Nicky sleep. He was lucky he'd missed the last part of the movie. I held my stomach with both hands. What went through a man's head when he knew he was about to die? As he walked over to the chair, did he think *I will never walk again.* When the priests finishing praying did he think *Now I am going to meet God.* Or did he think *Now I will be going to Hell.*

GUILTY! DEATH!

That night, I was afraid to close my eyes. I felt my heart under the sheets, ricocheting against my small chest, beating the awful thrum of Something Is Wrong.

What. is. it? What. is. it?

I fell asleep listening to new sounds. Not the dryer or the vacuum that I couldn't hear across an ocean. I listened to Nicky's thick breathing, nasal and small. The quiet shuffle of my grandparents readying for bed. And birds chirping in the shadowy lightness of a Danish summer night, reminding me that life went on even in the dark.

15

GABAPENTIN

September 15th, 2016: Day 553

I sat in the waiting area at USC Keck Dermatology, summarizing 35 years of medical issues into tiny boxes, wondering why they only leave half an inch for your list of medications. I scribbled "please see over" unscored by a huge arrow. Then I checked my attitude and reminded myself to have Hope. Dermatologist #3 had experience in HIV and other immunocompromised patients.

Maybe this time.

Dr. A. walked in with a messy ponytail and no lines on her face. It's a surreal moment when your physicians start clocking in younger than you. I wanted to ask, "How are these big words spilling from your mouth because you look like you should be getting ready for prom."

"Before we start, I want to tell you how heroic your recovery is."

To recap, I was three years sober. One of my non-negotiables in recovery is to state on every medical form that I am not, under any circumstances — even when clinging to their coattails as they slap me with the triplicate pad I'm jonesing for — to be prescribed anything mind-altering. When Dr. A. offered her kudos, it landed with a curious weight.

"Are you in recovery?" I asked. "Do you know someone who is?"

"I had a progressive mentor at UCSF who suggested we go to an AA meeting. Alcoholism really hijacks the brain..."

Her open-mindedness was thrilling. Alcoholics Anonymous is a program that is often misunderstood. It's dismissed as religious (it's spiritual) or held in contempt by those who have never been to a meeting or worked the 12 Steps. And especially by those find the concept of God problematic.

She was everything you want in a physician. She held eye contact, listened without interruption, and actually read the 40 forms I had filled out. If they're making docs like Dr. A. these days, I'm all in.

"I'm going to start you on Capzasin."

Capzasin is an over-the-counter ointment made of chili peppers that could block pain messages from my nerves. Capzasin sounded like smearing lava all over my skin, which seemed like an odd intervention given the whole "do no harm" thing, but hey, I was already a big fan of Dr. A, who shall hereto going forward be known as Dr. A+.

"I wouldn't know where to put it. I burn everywhere except my face and torso."

"Start at the origin site. If this doesn't work, we can talk about a pill."

I wanted to say *Can we go right to the pill?* but I was willing to try. What was one more week trapped in the burning fires of Hell when pills were on their way? Ah, Hope. Is there anything like the bubble of hope you float away in after seeing the doctor? Goofily smiling at everyone you pass because you're inflated with the possibility you may not spend the rest of your life in pain?

The perennial patient understands this. We do not dream of shiny cars or leather purses or designer gowns, but of a day when we don't have to sleep on specially purchased sheets. A morning when we jump out of bed, not scanning our bodies for pain, or chafe-testing an item of clothing against our skin. A life of being able to take our health for granted. Which is ironic because if that day ever came, I would be the last person on earth who would ever take her health for granted again.

September 22nd, 2016: Day 560

All Capzasin did was literally burn my arm. Now I had burns on top of flares. A week later, I sat in the exam room, twitching for the promised pill. This would fix everything!

"It's called Gabapentin. I'm going to start you at 300 mg a day which is basically a homeopathic dose."

She explained that Gabapentin was first prescribed for epilepsy and seizures, but its use had been expanded to include insomnia, anxiety, back pain, nerve pain (from diabetes and shingles) and detoxing from narcotics. I picked it up from the same Rite Aid where I used to meet Her. My pulse thrilled at a quick glimpse of this new and sunny yellow bauble through the translucent container. Hello, Gabapentin!

Please let this change how I feel in my skin.

Do I wish I had researched Gabapentin the way I researched my very first medications? In 1983, when I was diagnosed with chronic kidney disease at 13, there was no internet, no Google, no cell phones. No "Hey Siri, please tell me what Prednisone will do to me." Nope. This flat-chested teen, my growth already stunted, too late to follow in the Glamazonian footsteps of my Viking Danish cousins, took the subway from my High Park home, knapsack on my lap, and walked to the Metro Toronto Reference Library, inhaling that particular musty odor — the precious scent of knowledge — then made my way to the medical section and asked where I might find the definitions of medications that, little did I know, I'd be on for the next 40 years.

Imuran caused hair loss and Prednisone caused moonface, weight gain, and anxiety. I Xerox-ed the pages and highlighted my future in yellow. Then I sheathed these facts about myself in plastic, stuck them in my knapsack, and hopped a train home into a bizarre new world of pharmaceuticals.

I had a complicated case of kidney failure — Glomerulonephritis with three different types of scarring on my glomeruli. (Glomeruli (tubes) are attached to tubules (smaller tubes) and are the filtering system for the kidney.) This diagnosis was so rare that my pathology (tissue sample) was taken to a conference where only a Polish boy shared my diagnosis. It was kinda like making the Dean's List of Diseases, except instead of an award, I got a transplant.

At 14, I lived in the shadow of my doctor-father's death. Medical Science had been our world: cough medicine for a cough, a polio vaccine to prevent polio, and insulin for his diabetes. When a doctor said something was wrong with me, I did what they said. If they told me these meds would slow the deterioration of my kidneys, I was swallowing. But what made Young Hen (who was admittedly more for the books and less for the partying — irony!) go scholastic on her disease? And where was she in 2016 when I needed her?

Do I wish I'd posted on Facebook "Guys! Anyone ever taken Gabapentin?" Do I wish I had found the 2010 lawsuit against Pfizer who fraudulently marketed Gabapentin for uses not approved by the FDA? Let me put it this way. If, out of all the bad moves I've made in my life, I had the opportunity to take one of them back, it would be the decision to start Gabapentin. I would never have picked up the bottle from Rite Aid. I would never have swallowed that pill. I would never have wanted to hear the word Gabapentin again.

Or would I?

~

PAIN LOG 2016:

Started Gabapentin at 300 mg qd (daily).

September 23rd, 2016: Day 561

September 26th, 2016: Day 564

Dr. A+ increased Gabapentin to 600 mg qd. Had my second skin biopsy.

October 1st, 2016: Day 569

Pain seems better!

October 14th, 2016: Day 582
Dr. A+ increased Gabapentin to 900 mg qd. Had a massage today.
October 16th, 2016: Day 584
Pain is 85% gone. I barely thought about it today. Pain a 1-2.
October 17th, 2016: Day 585
Pain a 2-3. I wouldn't want to live this way.
October 26th, 2016: Day 594
Pain a 5-6. I hate this.

October 27th, 2016: Day 595

"I want to stop taking Gabapentin. I want another steroid shot."

"A steroid shot can backfire if overused." Dr. A+'s smooth skin crinkled with concern.

I didn't care. I was out. Gabapentin lowered my Pain some days, then others not at all. Dr. A+ didn't know why. Docs go by the facts, sometimes sharing them with a flaccid shrug. She said she had seen it work for some and not others. I wanted to scream, "Why isn't it working for me?" but I liked Dr. A+ too much. To be fair, doctors know what they know based on what they've read or been told by other doctors or patient experience or been tricked into believing by pharmaceutical reps.

Gabapentin is not a painkiller, it's an anti-convulsant. I didn't feel anything on Gabapentin, so I didn't understand it. Opiates I understood. When I took one Percocet I felt better. Two, even better. Three, fantastic. And so on. Gabapentin made no sense. When on it, I could enjoy hours with low-level Pain, only to feel It shift and flare as bad as ever.

"And you haven't been doing anything differently?"

"No."

I wanted the shot. Kenalog (a corticosteroid) had been the only thing over the past two years that brought any relief. Pain needed to be blasted out of my life, if only for a few months. What did backfire mean anyway? How could a shot make it worse?

Five shots in 19 months was bordering on excessive, but Dr A+ reluctantly agreed. Nurse Carlos would be in shortly.

Because it was my fourth appointment, Carlos knew a little bit about me, and I knew a little bit about Carlos. He was young and quiet and didn't use social media. He asked me to lie on my abdomen, and I apologized for my lack of undergarments. (Never got the hang of underwear.)

"We're all pros here." That's for sure I thought. Henriette is Sick Inc., still going strong after 35 years.

As he prepared the area, he asked what I was up to that evening? I hoped he was as deep into this distraction technique as I was. I mean, I barely wanted Kevin looking at my 48-year-old butt, never mind Carlos, even with his nursing license.

"I'm going to a meeting with a sponsee." And wham-o!

After it was over, I could tell it wasn't over. It was in the way he leaned against the cabinets and looked at his feet. Nurse Carlos was off the clock.

"So...when did you know..."

"That I was an addict?"

"My brother..."

Ah.

I told him the disease took me down quick — from dabbling to dependency to desperation in a few short years. I lost the power of choice at 40, and by 42 I was in rehab. I told him there was nothing he could do to make his brother want recovery. You cannot gift willingness, but that by not enabling him, he might get there quicker.

"Don't take how your brother behaves personally. I lied into my husband's face when he stood in the way of my addiction." Carlos looked at me mesmerized, like I was speaking another language he wanted to learn. "I drank rubbing alcohol on my husband's kidney."

"Your husband gave you a kidney?"

"Yes!" I yanked my hospital gown high for him to see, suddenly unshy, pointing to my abdomen that bore two long scars on either side. "This is my husband's kidney and this one is my mum's." Carlos inhaled through his teeth.

"Woah! You're like...the million..."

"The bionic woman?"

"Yes!"

"You're too young to know that reference."

"I'm up on my pop culture!" And we laughed. I told him there was help for family, too. His eyes softened.

"Thank you, Henriette."

"What's your brother's name? I will say a prayer for him tonight."

"Kevin." Now it was my turn to inhale.

"That's my husband's name." We both smiled.

As I drove home, I realized I'd shared about drinking rubbing alcohol with a freedom that startled me. I felt no shame about it, only gratitude at the possibility of helping another alcoholic.

And then a wave of self-pity rolled over me as my arms began to flare. Visualizing the Kenalog bubbling in my veins, I said a little prayer.

Please. Make this work. Take this Pain away.

~

October 28th, 2016: Day 596

Pain was a 6 while swimming.

November 3rd, 2016: Day 602

Hurts to lie on a sheet. 9. Talked to Dr. A+ for half an hour.

November 14th, 2016: Day 613

Started acupuncture today. Burning went through the roof. 7-8.5.

November 19th, 2016: Day 618

Barely slept all night. 9.

~

The steroid shot backfired with a sonic boom that rocketed me through the roof into the atmosphere. I was spinning, orbiting Earth, looking down at the tranquil blue and green sphere, wishing I could go back there, to a life of peace where Pain didn't rule my world — but I was stuck in deep space, with no way to return.

I ASKED to go back on Gabapentin. I know I made no sense, but with the increase in Pain from the steroid shot I was desperate for relief, even if it was only a few hours a day. And I'd only taken Gabapentin for a month. Maybe I hadn't given it enough time? Dr. A+ agreed. No more steroid shots, but she was happy to restart Gabapentin.

"Because Gabapentin has almost no side effects!"

NOVEMBER 23RD, 2016: Day 622

Went back on Gabapentin.

November 24th, 2016 – December 11th, 2016: Days 623 – 640

Better. I do not need to coat myself with Aquaphor (like fluffy Vaseline) at night. 4.

December 16th, 2016: Day 645:

Very uncomfortable. 7.

I DIDN'T YET REALIZE the impact Gabapentin was having on my CNS (Central Nervous System). Every time we increased Gabapentin, my Pain would drop for a few days, maybe a precious couple of weeks. But the reprieve would pass and Pain would return, an erratic creep upwards into the middling zone (4-5), and then at night spike even higher (7-9). Our kneejerk response? More.

Made sense to this addict. I had always been a fan of more.

In September, I started at 300 mg and by January the 3rd I was taking 1800 mg a day, which was considered a high dose. Dr. A+ would not go any higher.

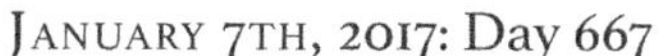

January 7th, 2017: Day 667

1-3 during the day. By evening it was a 5.

January 10th, 2016: Day 670

Worst day since Nov. 19th. Feels like my wrists are handcuffs of fire. 8-9.

Feb. 16th, 2017: Day 707

Good all day. 1. Flare at 4 pm. 4-6. Took Gabapentin at 5 pm. BRUTAL flare at 8pm. 8.

February 26th, 2017: Day 717

Brutal. 7. A bit better after prayer and meditation. 5.

Occasionally, someone would mention that people abused Gabapentin, to which I'd ask how? I took it at night, because it was supposed to have a sedating effect, but I never noticed feeling altered or different in any way I would be triggered to abuse. All I ever focused on was my Pain. Was It here or not? Was Pain staying or going?

Then I stopped keeping a pain log.

The way my pain bounced around made no sense, at least, not then. And I didn't want to think about it anymore. What's that saying, "Whatever you focus on grows?" Charting Pain felt like a daily affirmation of the Groundhog Day I kept experiencing. I just couldn't keep writing it, feeling it, living it. Hot. Brutal. Burning. 8. 9. 7. 9. Maybe stopping the pain log was the only way to feel like I was controlling a situation over which I had utterly no control.

16

NECKLACE

utumn 1977: Age 8 3/4

Nighttime.

Voices came from Mummy and Daddy's bedroom. Nicky was asleep in the top bunk, so I tiptoed over to our bedroom door like *Harriet the Spy*. I loved Harriet. She watched everyone, and wrote everything down, and threw temper tantrums like I wanted to sometimes and didn't know why. She also learned from her nanny Ole Golly that it was sometimes okay to tell a lie — like when someone made a meal you didn't like. I slipped into the hallway. My parents were rarely together and I wanted to know what they were saying.

The apartment stood in shadow. It seemed darker at night when it was just Daddy and Nicky and me. Daddy forgot about Mum's soft touches — lighting candles or opening a window for fresh air or setting the table with placemats she'd crocheted. It smelled stale without her strong perfume in the air. I missed her. She was like a surprise guest on a talk show I never got to watch.

Their bedroom door was cracked. Not for the comfort of light and sounds like I needed, but like someone had been in a hurry and forgotten to close it all the way. I got as close as I could, not caring about their privacy.

"I think I had a heart attack." Daddy's voice sounded tight. A heart attack! Why wasn't he in the hospital?

Mum made a strange blowing sound from her mouth. A scoff! She didn't believe him! She sounded annoyed. I didn't understand. Why didn't her voice soften? Then their voices got quiet. I squished my ear right up against the door, careful not to push it open. I couldn't bear this. Was she at least holding his hand?

I leaned against the doorframe, weak. My heart thudded, pain twisting it like a rag as I slid to the floor to catch my breath. Was this what a heart attack felt like, or just a broken one?

A YEAR earlier Mum graduated from secretarial school. Her diploma had a huge gold seal on it that said Honors, which made me proud. One night she had her classmates over to celebrate. They crammed in on our long couch, giggling at how many of them could fit. Mum wore leather boots with heels. She floated around the apartment offering drinks and swinging trays of pickles and cheese and crackers through a haze of smoke. She was the hostess with the mostess, shining like an unreachable movie star I wanted to know.

Someone asked, "Peter, what do you think of your wife?" She threw her arm around him and realized in those boots she was taller than him. She started laughing and laughing, bending her arm into the shape a man makes flexing his muscle.

Did Daddy laugh? I don't know. I wasn't supposed to be there. I'd been sneaking down the hallway to spy like Harriet, hiding behind furniture, avoiding bedtime. Maybe he did laugh and I just don't remember.

I remember it was the last time I saw them touch.

DAYTIME.

From behind their bedroom door came rumblings. Daddy's voice was low, not deep. Mum whispered her words. Then voices so quiet I strained to hear any sound for long minutes. Were they even talking?

I could picture them through the door. Mum standing tall in her distress. Her rouge-stained cheekbones, now blotchy with emotion. Daddy looking tired, the back part of his short-sleeved shirt untucked. In the pocket, the top of a Bic pen and paper sticking out. After he came back from the hospital, he always carried these in his pockets.

I leaned right up on the door, fearless about getting caught. I needed to fix this. Didn't Mum know we had to protect Daddy? We had to help him, not fight with him.

Just then the door flew open. I squinted against the brightness. Daddy stood backlit in the doorframe. Mum shifted away in the background. Was she hiding from me?

"Are you standing there?"

"Yes, Daddy."

The energy in the room hit me like a slap. I wanted to yell, "You love each other! I know you do!"

"Do you want this? In his palm he revealed a tangled mound of silver. I pinched at the pile and threaded out a fine strand. Swinging from its base was an elegant heart studded with tiny diamonds and blue sapphires.

"Your mother doesn't want it." A sourness rose in my throat.

I watched it swing; a delicate metronome marking time. Why wouldn't Mum want this beautiful necklace? What had Daddy done to turn her away from it? It sparkled like how a tear on a cheek catches the sunlight.

"OK." I said, not really sure. Daddy slipped into his office.

I didn't talk to Mum. I knew she wouldn't give me an answer that was real. For as much as I loved playing dress-up with her gowns, I was tired of pretend. I was tired of not knowing the truth. And so I told the truth. At least to myself.

Like Harriet, I'd told Daddy a little lie. I didn't want the necklace. Daddy hadn't bought it for me, he wanted Mum to have it. It would feel strange if I ever wore it. I walked back to my room and gently placed it in my tin container of treasures and shut the lid. That Mum didn't want it made it unpretty, but someone had to love this beautiful piece of jewelry. It wasn't the necklace's fault that no one wanted to see it shine.

NOVEMBER 1977: Age 9

I had just turned nine when they called us into the living room.

"Mum is going to move into her own apartment..." And that's all I heard. I screamed *NOOO!!!* and tore down the hallway, away from them, away from the living room where we decorated a real spruce tree for Christmas with real candles and a bucket of water standing by, just in case. Past the teak sideboard with the sherry glasses that were only brought out on special occasions. Past the main bathroom where Nicky and I played in the tub together, Daddy splashing us and Mummy filming with the Super 8 camera, documenting silent memories of children squealing, Daddy's pride as he looked into the camera smiling, always smiling.

I landed on my bed, tears flying off my face. Mum would live a couple buildings over in the apartment complex. We would live with Daddy and see her all the time. I curled into a ball with my back to the door. I didn't believe either of them. They had learned to lie like Harriet.

MARCH BREAK, 1978: Age 9 1/2

For March Break Daddy, Nicky and me went to see the cherry blossoms bloom in Washington D.C. Daddy's sister, Auntie Teresa, and her husband Yair, were on sabbatical in D.C. from their doctor jobs in Israel. But Daddy said we would stay at the Holiday Inn instead.

I have a vague memory of the cherry blossoms. Soft pink and fluffy. Oh, they were pretty. I wanted to fill my arms with the delicate flowers and bury my face in them, even though they had no smell. Daddy said I couldn't. The Americans were very strict about picking any, especially in the nation's capital! Cherry blossoms die at the peak of their bloom. Their gorgeous frothy pinkness meant they were just days from falling to their deaths.

Mostly I remember Arlington National Cemetery — rows upon rows of white marbled death sprawling across wide and green lawns. Daddy showed us JFK's gravesite with an eternal flame. His grave was a simple iron plaque with his name on it, with the flame coming out of a stone nearby. JFK was handsome and intelligent and died very young. I thought it was beautiful he got a flame that never burned out. Daddy told me it had something to do with natural gas, but I believed it was more magical than that.

THE HOTEL ROOM felt dark and small. There were two double beds and a TV screaming in the corner. We loved the jangly American commercials that were glitzier than ours. My brother and I were fascinated with all things American, like the sugary Kellogg's cereals that were such a special treat when we got them. I loved it when we were allowed the multi-packs of small boxes, but only when we were very good.

Nicky sat on one of the double beds watching TV and Daddy wandered around naked.

There was a knock at the door. "Room Service!" Daddy opened his wallet to reveal uncolored, UnCanadian bills. He pulled one out and held it up to me.

"Is this a ten or a 100?" I flinched like someone punched me in the gut. Why could he not tell the difference? And why didn't I ask?

"A ten." He didn't thank me.

Daddy put on a robe and answered the door. Did he even speak? On nights like this it was like he floated above Earth. Here, but gone. He wasn't with me. He wasn't on the bed eating burgers, squeezing the small packages of ketchup with aggression, watching the blood-red thickness smear all over my fries. Where was he?

He had just turned 38. His choppers were in a glass on the bedside table. He wore a compression stocking on his left leg. There was a plastic hearing aid in his right ear, and vials of insulin on the bathroom counter. And bottles in the shadows, in the car, in him. He was everywhere, but nowhere.

He was inside my heart, an irregular heartbeat.

This trip didn't feel like our other March Break trips. Three years ago, we three took the train to Ottawa. We'd watched the sunrise as we pulled into to our capital, sipping hot tea. We visited the Parliament Buildings and the House of Commons where elected Canadians would argue. From the public balcony we watched the prime minister, Pierre Trudeau. I didn't understand what he was talking about, but I did like the red rose in the lapel of his brown suit. Daddy whispered that Trudeau wore a rose every single day. Trudeau loved flowers like me!

We stayed at the CN Chateau Laurier — a huge and fancy hotel built in 1912. I thought the green towers were a little ugly until Daddy explained they were copper towers that had tarnished over time, the way pennies did. We had waffles and pancakes with syrup and bacon brought to us every morning. Then Daddy took me down to the hair salon where they'd put my hair in a ponytail. We went to the philatelist society, the Postal Museum and watched the waters of the Rideau canal melt. We bought presents for Mummy and wrote her notes on the train ride home to Toronto. It was lightness and learning and walks together.

There was peace.

It was love.

17

POPPIES

March 11th, 2017: Day 730

5 am and I haven't slept. Pain rages. Thorns poke so sharp and hot I can't lie on my back. Most of the night I've balanced on one inch of my body — from my shoulder blade along my ribs to my kneecap — on the bony parts with the least contact with the bed.

Kevin sleeps beside me, a wee smile on his lips, the one that fluttered away during Her dark days, and returned to land now that I am sober. Wahlter curls at his feet and I wonder how my boys have escaped the flames that consume me? And how glad I am that they have.

I slip out from under the third sheet I tested against my skin. *This one's too thick. This one's too thin. This one's not right at all.* I don't weigh much anymore, being burned alive and all. Wahlter's eyes pop open as I tiptoe away, dragging the sheet with me. They shut and he soon snores. It's a low moment when you realize you're jealous of your dog.

I move the couch cushions and lay down. *A change is as good as a rest. I'd prefer a rest.* I balance on my shoulder, trying not to think about the lava bubbling beneath my skin.

In four hours I am leading a workshop on the Fourth Step. (*Step 4:*

Made a searching and fearless moral inventory of ourselves.) In this step, alkys write out resentments towards every person, place, thing, or institution, and then our part in that resentment. I am useless without sleep, barely able to button my shirt without having a meltdown, never mind guide 20 fellows through a spiritual tool.

I stare at the back of the couch. Who do I resent for Pain? Medical Science? Kevin? My cousin? The pumice stone? Me for using it? All of the above? And what about the one that begins with a small g? Maybe I needed this workshop more than anyone.

I roll onto my other shoulder, trying to induce sleep by keeping my eyes closed. They pop open. Light is slicing through the canyon dark. It is 5:30 am. My pain is a 9.5. This is the first time I have been awake all night because of Pain.

I have to cancel. How can I cancel? Short of going to the hospital, I have nothing. And what would I say when I check into the ER? *I didn't sleep. I'm tired. I'd like a note to get me out of spiritual growth.* I hear the doctor's argument now. "I didn't sleep through medical school!"

I need to meditate. I need a mantra. I try the Third Step Prayer. *(G)od, I offer myself to (T)hee...To do with me as (T)hou wilt...* I flinch. I do not want (H)im to do with me as (H)e wilts!... *Zap. Zap, zap.* My body is sparking. Pain consumes me as a wave, a tumultuous salty wave stinging like the venom of a thousand jellyfish before dragging me into the undertow.

Fuck meditation.

I go to the workshop.

My heart fist-slams me for all twenty minutes I speak. I am jacked up on caffeine and panic, and feel like I am speaking in tongues, negotiating with Pain the entire time. *Please stop sizzling. Am I talking? I can't think.*

Lay off.

Fuck off.

Someone help me.

I leave the workshop with my resentment to Pain intact.

MARCH 16TH, 2017: TWO YEARS

"I have no idea what is going on with you."

For as much as I hated being at USC, I loved Dr. A+. She told me she'd spent over an hour studying my case the night before. The biopsy in November had revealed nothing. It was not a virus. It was not an infection. It was not an autoimmune disease. It was not an allergy. It was nothing immunological, or related to my kidney transplant. Gabapentin was not helping. Acupuncture was not helping. I had introduced CBD with a non-psychoactive amount of THC, and that was not helping. What had her eyes seen?

"What does it look like to you?"

She sighed the sigh of a thousand doctors who have been rendered helpless by the mysteries of the human body. It made me like her even more.

"It has components of various skin diseases, but nothing I have ever seen." I looked at the floor. "I'm going to set up a Grand Rounds for you."

Grand Rounds is a once-a-month medical event where 30-40 dermatologists review puzzling skin conditions. My heart skipped, excited, a teenager going on a first date, like I'd been waiting forever for Dr. A+ to ask me out and she finally had. I looked up through my eyelashes and smiled at her. With a second set of eyes on my skin they would find something. What it's called when it's 40 sets of eyes? Hope.

Maybe this time.

"Until then here's another ointment to try."

~

MARCH 27TH, 2017: Day 746

The word on California's street was the wildflowers were blooming! Kevin is not a flower lover. He does not stop to admire, nor does he stop (much) to purchase. It's a banner day when I receive a bouquet for "no reason." Me? I like to stick my face inside a bunch of lilacs, or any other stinky-smelling bloom, and huff. Instant calm.

Nostalgia and heartbreak as balm. *If you love flowers so much why don't you marry them?* I would. Happily. Almost nothing makes me happier than flowers, and I wanted to see the poppies.

Pain was telling me to stay home and be miserable, but I wasn't listening. I hopped onto the freeway and up to the Antelope Valley Reserve near Lancaster. The drive was spectacular. Fifty shades of green (sorry!) sprayed with bright yellow blooms, and the boldest of blue skies. Sometimes California is a big show-off.

It was impossible to observe such clean-cut beauty and not feel the presence of something bigger than me. When I wasn't at home, I would pray anywhere — bathroom stalls, parking lots, and especially inside the car. We'd built a rapport, me and (G)od, the divine bucket to my emotional vomit. I talked to (H)im anyway I wanted, and (H)e met me wherever I was, absorbing the venom I spat, deflecting the swears I slung, always game to meet my brokenness at the table.

Prayer was like a baby blanket or pacifier I whipped out whenever I felt unsettled, never relieving me of Pain, but offering calm to ground me. As if (G)od held one handle of my load, and I held the other, carrying my Pain together. A feeling that I was not alone.

I craved this feeling like a drug. (H)e was becoming my big connection, replacing the doctors and pharmacists who had served me pharmaceutical relief for so long. I needed it.

I looked through the windshield at the crystalline sky highlighting the rocks of Agua Dulce canyon.

"...I believe (Y)ou know everything about me, (G)od. I don't have to say it out loud, but I need to. Then (Y)ou become real. I need to feel (Y)ou. I'm so sad. I'm probably depressed, but I can't tell my doctors that because they'll say depression is causing my Pain. I want to say, "You'd be depressed, too, if you'd been in Pain for two years!" With Undiagnosis you can't suggest that you are anything except mentally solid, which is ridiculous. Who wouldn't be at a breaking point? I am. I know I am.."

It was a long drive and (W)e talked about all of it. About the laundry list of interventions that had not worked, from oils to ointments to shots to drugs: Capzasin, Singulair, Doxycycline, Amitriptyline and now Gabapentin. I clutched the steering wheel, remembering. I was now smearing a ketamine compound on my forearms.

"...My acupuncturist is lovely. Needles jut out of me like tiny javelins, as she holds my head in Reiki, and I break down and cry. She tells me YOU ARE GOING TO GET BETTER. I eat black tahini in the morning and place crystals on my chest at night. I feel like an idiot, but I will try anything..."

Leaving the freeway, there was an angry knot in my chest. During prayer, I always felt a shift, a crack and relief flowing from my heart into my veins, much like drugs. But not today. (H)e had not shown up. As I pulled into the California Poppy Reserve, I wanted to kick at the walls of my closed-in chest. To demolish the fear of feeling utterly alone.

I walked up narrow paths that snaked between patches of marmalade-colored blooms. The poppies were spectacular. How could I not be cheered by clusters of orange exploding in defiance against the dreary sand? I once heard that everyone should own something orange to wear on days they feel blue. That the color orange evokes feelings of optimism and energy. A wry smile curled at my lips. This sounded like a very California woo-woo way to deal with Pain.

I was mostly alone, passing the odd tourist lying on the flowers, crushing their delicate skirt-shaped heads, grabbing their selfie, despite signs everywhere that told them not to. I made my way to the top of Antelope Butte Vista, pushing myself into a surprisingly strong headwind, battering the air with small fists, panting as I reached the top. I stood with my arms on my hips catching my breath. Regular workouts were not keeping me in shape. I felt old. And defeated.

The 360-degree vista of the Antelope Valley stunned with patches of gold and yellow and faraway clusters of purple and blue. And wind. Cold gusts swooped in, startling me, whipping my short hair back and forth, better, fuller, faster than any of the new blow-dry bars that had sprung up on Ventura Blvd. I closed my eyes against the sand being flicked into my face, cementing my feet against the wild and comedic blasts.

Inside the wind, I could not feel my skin. No Pain. I let my body roll inside gusts that moved like interpretive dance, that threatened to take me down, but never did. I knew I wouldn't fall. I raised my arms as if on a ride, laughing out loud, to no-one, for myself. And for a few minutes, I was happy.

~

THE NEXT MORNING, I told Kevin I was going outside to write.

"Are you going to write about the irony of being in a poppy field? So close and yet so far."

"They are not opium poppies." I laughed.

"I had a nightmare," he said, rubbing his eyes. "You were being held hostage."

"I am being held hostage."

I sat overlooking La Tuna Canyon, lifting my face to the sky. A hawk flew by at eye level, downshifting to glide along a warm spring wind. I watched him cruise the canyon, wings spread wide. The hawk trusted the wind would support him. It was his invisible strength. He never doubted the wind would help him let go and soar.

The winds. Were they a nudge? To surrender to the tempest of my life?

The tears that wouldn't fall yesterday fell with something deeper than release. My first shiver of trust.

Let go of your Pain.

You can let go.

Give it to (M)e.

Maybe, if I could just let go, I might find my footing a little bit more.

PART III

GOD IS NOTHING

18

GREASE

November 1978: 10 years old.

In September of 1978, Mummy, Nicky and I moved into a rented bungalow in the north end of Toronto where Orthodox Jews came out to pray on Fridays with their black hats and curls. It had three bedrooms and small spiders in the bathroom. Our bunk bed was now dismantled. Nicky had one section in his room, and I had the other in mine. I liked having my own room, but kinda missed talking with Nicky at night, promising not to tickle his feet as he ran up the ladder to bed.

We had almost no furniture for the living room, with wooden floors that stretched long like a cold slab of beach. There were two wicker armchairs and a coffee table from our balcony at home, and a massive teak cabinet with a record player on top. When we played music it echoed as if we lived inside a theatre, with one braided rug our Guinea pigs loved to run across.

We didn't even have a couch, like the black one left behind in the apartment, the one Nicky and I made into forts to shield us from the world. I didn't want Mum to buy one because that would mean we were staying. This place would never be my home.

Nicky and I learned how to take the subway by ourselves a year earlier, at nine and seven. We shadowed Daddy, taking a train from High Park, changing trains at Bloor & Yonge, then catching a bus from St. Clair to school. Nicky got off one stop before me at UCC, and I got off at BSS. We became latchkey kids, first letting ourselves in at the apartment before the separation, and then the bungalow.

Living on Glencairn Ave., it took us a lot longer to get to school even though we were actually closer than when we lived in High Park. The subway didn't run through the upper section of the city, so we depended on two buses that stopped more often than an underground train. My brother and I were no longer piled together inside the luxury of the Jag or the goofiness of the Pacer, slurping our chocolate milks as Daddy bounced across train tracks at our command.

I got on the Forest Hill 33 bus north through Old Toronto, tucking my knapsack under the seat. The bus ride back to Glencairn was long and bumpy. The cranberry and pumpkin and mustard-colored leaves fluttered across the bus's windshield and into rush hour. I rested my head against the smudged window, heavy and tired. Their beauty felt punishing, a delicious display meant to fill me up, but I felt nothing. My heart was stunned, like when the Guinea pigs got scared. They would freeze and wait. That's how I felt. Paralyzed. Waiting for this pain to lift from my heart. I put my headphones on and searched for music on my tiny radio. I could sometimes find a song if the frequency was just right.

The air was already cool, almost cold. "Time for a hat," Mum said. After another Danish summer of long bright nights and cards and cola, and every second of every day with my brother, it was over. Now Daddy lived at High Park, Mum wasn't home until after 6 pm, and Nicky and I each had a key to the house. Four satellites spinning in four different orbits.

Mum had full custody of us because Daddy hadn't shown up to court. I kicked the leaves around with my faux fur boots as I crossed through the parking lot at the corner of Eglinton and Glencairn. Why didn't he come? He always wanted to see us. There had to have been a good reason. A really really good reason. I wasn't angry. I just missed him. Like I missed everything.

I slipped the key in the lock and pushed the front door open. It smelled like paint. Every room was white and bare. No pictures on the walls, a couple of plants. I knew Nicky wasn't home yet. The house was beyond quiet, just the faintest rustle from one of the Guinea pigs inside their cage. I poured some apple juice.

To be separated from my father felt like a part of me had been amputated. I was still going to school and doing my homework and tying my Oxfords and swallowing my food, but everything felt off balance, like I might teeter into the darkness around me. You couldn't see it, not in this cold and empty house with its bright white walls, but darkness is more of a feeling anyway. I could feel it in the way my breathing felt tight, in the way my stomach was always upset, even when I hadn't eaten, in the way it was hard to speak when I pictured Daddy at home alone.

The spark of him was my pilot light. Without him, it was out.

But I kept doing everything I was supposed to, wondering when I would go back to feeling okay.

I put the empty glass into the sink and walked away.

In the summer of 1978, *Grease* was the word. Nicky and I missed riding the Brylcreem wave because we'd been in Denmark, their cinemas months behind North American movie releases. By the time we started school again, singing from the *Grease* soundtrack at recess was ritual. Everyone knew every song. I got the double album when I turned 10 at the end of October.

I was obsessed. Just like my schoolmates, I knew every lyric to every song. When you opened the album it looked like a scrapbook — pictures from the movie were laid out on a Formica countertop from *The Frosty Palace.*

I wanted to be like Rizzo. She was the boss, prancing around the *Pink Ladies* slumber party with her take-no-prisoners strut. Sandy was so beautiful, but all she did was swing her silky hair around and toss writing paper at Danny's smarmy smile in the water. And oh, how she would cry...

Hopelessly devoted to you...

Why didn't she just ask him out? It seemed obvious. Mum said girls could ask out boys. I would do that when I was old enough.

I wanted to discuss this with Daddy. He had dropped by with a gift for my birthday, but Mum seemed annoyed. When she said he wasn't staying, my stomach dropped. *But I want him to stay. It's my birthday.* We were all here. The four of us were all here. Couldn't we just try?

Daddy moved towards the door. I felt sick. He couldn't leave yet.

"Dad! I'll just play one song!" We had to sing one time the way we used to in the car. Smiling, I placed the needle on the shiny disc starting with my favorite track, the fourth track, "You're the One that I Want."

Yoo, hoo, hoo, Honey / The one that I want!

My hips popped to the bass. It was irresistible! But Daddy just stood there. He looked at the album, but he wasn't seeing it.

"Daddy?" He stared right through me. His tie hung slack, like a noose around his neck. His pants drooped in the bum, and the light checker print was marked with dark stains. Were they chocolate stains from his blood sugar crashes? Or dirt? Or from the time I passed the bathroom and saw him strain on the toilet and his poo hit the floor? I had scurried away thinking I should help, but didn't know how.

I tried the seventh track — Rizzo's showstopper.

Look at me, I'm Sandra Dee / Lousy with virginity!

If I could just get him to sing, he would smile. I had to see him smile before he left. I wouldn't care if he had forgotten to put in his dentures. I would brave the gummy grin that scared me the first time I saw it. A smile that made sad me the wider it grew, but I would be happy to see it now. I would! I was dying to see it.

I get ill from one cigarette!

I held the double album open in my arms, offering it to him as sacrament. Music was us! Remember the Beatles? *We all live in a*

Yellow Submarine! Eat from this. Drink from this. Sing from this. Smile from this. Heal from this. Take from this. *Take it. Take it, Daddy!*

This was all I could offer. And I willed him to have all of it.

All of me.

Please God. He's the one that I want.

I remember we didn't sing. I don't remember if he smiled.

19

GRAND ROUNDS

March 30th, 2017: Day 749

How USC describes Grand Rounds:

Grand Rounds USC Keck School of Dermatology

Held the 1st Tuesday of each month (August-July). Consists of Patient Presentations as well as a didactic lecture from internal and invited speakers. This conference regularly attracts 30-40 dermatologists from the surrounding communities, as well as the USC dermatology residents and faculty.

How I described Grand Rounds:

Hope.

My point person for the event was a PA (physician's assistant), a Dr. S. He explained the dermatologists would be given a one-sheet that detailed my medical history ahead of time. They would examine my skin and ask questions. Finally, they would hear a presentation and offer feedback.

I received an invite in the mail:

1) ***Come to the event.*** *This meeting enables multiple dermatologists from the community to see your skin condition and provide input on how to best diagnose and treat it.* Why would I not come? Was it because

without me present USC wouldn't be able to charge my insurance? I had no reason to stay home. At home there was Pain. At least on the drive down there was Distraction, and inside the examining room, there would be Hope.

2) ***Be on time.*** D-uh?

3) ***Wear clothes that will make it easy for them to examine the affected parts of your skin.*** I've had blood labs drawn for 34 years. I know to wear tops with sleeves that push up. On dialysis, I wore scoop-neck blouses to access the PermCath in the middle of my chest. Layers are good for room temperature drops and multiple pairs of socks protect against stepping in bodily fluids or medical waste. I could teach a course on what to wear when disease is coming at you.

"Can you bring some pictures?" Dr. S. asked.

Could I bring pictures? Please. Behold the bespotted arm like the limb of an infected tree! Observe how a swath of rage sweeps across my face like the Joker's grin when I use hair removal cream on my upper lip! Gape at the red-red-redrum arms and thighs damp with droplets from the tub it's been suggested I never enter, but was psychotically drawn to, because of the brief relief found underwater before being pickled by Pain! Yes, Dr. S., I have pictures.

I forwarded my invite to Kevin. *Yay* he wrote back. We did not get excited by invitations to art installations or book signings or movie premieres. We got excited by 30 dermatologists inspecting my medical underbelly. We got excited by Hope.

April 5th, 2017: Day 755

Kevin and I sit in an exam room at Keck School of Medicine of USC. I perch on the end of a reclining chair covered in crinkly paper. My baggy floral top lies in a ball beside me. I wear a blue tank top with spaghetti straps and jeans.

I bounce my clogs against the side of the chair. I'm told I don't need to wear a hospital gown. Why wouldn't the dermatologists want to inspect my skin? Shouldn't they inspect every part of me? I look at my arms. They are flesh-colored calm, unlike my insides that twist in frustration. Suddenly, I can't catch my breath.

"Kevin. My arms don't look red." I manage.

"We have the slide show." Yes. Thank you, Sweetheart. I exhale. We have our PowerPoint presentation. We debated how long each photo should remain on the screen. Three seconds between images felt too short, but five seconds too long. Would four seconds be just right? Long enough to make an impression, but not too long to bore? Long enough to testify my life navigating the fires of Hell? It plays on a loop on my laptop on a stool beside me.

I hear them before I see them, a low-grade rumbling through the door. The odd *Hi? How are you?* The high vibration of pleasantries. Wait. Is this fun for them? Social? I glance at Kevin , who paces the room. He catches my eye and half-smiles. *Doctors, am I right?*

Dr. S. comes in with Dr. A+. I see her and want to burst into tears. She looks so nice. Her tendrils are sprayed back and she wears a formal blouse beneath her white coat that is starched a blinding white. Is this the one she pulls out for special occasions? Am I a special occasion? I want to hug her. I feel myself trembling.

"Some will ask questions. Some won't."

"OK." I rub my hands on my thighs.

"And then we'll talk about you."

Kevin has the laptop on pause. The first image is my thigh, screaming red. Screaming to be acknowledged. Red like a stop light. Stop. See me.

"OK. Let's go." I get a wave from Dr. S. who thanks me for all my help. Seems odd. Thanking me for showing up to a potential solution for my Pain. But then again, after 34 years living in these cubicles, it always surprises me how much I want to leave.

Kevin clicks play and the door opens. The first White Coats pop around the door, holding the one-sheet. They approach tentatively or is it respectfully? They bend and stare, not poking at my arms that look fine, then look at the screen for five, 10 seconds max. They look at their one-sheet again. For a moment, I think they are going to ask me for my autograph. Please sign this Rare Disorder Woman! I can't read them. Their faces are blank. Are they bored? Are they focused? One of them bends over and squints at my chest.

"Is that it? Or is that skin damage?"

I glance at Kevin, panicked. *They can't see it!* Kevin hovers behind me, armed and determined with his Coke Zero and iPhone, arms tucked into his arm pits, dying, dying to say something, to explain how bad it is for me, that he hears me cry at night, scream across the canyon, beg on my knees, but he has promised not to. First-hand agony has the most impact. The story is mine to tell.

I gesture to the photos flickering on the screen.

"They're not as red as I'd like today," I manage. Which is ironic because I would like them not to be red at all.

Four more derms roll in, smiles fading as they find me hunched, holding myself, their demeanor shifting from social to professional in a practiced blink. Stop. Inspect. Question.

"Have you tried Gabapentin?" asks one of the doctors I recognize from clinic.

"Yes. It's not working." I squeeze my thigh against a tongue that wants to lash out. *Is that all you guys can offer? A pill?* then realize that's pretty rich coming from me.

They spend a few moments watching the red images flash by. One of them asks, "What does it feel like?"

This is my cue. My lines are memorized. *And action...!*

"It feels like the worst sunburn of your life with an electrical current running though it all the time. Then I rate it on a scale from 1 to 10."

"What's your number today?"

10! I want to scream. *10, you fuck faces! I hate this so much!!!*

"6. 6 ½," I swallow, forcing my voice to stop quivering. "I would give you years of my life if you could make it stop."

Their expressions run the gamut from inquisitive to piteous to blank. I feel a horrible darkness moving in. Like I've lost before the race is even over.

For a couple minutes we are alone. I feel my husband beside me, his loyalty warming my back. I cover my face with my hands, rubbing at my Cover Girl-less skin. I never wear makeup to a doctor's appointment. You have to paint the picture without paint.

"Kevin," I beg. "What is this like?"

"Like a screen test. You are auditioning for your health."

Yes. That's exactly what's it's like. Even if we picked the right photos, even if I say my lines perfectly, even if I'm Dr. A+'s favorite patient (because I am sure I am), I may not get the job. I may not get an answer.

An older derm leans into me, leading with a kind smile.

"What do you think it is?"

I am startled. Gratitude softens my frown. "Oh. Well...we thought...Complex Pain something?"

"Complex regional pain syndrome. Yes, I can see that. But not quite."

"No. Not quite." She is right. CRPS is prolonged pain after an event such as an injury or heart attack. Pain then occurrs in an area away from the origin site. *Not quite.* She smiles and wishes me luck.

Luck? Luck is for lottery tickets!

The remaining derms drift in and out of our frustration, leaving traces of aftershave and indifference, reminding me of Hallowe'en stragglers, older teens chaperoning their younger siblings around, showing up half-heartedly invested in a witch's hat or cowboy boots because they were made to go.

I squeeze the migraine building behind my eyes. Dr. S. pokes his head in and assures me it was a great turnout. Now they will meet another skin patient, adjourn to hear presentations and brainstorm through the night. Then they will call me.

Don't call us, we'll call you.

And just like that, I am released from this episode of my Medical Mystery Tour. The dermatologists will now review: Glomerulonephritis at age 13. Two-time kidney transplant patient. Chronic migraines. Three years in recovery from drug and alcohol addiction. Non-Specific Perivascular Dermatitis presenting as chronic skin pain.

Pain. Pain. Pain. I swear I can feel their big brains burning through the story of my life as we walk the hallways back to our car.

Kevin takes my hand and looks at me with all the love.

"Do you want to get sushi?"

And I burst into tears.

20

RAVIOLI

December 1978: 10 years old.

The four of us stood outside the bungalow. The Pacer idled. Mummy and Daddy were yelling. The wind was yelling. Bare branches flicked at the dark sky. I couldn't see any stars. Nicky and I stood between them, waiting, always waiting for the fight to be over.

"You can't take them like this," she insisted, beautiful and tall, her eyes flashing jewels. She shone brighter with every word. I felt bad for feeling proud. Daddy seemed so small. That's all I remember. A small man, trying so hard not to be small, but unable to stand tall.

I don't remember if we stayed with Mum or went with him that night. Does it matter? How many times had we gone with him when he was "like this?" I would have gone anywhere with him. I would always be safe with my dad.

I didn't want him to lose.

DADDY PLUNKED down two bowls of Chef Boyardee ravioli. This was supposed to be a treat. Mum would never let us have this unless we were sick, but the pasta looked weird. I poked at it. It was cold. A small pot stood on the stove with a wooden spoon sticking out of it. Had he not heated them up long enough? Or had he forgotten to turn on the burner at all? I looked up from the gloopy squares to tell him, but heard the click of a door. He was already gone. Inhaled into his den by some force I couldn't name, but had marked us all.

Nicky looked at me, big eyes. I looked over at the closed door. Was Daddy coming back? Should we start without him? I knew never to knock unless it was an emergency. Was cold food an emergency?

Why had he left? Nicky and I didn't say anything. The hush in the apartment hurt, but neither of us could bring ourselves to speak. To speak would acknowledge that our father did not want to be in the same room as us, and that was unspeakable.

We sat at the table where we had grown up. Where we'd built shoe box homes for the Guinea pigs, negotiated bites of liver with Mum and tossed the napkin-covered remains beneath, and played rummy. This beautiful teak table purchased because it was Danish and functional, and perfect for a family of four.

It was dark in here and dark outside. Early winter blackness. I looked around the living room. It felt like a waiting room. There was one light on in the corner. A standing lamp that cast an eerie glow. There were gaps in the room, pieces of furniture Mum had taken to Glencairn. And it was silent. No radio playing in the kitchen. No TV mumbling the latest chaos from the Middle East. The feathery touches of family were gone. No candles flickering. The smell of something cooking. The absence of love turned my stomach. Should I turn on some lights? Could their light burn away the darkness in every corner?

Now I could find the word evil. It was here. It was easy to find.

I looked down at the table. Daddy had forgotten drinks. No Grape Crush from the vending machine at his office. No after-school chocolate milk, flourished with a bendy straw. No strawberry milk. Had he forgotten how to make it? *I could show you, Daddy.*

Nicky picked up his fork. The overhead lamp ensnared him in a triangle of light, as if subjecting him to interrogation, a prisoner of something. We both were. I'd always thought a prison was an inside room with bars. Prison was the *feeling* inside when the person you love leaves you behind.

I looked at the closed den door again. Daddy wasn't coming back from the stamps and TV and brown bottles. The fork wobbled in Nicky's hand. He wanted to eat, but couldn't.

With a surge of love, I pushed myself back from the table, and walked into the kitchen. I flipped on the light and looked around. It was just a room with a stove and a fridge and a counter I used to sit on. Where Daddy had demonstrated the art of the tomato and mayonnaise sandwich — a dash of salt on the tomatoes and a pinch of pepper on the mayonnaise. Where he'd made me "baby tea." English Breakfast strong, but creamy thick with milk, one square of sugar (sometimes two), then cooled by his paternal breath. *You don't want to burn your tongue!*

I dialed our new number and waited. Nicky didn't take his eyes off me. I gave him a small smile I could not feel.

As I twisted the long cord, Daddy's pager caught my eye. A big, weird box he'd hold up to the phone and punch numbers into when he was "on call." My stomach dropped, realizing. He wasn't on a house call! He was still here! He was right behind that door! With his melodic laugh and empty grin like a defective doll no one wanted to play with.

I'll play with you, Daddy.

The phone clicked. "Hello?" The song of her voice flooded me with relief.

"Mum," I breathed.

"Pussepige?"

"Daddy left us alone." She sighed, air escaping a collapsing soul. "Can you come and get us?"

Her pause told me everything. In the gap between our words, drops of agony fell. A rainstorm of pain. We were awash.

"Please." I whispered.

"I can't. It's your father's turn." Nicky and I were stranded. Caught between two worlds, and neither felt like home. "I will get you in the morning."

I hung up the phone picturing Mum alone in that blank kitchen, sitting at our makeshift dining room table — an unvarnished desk with two benches you could stain or paint to your liking. *Won't that be fun?* Was she as sad as I was? Or was she a little happy that she didn't have to be here anymore? And was I sad that I did?

I never wanted to leave, Daddy.

All we had to do was eat and sleep and tomorrow would be here. I looked inside the fridge. There was no milk. I turned on the tap and filled two glasses of water. I opened the freezer, removing two ice cubes from the tray. As I dropped a cube into each glass, they landed with a hollow plop. Trying to make something out of nothing.

My baby brother was waiting. He hadn't moved, his beautiful brown eyes tracking me wherever I went. I set the glasses down and looked him in the eye.

"It's just one night." I still couldn't feel my smile.

I SAT and looked at the slimy pasta and sauce. My chest burned with pain. He bought Chef Boyardee because he knew we loved it. He made us this special meal because he loved us. I didn't care that it was cold. *I'd eat a hundred cold raviolis if you'd come back. I'd eat liver and onions for a thousand nights if you would sit with us. Come back and sit here.*

Be here.

I looked at the door one last time.

21

ERYTHROMELAGIA

April 7th, 2017: Day 757

"The results are very unsatisfying." Dr. A+ was on the phone. "There were large experts in the room who were struggling."

After Kevin and I left, the dermatologists talked skin until the wee hours of the night. Although several theories were mashed into medical pulp, not one was palatable.

One dermatologist postulated my Pain might have something to do with my original diagnosis — Glomerulonephritis and the unidentified virus that caused my kidneys to fail. "Do you think you could find that paperwork?" I rolled my eyes. *From 1983? You mean from before the time of computers?*

Another dermatologist speculated it might have something to do with the years I drank and used.

"I don't see how that's possible. I haven't had a drink in almost six years. The pills almost four." I offered.

"I agree." I wanted to hug Dr. A+.

"Someone else wondered if it was all in your head."

I felt myself flinch. *Stay calm. You knew this was coming.* I did. The

I-can't-see-it-so-how-can-I-believe-it skeptic. I was only surprised I hadn't been faced with it until now. I steadied my voice before answering.

"Well, that is not the case."

"I know." Dr. A + was tops.

"The only diagnosis that makes some sense is Erythromelalgia." Now because Dr. A+ is such a tenacious mofo, she had theorized this condition to me back in October. Erythromelalgia occurs when blood vessels in the skin are deregulated — they constrict and dilate more than they should causing excruciating pain. This condition of vasoconstriction and vasodilation occurs only in the hands and feet, the only places where I had zero Pain.

"Medicine just isn't advanced enough to give what you have a name, Henriette."

My eyes welled up when she said my name. *Stop it. Focus.* I shifted on the bed, pausing my pen. I closed my eyes to ask. "So, was this like my Mayo Clinic?"

Should I still have Hope?

And this is why Dr. A+ earns her modifier. She told me for as great as her current employer is, the Mayo Clinic or the NIH (National Institutes of Health) might be the next stop on the Pain Train.

"You might consider them..." But Kevin had shut down the Mayo as an option.

My hands shook as I hung up the phone and Googled Erythromelalgia. I found a 17-page document at www.rarediseases.org prepared by Dr. Davis, Professor of Dermatology at the Mayo Clinic. I had some of the hallmarks: intense burning, severe redness and increased skin temperature that was continuous in nature. But not swelling. I did not have swelling. Erythromelalgia affects the feet, and sometimes the hands. Pain affected my arms and thighs, my upper back, lower legs, and tops of my ankles. But not my feet, or hands.

I turned the virtual page, scanning my possible future. Erythromelalgia primarily affects women in middle age. It affects 1.3

out 100,000 persons, or 13 out of 1 million people. And *...although treatment response is variable, experts indicate that many achieve significant alleviation of symptoms with appropriate medication regimens: In addition, although uncommon, remissions have been reported in some patients.*

Alleviate, not eradicate. Uncommon remissions. But I didn't have Erythromelalgia, just something that kinda, sorta looked like it some of the time.

I slammed my laptop shut, my blood pulsing. Kevin called out from the living room, "How did it go?"

"NOT GREAT!" I broke, slamming our bedroom door over and over, daring the door to pop off the frame, a toddler-worthy tantrum. Kevin came around the corner, and I unleashed, still bitter about the Mayo.

"If this was happening to you I wouldn't care about money!" My skin screamed along with me.

Kevin's lips formed a tight line. "There are medications you can try."

"I don't want another pill! They don't work!"

Dr. A+ wanted me to run three drugs by transplant clinic: Misoprostol which smooths the blood vessels (and sounds like cheap Russian vodka), Carbamazepine (used for bipolar and epilepsy), which can help nerve pain like trigeminal neuralgia. (This is known as the suicide disease. Do not Google if you want to sleep tonight), and sodium channel blockers. But I already knew Erythromelalgia wasn't what I had, and these weren't the drugs to try.

I fled across our cobblestone patio toward the sunset. I was so grateful for Dr. A+, a kind and determined physician who never gave me anything less than her respect. She had worked so hard. She had to have been disappointed, too. I felt a small comfort in realizing this, like my Pain level coming down from an 8 to a 7. It was something, but it wasn't enough.

I watched the California gold melting across our sky, across the San Fernando Valley towards Malibu. In the distance, I could hear bagpipes. It wasn't Kevin, but I knew who it was. We'd spotted him circling our Shadow Hills neighborhood playing the pipes — badly, as Kevin liked to point out — while riding a unicycle. We'd laughed and called him the Unipiper.

The first time I heard the pipes live was when Kevin played at our wedding. He had a crew cut for the 50's show *Forever Plaid* he was performing in, and I had moonface from Prednisone. I clapped along with everyone, astonished by his talent, enamored by the "Aw, shucks!" grin that swept across his face when the room exploded with cheers.

My life made sense then. I had the man, the career, the house, the dog, and a green card. But above all, I had my health. Seven years post-transplant, my kidney thrived. I tolerated my medications, my migraines were controlled, She had not arrived on the narcotic scene, and I did not know Pain.

Sunset flooded the canyon, rivers of rich orange and lavender blue. They didn't have sunsets like this in Toronto. Not soul-rattling events that mesmerized until the evening star popped out to say hello.

Had I ever truly been grateful for those first years of post-transplant health? How could I know to be grateful for a Pain-free life when I could never have comprehended this monster under my skin? No one deserved this.

The sun disappeared beneath the horizon and a slight chill settled in. Still, I was in no hurry to move. And besides, wherever I went, there It was. *I wish they had found something.* I once read that when you say "I wish..." you are not accepting your circumstances.

No matter. My wish had not come true.

I stayed for a while, evening blanketing the hills, feeling my insides harden as night closed in. I felt no gratitude or urge to pray. I had read to "do it anyway," but felt locked. Had the gurus chanting on their mountain tops, or the scribes who wrote about gratitude ever experienced such Pain?

I pushed my T-shirt sleeves up and patted the arms that burned.

Beauty like this was reserved for people who could be present and undistracted. I thought about how much my skin hurt. I was always thinking about it. I was alive, but never fully here, every experience smeared with despondency, my life not mine to fully enjoy.

Because my life wasn't just mine, it also belonged to Pain.

22

DEATH

December 13th, 1978: 10 years old.

The front door slammed. Crisp air whirled in and gripped my shoulders. My godmother's voice rang out.

"We're home!" And then she just kept nattering.

I looked at Nicky. Why was she here? And why was she talking so much? She was always chatty and loud, but now she was fake chatty. Mum didn't say anything. She didn't have to. The fact that they were both here told me everything.

We followed Mum into the living room. She walked stiffly, like a queen. The uncluttered floor stretched out for miles. I found the empty space comforting. The lack of furniture promised the room would never belong to us. I looked at the record player. I thought about placing the needle on a record, any record, and letting the crackles of suspense distract me from what I knew was coming.

"Sit down." Her voice was hoarse.

Mum sat in one of the wicker armchairs, tucking her skirt beneath her. Nicky and I floated to the floor and sat cross-legged like schoolchildren awaiting the day's lesson. She looked radiant, her skin a romantic alabaster. Her eyes downcast, as if lost in a spell from which she could not wake up.

She did not speak. She didn't know how the story was supposed to go. She was to take our hands in hers, or lay our heads in her lap, and lie. I wanted lies wrapped around me, like arms in a bathrobe, dreamy and warm, that I might fall into a 100-year slumber like Sleeping Beauty. Or maybe longer.

I looked at her face. Her beautiful face.

"Daddy's dead, right?" Did it sound like an accusation?

Mum nodded. Nicky screamed and ran from the room, unable to remain in a space tsunamied with too much history too soon. I watched him leave; my soul punctured by his cries.

Leaving. Everyone is leaving.

I didn't cry. I didn't move. Moving would have been like moving on. *Going to pee. Daddy can't pee. Going to eat supper. Daddy can't eat supper.*

Mum just sat there. I wanted her to go away. I wanted her to stay. I lay on my back, feeling the thin warmth of winter's sun on my face. I curled onto my side, not feeling the chill in the room, but a radioactive burn in my bones. It was our fault. He had been alone.

"What happened?'

"He went to work and collapsed."

"How did he die?"

"Pneumonia."

I knew that wasn't true. It was diabetes. It was the brown bottles. It was the Something Is Wrong that had shadowed me my whole life. It was the light that had gone out in his eyes.

But Daddy, you were my light.

That night, I lay in bed, listening. Mum was in Nicky's room, soft words of comfort floating in the air. Soft cries too. I pulled my thumb from my mouth. I had been sucking my thumb my entire life. I kept it a secret at sleepovers, thinking ten was a bit old to still be doing this. I lined my thumbs up, side-by-side and studied them. The left one was healthy and plump, the right one shriveled and old. Mum had warned me about my teeth, too.

I curled my legs into my chest. Daddy's name was Peter. It meant "rock" from the Greek. I loved collecting rocks — from the landscaped garden beneath our apartment building to the beaches of Denmark. I was fascinated with their composition and colors.

This year I had learned about the three types of rock formation — Igneous, Sedimentary and Metamorphic. Every rock was a piece of history captured, compressed between layers of formation and color over staggering amounts of pressure and time. All those ancient stories no one would ever know.

I would keep rocks in shoe boxes and display my favorites. I never mastered skipping a rock across the water, that magical dance-like skim. I never thought of rocks as something strong and enduring. They were treasured objects, that if thrown, sank rapidly to the bottom of the sea.

That night, I stopped sucking my thumb.

DECEMBER 14TH, 1978

We went to school the next day. I must have worn the Oxfords that Daddy taught me to polish. I must have tied the tie that Daddy taught me to tie. Nicky and I took the buses that Daddy taught us to ride. The sun came up. I had some tea. Baby tea. I wasn't a baby anymore.

Today was the Junior School's Christmas concert. We'd been rehearsing carols for weeks. Every year I would practice for hours, humming on the bus, singing in my bedroom or in Mummy and Daddy's bathroom, raising my arms to the sky, feeling the melodies give wings to the rumbly upset living inside my tummy.

I had two favorite carols. "Once in Royal David's City" because it landed in a minor tone I found enchanting, and a little melancholy. The lyrics made me wonder about what happened in Heaven and who you might see.

We shall see Him / but in Heaven / Set at God's right hand on high

Where like stars His children crowned / All in white shall gather round

I also loved "'Twas in the Moon of Wintertime" because of its haunting tones. I pictured a shadowy landscape, and thin tree branches stretching up like ballerina arms for the moon. It made me feel like something was always out there, even if it was cold and dark.

Before their light the stars grew dim / And wandering hunters heard the hymn

I loved these hymns because they weren't popular like "Away in a Manger" or "Joy to the World." Those were simple and boring and too on the nose about the whole Jesus thing (*Joy to the World! / The Lord is come!*). My hymns sang like poetry and weren't played much. Sometimes I liked being different, but I also wanted to belong.

I didn't belong today.

Daddy's favorite carol was "Good King Wenceslas." I loved that one, too. It was a terrific story, especially the part when the King and page walk through the storm together. The page cannot go forward anymore (*I can go no longer!*) and the King tells him to walk in his footsteps. The heat of his footprints helps the page go on.

Mark my footsteps, good my page / Tread now in them boldly
Thou shall find the winters rage / Freeze thy blood less coldly

Daddy had been alone for his last footsteps in his office. His secretary had called the ambulance. We hadn't been there.

We were lined up by grades in the hallway outside Chapel. It is a peaceful space with stained glass windows and concrete archways and an altar where a minister sermonizes. I only remember one thing he ever said. "Whenever you say the word **but** in a sentence, you are cancelling out everything that came before..." Was he saying we should never use the word **but**? Was it bad if we did?

We entered our pew as a class, one row down from the altar. My friends tittered behind their veils. I pulled mine forward like curtains so no one could look in. I glanced up at the altar, noticing faraway Jesus on the cross, **but** not giving Him the kind of attention I gave Him when I was with Daddy.

The Chapel echoed as everyone sat. That morning, I told two friends Daddy died. I didn't really want anyone to know, yet by the afternoon it seemed like everyone did. I shouldn't have told Victoria. She was a bit gossipy. My shy friend Andrea was incredibly sad.

I wasn't angry at them. I figured it would happen. How could it not? It was a fact of life now like: The sun is hot. The moon is round. Daddy is gone. No, he wasn't gone, he was dead.

The concert began. Up to sing. Down to sit. Kneel to pray. Nothing came out when I tried to sing, the melody curdled in my throat. I glanced over at Ms. Santer. I didn't want to get into trouble, so I mouthed the words, offering air. Air I could muster. Sound was impossible. Sound was the *Yes, my Darling* I would never hear again.

As I breathed inside my veil, melodies soared to the rafters alongside the organ's wail, long notes held by radiant faces, my friends, teachers, and minister. It was beautiful. It was all wrong. My stomach stabbed by a million needles. This glorious sound that was my release to sing, to share with family, *Daddy can I practice on you on more time?* made me want to plug my ears. Suddenly nails on a chalkboard.

Nails through my heart.

YEARS LATER, my sensitive friend Andrea would remind me she came by Glencairn that night. As she left a card in our mailbox, she looked up to see a harvest moon. It had been glowing, impossible to ignore.

Thursday December the 14th, 1978 was a full moon. Harvest moons occur in September, so what Andrea remembered was incorrect, yet right. She recalled the moon as radiant in its power to light up the dark, glowing at full capacity, lighting Daddy's voyage into the stars, around the planets and through the galaxies he'd helped me see.

I wish I had looked up to see the moon that night, but I was lost without my sun, the warmth of him, his soft hair falling as he bent to listen to me. Without him, my world was off its axis. It made no sense. *I was going to tell you about the concert, Daddy.* How could there be no more car rides? No more questions? No more song.

I folded my veil and put it into my knapsack for the bus ride home. The next year BSS discontinued the veils. The timing was perfect, because after that day, whatever god I knew stayed with the balled-up veil and a wrinkled copy of the carol concert program in the bottom of my bag.

Carols I could never sing again without picturing my Daddy as stardust in a dark winter sky.

~

Ottawa Mar 18-21, 1975

You see them sleeping side by side. No! it is not pride, but quite the opposite...humility that hits you. The almost incredible realization that you yourself, even though accidentally, were involved in the creation of such beauty. You drop to your knees and sob on the bed-cover: -

"Dear God...thank-you dear God, that if only now and again, you still have given me the opportunity to experience joy beyond the powers...my powers...of expression and description."

My chest, almost literally, is bursting with love and joy and happiness to see them in their sleep...so beautiful, so tranquil, so innocent and sweet and "ours" — 'cause here their faces & sweet breath mix in my thoughts with my feelings for "dear wife, Birgitte." So much love to be felt — even in short bursts — I surely do not deserve. But again:

"Dear God, thank you for the opportunity."

Truly, how many men on earth have this, my good fortune, to be literally bursting with happiness in seeing Henriette and Nicholas, and feeling Birgitte's warmth close by. As I smile, I cry too.

A senseless ? note — maybe — but only to those who do not know me, nor know the ascent of man's soul.

PART IV

GOD IS

23

HILLENBRAND

One morning, I woke up to find my limbs leaden...I couldn't hang on to a thought long enough to carry it through a sentence...He once said that he could sense the disease on me. I knew what he meant. I was disappearing inside it.

In 1987, at age 19, Laura Hillenbrand (*Seabiscuit, Unbroken*) was diagnosed at Johns Hopkins with Chronic Fatigue Syndrome. CFS is one of the most frustrating diseases. It incapacitates and there is little viable treatment available.

Hillenbrand was bedridden for weeks, then months, then years. A writer, she would write for magazines when she could.

Because looking at the page made the room shimmy crazily around me, I could only write a paragraph or two a day.

I discovered Hillenbrand's 17-page essay "A Sudden Illness" about her medical journey through Undiagnosis and pain. She sustained these symptoms for years yet wrote two books. I read *Unbroken*, but when I read her words about herself, I hung them over my desk.

My illness is excruciating and difficult to cope with. It takes over your entire life and causes more suffering than I can describe.

If I tried for a thousand years, with a million pens and a billion sheets of paper, I would fail to articulate with such sublime accuracy the life of the chronically ill. She became my muse because of her mastery of words, and her fate living with the condition catalyzing them from her.

She wrote *Seabiscuit* one paragraph a day. So, on the days I sat writing with icepacks on my arms or a fan blowing on my skin, I thought about Hillenbrand. She'd been crippled by vertigo, her Unidentified Virus dominating her body, cranking up the feedback in her head to frequencies she almost couldn't bear.

Almost, but not quite.

~

April 11th, 2017: Day 761

"You don't have an appointment."

She was a total beeyotch. I was here for my annual transplant follow-up, but this b. kept insisting it had been moved to August. It was true, last August I'd met with Dr. J., my transplant physician, regarding the Pain situation. He ran immunological and viral blood tests, looking to identify something he could treat with IVIG, the groundbreaking antibody therapy he pioneered, but all the tests had come back negative. Today, I was here for The Kid.

I knew the look. Disdain smeared across her face like baby food. I have no idea why. Maybe it was the polite way I asked her to accommodate me, even though I wasn't on the books. Maybe it was my comprehensive explanation as to why I needed to see Dr. J. *I just had a Grand Rounds at USC and need a list of potential medications reviewed for dermatology* (i.e. I was smart). Or maybe it was because I have red hair.

"I'll check," she snapped. I made bewildered eye contact with the other receptionist who, quite frankly, looked scared.

Cedars' Comprehensive Transplant Center was new and improved, now located on Beverly Blvd., all sunlight streaming in through floor-to-ceiling windows. The latest daytime talk show played muted on a flat screen in the corner. I inspected the shiny plastic plant on the glass table beside me, scrunching up my nose. I hated fake plants.

You know, despite all of Cedars' bells and whistles, there's just no way to dress up illness. You might be sitting half-perched on a slick leather couch, your feet tapping a gleaming floor, but it's still a waiting room. And waiting by definition is existing in the unknown. Transplantation is a game of waiting. Waiting to get blood drawn. Waiting for your latest creatinine. Waiting another three months to get labs drawn again. And waiting for the day when the waiting will end. Because one day, the kidney will just stop working. And then a whole different waiting game begins.

"Your follow-up is in August," she shouted from across the room. The wings of her lab coat fluttered as she strode away. Okay then. I locked eyes with the other receptionist.

"Does that mean you're going to be seen?" she asked. I shrugged.

Where was Old Hen? The pharmaceutical whore who spread her scrawny body across pharmacy counters and demanded justice.

"Can you check again?"

"It's too soon to refill."

"But I called my doctor!"

"Sorry. Next!"

"Well, screw you!"

Sigh. Thank God she was gone. Instead, I waited, confused, wondering why people who don't seem to like people work in health care where people like me could really use a bit of support.

Eventually, I was seen.

My life has been filled with medical forces, and Dr. J. is one of them. He is the head of kidney and pancreas transplantation at Cedars-Sinai Medical Center. He pioneered IVIG treatment — an IV antibody treatment that boosts transplant recipients' acceptance of multiple organs, mostly kidneys. It's all about desensitizing the antibodies between your immune system, your original kidney transplant and any kidney transplants to come thereafter. IVIG is also used to manage other immunodeficiencies (autoimmune, inflammatory, and infectious), which is why we'd been searching for a virus to treat last August. Also, I wish so bad that I could show you a picture of him. The guy is a dude.

"No to the channel blockers. Your blood pressure is already low." He scanned the sheet. "Carbamazepine and Misoprostol are fine. Phototherapy is also fine."

The center was quiet, the last of the transplant patients gone home with blood results to digest and scripts to fill. Dr. J. shifted in his chair, listening. He knew a bit about Pain, and I was filling in the gaps.

"This is terrible."

I told him about winning an award for the book I had been writing for over two years. That some days I could only write a few paragraphs. On days when my Pain was a 6 (interferes with concentration), I couldn't focus. I didn't have to tell him how it was destroying me. Empathy was smeared all over his face, not like baby food. Like a fucking grown up.

He leaned back on the stool, folding his arms across his chest. "There's an author, who wrote Seabiscuit...Hillenbrand..." I looked at him, stunned.

"I think I might cry." I told him about Hillenbrand's essay, and the quote I pinned to my wall. He added:

"I've seen a lot of strange things in transplantation, but nothing like this." I sat quietly, feeling a piece of me collapse, like a log on a fire when it shifts and crumbles into white ash.

"It is the hardest thing as a physician. When you see someone is suffering, and you don't have the means to help them." I gave him a small smile, my stomach plummeting. Where do you go when Grand Rounds and the head of transplantation at Cedars-Sinai can't help you?

But hadn't he? It would have been easy to dismiss my Undiagnosis, especially when there was no proof aside from the occasional red patch. Mentioning Hillenbrand showed me he'd not only been listening to my journey with Pain, but to the dreams Pain was preventing me from achieving.

A teenage Hillenbrand was once told her illness was all in her head. *You'll grow out of it in a few years. Come back in six months.*

I hadn't been told that. I had been believed.

~

I STEPPED into the elevator going down. The doors opened on the second floor and guess who walked in? Ye ol' beeyotch herself. She noticed me and turned her back. Apparently, she is very good at this. At the lobby level a teeny woman got on, her brow scrunching as the elevator continued down to P1.

"Oh, is this going down?"

"Yes, but don't worry," I grinned, "What goes down always comes up!" And then the two of us bust out laughing. And the b.? Not even a smile. My skin might have been burning, but I was glad I wasn't living in hers.

~

APRIL 13TH, 2017: Day 763

"You need a good neurologist now."

Dr. A+ was titrating me off Gabapentin. The only problem was she didn't know how. What was I supposed to think about a physician prescribing a medication she didn't know how to titrate? With this startling admission, I almost removed the + moniker from her title, except my neurologist is also a Dr. A., so to avoid any confusion I kept it, although I wasn't quite sure she deserved it anymore.

We discussed the potential side effects of Carbamazepine and Misoprostol. I paused. The Erythromelalgia diagnosis was no medical slam dunk. With a funny flutter, I realized I was not interested in anything systemic. No more pills.

Instead, I told her Dr. J. was fine with phototherapy. Also known as light therapy, it uses the less dangerous UVB rays on your exposed skin to treat conditions like psoriasis and eczema and Undiagnoses, too. The UVB rays only reach the epidermis, while UVA rays are associated with some skin cancers. This intervention is reasonably safe for immunocompromised patients with our susceptibility to skin cancers.

Leaving USC without another prescription in my purse felt like letting go of a parent's hand. My pills for transplantation, birth control, headaches and migraines held me in their palm my entire life. I didn't want to do this on my own — not without the hand of Medical Science on my back. Is this how Hillenbrand felt when they told her CFS was not treatable?

He could offer no treatment. Eventually, he said, some patients recovered on their own.

"Some don't?"

"Some don't."

~

April 14th, 2017: Day 764

I tried floating. Once I talked myself down from the claustrophobia I felt sealed inside the tank (irrationally concerned about being trapped by a fire, because why would a fire break out inside a tank of salt water?), I enjoyed it. Sorta.

I bobbed for an hour in eight inches of water. It hurt. Like every cell had been scrubbed with steel wool and rock salt and left stinging. I tried to frame it as the good kind of pain, the healing hurt of hydrogen peroxide on a cut or the sting of antibiotic on a tooth infection. I relaxed my brick of a neck against the firmness of a salt wave, and bobbed like a jellyfish in the Danish sea, relaxing enough to doze off, but ever aware of my skin protesting.

I thought of the shrieking metal-on-metal sound Hillenbrand heard between her ears.

The vertigo wouldn't stop. I didn't lie on my bed so much as ride it as it swung. There was a constant shrieking sound in my ears. Every few days there was a sudden plunging sensation, and I would throw my arms out to catch myself.

I breathed in and out, my breath slowing. My body was still a hard-candy shell of Pain, but my center became ooey-gooey calm. Calm within the chaos. Which reminded me this was how I felt in prayer.

When I prayed.

April 17th, 2017: Day 767

I met with my neurologist, Dr. A. and explained Dr. A+ was not confident titrating me off Gabapentin. On 1800 mg I became a zombie, but oddly, now at 900 mg daily, my side effects were worse. Very large and exotic red patches appeared with frequency. A concentrated burn sensation would start, as if someone was branding me with an iron, and a red patch would appear from beneath the epidermis like a creature showing its face behind you in the mirror. My appetite was dead, and my ears, oh, how they screamed. And through it all, Pain remained the same.

Dr. A's taper was straightforward. Reduce Gabapentin by 100 mg a week. Nine more weeks! That sounded like forever. Now that I had committed to breaking up with this hellion, I wanted it to be over. I had no patience for any of this anymore.

Hillenbrand was in bed for two years, and one day could walk to the end of her street.

April 23rd, 2017: Day 773

When my acupuncturist suggested I look at my diet, I knew we were done. My Pain had not improved with six months of needles, low lights and Reiki. I was fine with it. She was located an hour away, and expensive. I came to her with red skin, intense burning, and an open mind. I left with red skin, intense burning, and some pretty rocks to lie on my chest at night. Acupuncture worked for people, but not for me. Also, she lost me when she told me to make a vision board for my Pain. This suggestion reminded me of *The Secret* and its pernicious implication that if you laugh at Charlie Chaplin movies you can cure yourself of cancer, suggesting the patient has failed if they cannot heal themselves with "good vibes."

Hillenbrand was once told she had an eating disorder when she had swollen glands, mouth sores, and strep throat for three months, but sure, I'll look at my diet.

April 25th, 2017: Day 775

I went to my second meeting of Chronic Compassion, a support group for patients with chronic illness and their caregivers, led by a young therapist with RA (rheumatoid arthritis). Eight of us sat in a circle on a church floor, Palo Santo incense burning in the corner. After two weeks titrating off Gabapentin, I noticed difficulty sleeping and an increase in ear-ringing. Having a conversation was like being inside a club, screaming to speak, straining to hear.

A woman shared her recent MS diagnosis. She was shy and looked dazed. I recognized her slump, the *why did this come for me?* defeat.

"Don't give up hope!" I cried out. "The best doctors believe medicine is art, not science." Her eyes grew shiny.

"I really, really believe they will figure out what's wrong with you!" she replied. Then we were both crying.

Cherilyn, a delicate California blond and the group's other leader, was a caregiver to her mother who suffered with autoimmune disorders. She told us to lie back on our yoga mats.

"I'm going to offer you a mantra. Other people feel this..." she breathed.

"Other people feel this..." we breathed.

Okay. I rolled my eyes. When I'm in Pain, I don't find it helpful to be reminded that other people are "going through it." When I was a kid in the 1970's it was the "Finish your food, there are children starving in China!" pitch. Well, I'd never been to China, and I'd never been starving. When Mum nagged me to finish my meal, I would have happily shipped off my piece of liver to China. You couldn't force me to be grateful.

But this was different. Cherilyn wasn't asking me to have empathy for something I had never experienced. She was asking me to remember other people were suffering the way I was suffering right now. That I was not alone.

"In for four. Out for four." My breath came in patchy gasps. "Place your hands on your heart."

I held my hands against my rice paper-thin chest. I shook all the time now, anxious, as if I'd guzzled a gallon of caffeine and been forced to lie awake all night in Clockwork Orange-tooth picked terror. In my insomnia, I visited online support groups for patients coming off Gabapentin, reading hundreds of withdrawal experiences from around the world.

As an anticonvulsant, Gabapentin down-regulates or suppresses your Central Nervous System (CNS) — a kind of numbing that explained my brain fog and fatigue. Unlike an opiate that tells you not to care by releasing endorphins, Gabapentin told my brain not to respond to Pain by suppressing the CNS. Gabapentin has a very short half-life (five to seven hours). After a dose wore off, my CNS would be reminded it should be responding to Pain. Taking three daily doses, my CNS was being suppressed, then alerted, suppressed, then alerted, suppressed, then alerted, three times a day for eight months. This explained the roller coaster of Pain I'd been riding. Dazed and confused, my brain no longer understood how to respond to Pain. (This is portion of the evening where I remind you this was my experience, and I do not have an MD after my name.)

Now that I was titrating off Gabapentin, my CNS was being upregulated. Jacked up. Way way up. This explained the punch-in-the-chest panic attacks that had me pulling to the side of the road. Shitting my pants at night. Crying uncontrollably on the toilet in the middle of the day with a ferocity that startled even me, The Emotionalist.

But Gabapentin doesn't have any side effects!

Cherilyn breathed. "Other people feel this." Tears slipped down my face. Hillenbrand.

If I looked down at my work, the room spun, so I perched my laptop on a stack of books in my office, and Borden jerry-rigged a device that held documents vertically. When I was too tired to sit at my desk, I set the laptop up on my bed. When I was too dizzy to read, I lay down and wrote with my eyes closed. Living in my subjects' bodies, I forgot about my own.

I kept breathing in and out, my body trembling. I didn't want to be here, but I was. And so was Hillenbrand. An author. A woman. A soul. Out of nowhere, a sudden illness had come and robbed her of her health. And she was surviving.

Other people feel this.

24

SCOMBROID

May 4th, 2017: Day 784

Not long after my acupuncturist suggested I look into my diet, I found myself nibbling the paper rim of a cup of camomile tea, waiting to meet Dr. G., a Silver Lake midwife with a PHD in naturopathic medicine. Music tinkled above me as the flowery liquid dribbled down my throat, warming me with possibility. I mean why not? If she was good at delivering babies, maybe she could deliver me from Pain?

Maybe this time.

"Wow...Grand Rounds..." Dr. G's voice drifted as if to suggest "I'm gonna try my best, but those are some big brains to follow."

I liked her humility. I would have gone suspect if she started waving oregano oil around and claiming she had the cure. Right away, she postulated there was no magic bullet. She would treat Pain like a dam with 15 holes, and if we could find interventions to fill a few of them, I could get some relief.

I loved her enthusiasm. We started with B12 shots, a symptom survey, and a poop test. With my lack of sleep from the Gabapentin detox, I was willing to eat my own poop if she suggested it. She put me on Pulsatilla and Theanine for who-the-hell-knows. Shots of

ACV (Apple Cider Vinegar). She increased my Alpha Lipoic Acid from 600 mg to 800 mg which Dr. J. had prescribed because it helped his neuropathy (nerve damage-like numbness). For some reason this connection between Eastern and Western medicine comforted me. Medical Science goes hippie! Somewhere between the interminable distance between East and West there had to be relief.

She studied my viral and immunological tests from last August, and my autoimmune labs from 2015 and 2016. Then we drew blood for IgG / IgA food intolerance testing. Not an allergy test, this bloodwork identifies the foods my body creates antibodies towards on a scale of 1-6 (1 being the lowest intolerance and 6 being the highest). When she walked in with my results, she sounded impressed in the way nerdy medical folk geek out at curious data.

"This looks like you're a seven-year-old boy with psoriasis all over his body." I wasn't exactly sure what she meant by that, but I was pretty sure I didn't want to be it.

Dairy, sugar, and gluten came back as big offenders, but soy and almonds, two foods I considered a "superfood" and gobbled with unfortunate enthusiasm, came back as the highest intolerance. I eliminated these foods and we waited.

Seeing a naturopath felt a bit like the next stop on the Pain train, but she was intelligent and thoughtful, quirky and kind, which stoked my embers of Hope. Then she used "crikey" in an email, which Daddy used to say all the time. When I read it, I felt a flash of tenderness. I'd never known an American to use it. I chose to believe that meant something.

May 20th, 2017: Day 800

As a Canadian, it's almost sacrilegious if you can't get down with Bryan Adams' no-frills rock sound. I have loved Adams since I was 14 when he crooned from an empty swimming pool about how love cuts like a knife. If you look closely, you'll spot my high school BFF and I banging our 16-year-old heads in the front row of the video for Adams' rock anthem "Somebody."

It was a Saturday afternoon in our cabin in the hills. Kevin had just purchased two tickets to Adams' concert for date night at the Greek Theatre. I wiggled around the kitchen to a Best of Adams CD, nuking a plate of leftovers for Kevin.

Yeah / I'm gonna run to you...!

"Sweetheart, it's happening again."

Kevin stumbled into the kitchen clutching his head. His eyes were bloodshot, his skin bright red with blotches. He held his upper arm in an ominous grip.

"My head...the pain in my head!" He was making sounds I'd never heard. We raced to St. Joe's in Burbank, just 12 hours after we had left. How was this happening again?

At 10 pm the night before, Kevin was admitted for chest tightness and severe head pain. Six hours later, after an EKG and head and neck CT scan, he was diagnosed with cluster headaches. *See a neurologist.* Hmmm.

I've had chronic migraines from about the same age I began rockin' out to Adams, and something about these diagnostic dots did not connect. As a professional migraine-sufferer with 30 years of experience, I'd never been covered in blotches or had chest pain. But after 40 mg of prednisone, Valium, morphine, and Reglan, Kevin was no longer screaming, so we took the win and added the neurology suggestion to our ever-growing physician list. By 4:30 am we were back in bed with one mightily confused basset hound.

"Time to get up? What? No? Time to sleep? OK! Zzzz."

This second attack happened so quickly we hadn't picked up the steroids and pain meds prescribed the night before. As we pulled into the hospital, Kevin's symptoms escalated to full body itching. He couldn't decide what to do with his hands — clutch his head or scratch his legs until they bled.

After the nurse left, I turned off all the lights. I watched him for a while, his face glowing in the light of the IV. He lay, head cradled in his arms, an eerie reflection of the times I'd held my slaughtered body in withdrawal. He moaned softly. The nurse had administered IV Ativan and prednisone, but we were still waiting on the morphine.

"My head..." Kevin mumbled through a fog of agony. At home, he had collapsed on our bed, beating himself in the head to distract from the pain. What was happening to him? And where was his shot?

Please tell me you know the scene in *Terms of Endearment* where Aurora Greenway's (Shirley MacLaine) daughter Emma Horton (Debra Winger) is dying of cancer? Aurora walks out to the nurses' station and respectfully requests the nurses give her daughter the drug she is due. They nod and say they're on it, but it's not fast enough for Aurora. She pounds on the counter, paces it like a wild animal until she snaps. *Give my daughter the shot! All she has to do is hold out until 10 o'clock. IT'S 10 O'CLOCK! GIVE MY DAUGHTER THE SHOT!*

My inner Aurora hovered in the doorway, my half-body in, half-body out stance insisting there was unfinished business in here. I wanted to cup my hands around my mouth and make like a megaphone. *GIVE MY HUSBAND THE SHOT!* Instead, I reined in the tornado of Old Hen and whispered,

"They're coming, Sweetheart. I promise." His temple throbbed. My husband hurt.

I took in his contorted body, holding himself still against the pain. A surprisingly soft blanket covered his feet. A portrait of pain in repose. I knew that pose. Do not touch his forehead. Do not kiss his cheek. Do not adjust his blanket and disrupt the perfect imperfect comfort he has found.

Pain yanked my arms, insistent. *Pay attention to me.* I rubbed them aggressively. *No. I am not giving you this moment.* But I did think about how twisted life was. Here my husband lay suffering in his own Undiagnosis, and I was still in Pain.

The nurse slipped into the room. As he adjusted the drip, I suggested with dead calm, no raised eyebrow, or foot tap, that something had been lost in pharmaceutical translation. Kevin was due his morphine. The wide-eyed child nurse nodded. I smiled to myself. See? No need to be a tornado about it.

Minutes later, Kevin's morphine was administered. As relief slithered in, he turned his head towards me. Tears filled my eyes.

"Sweetheart..." he mumbled, eyes half-shut.

"I can't stand the thought of you in pain." We sat in the hush of our powerlessness. The IV beeped. "Didn't you ever feel this way?"

"Of course," Kevin croaked. "Dialysis...I couldn't...I had to go for a walk."

Yes. It had been Hell for him, too. I could see that now. How helpless I felt standing here, unable to fix what I perceived to be broken. But that was not my job. My job was to love.

Please (G)od, take his pain away.

The ER doc marched in waving a piece of paper.

"He has scombroid. I have to report this to the Department of Health."

Scombroid sounds like a turn-of-the-19th-century insult — "Oh, you scombroid!"— but it is a dangerous type of food poisoning, a rare toxicity that occurs when fish are improperly stored. The bacteria causes an overproduction of histamines that can cause death. Friday night, I'd served us tuna steaks from a supermarket that might rhyme with "doubts", from a city that might rhyme with "sperm bank."

Because I had no reaction, neither of us thought his "cluster headache" had anything to do with the tuna, so I served the leftovers for lunch. I'd cut two steaks into four quarters and unbelievably served myself the uncontaminated tuna both times.

"Who made them?" the doctor asked. I nodded. "Do not feel bad. There was no way to know."

I was grateful for this sprinkling of kindness. It's easy to feel like a cog in the medical machine in a high turnover place like an ER. Where time is often of the essence and diagnosis critical, the medicals can get swept up in the hamster wheel of it all. But all it takes is a listening ear, an extra heated blanket, or this kind reassurance that I hadn't done anything to harm my husband, a humanizing moment to remind us we are not just our sickness, but souls navigating it all.

A couple hours later, Kevin and I were on our date night, holding hands, strolling through CVS, wandering through that odd section in every pharmacy, the aisle with turkey basters, Hebrew bingo and Chia Pets.

This was the same CVS where Old Hen waited for her fix, thinking only of one thing. *What if they've run out?* I could see her zipping through the store, eyes wild, tucking her wine under her arm, shifting from hip to hip, pretending to look at her phone so the shamed soul inside didn't have to make eye contact with anyone, strategizing how she would pay with cash and destroy the receipt as evidence so her husband would never know, forgetting when she couldn't get out of bed the next morning, too sick to move or form a word without slurring, and he would see and be shattered. I didn't want to run into her ever again.

Kevin pulled me close, wobbling over the holiday chocolates. "We should get a sweet treat...thank you for taking care of me...or maybe a dumb magazine...oh, look! Fourth of July Snoopy!"

Kevin's altered stream of consciousness was adorable because we both knew it was temporary. It would not turn into begging or pounding or wailing for more.

"Bryan Adams. That would have been fun..." Kevin mused as we headed for home. It would have, so I put Adams on the car stereo instead.

You know it's true / Everything I do / I do it for you...

Halfway home from the pharmacy, I realized this was when I would feel Her kick in. Fiorinal. The three, maybe four capsules I gulped down in the parking lot, then I'd fantasize about the additional pills I would pop the second I pulled to the top of our driveway. The receipt I'd crumple into a ball. And how I would wish I was alone.

Kevin slouched in the passenger seat, relaxed. His blotches had come down a couple of notches. The prescription bags were by his feet. I wanted nothing to do with the chaos inside.

How did I get here? This place where I knew constant Pain, tinnitus that denied me sleep, Kevin's suffering, staying sober through it all? What force had brought me here?

Please (G)od, help me. Help me stay sober. I love pills more than anything.

More than my husband.

More than myself.

More than (Y)ou.

"Thank you for taking care of me." Kevin smiled.

I put my hand on his cheek and held it there a moment. There was no place in the world I would rather be — not even fourth row at a Bryan Adams concert. My favorite Canadian was beside me, safe and smiling. And me?

Tonight I was free.

25

LEXA

The first time I heard Lexa share was at an AA meeting after she completed chemotherapy for ovarian cancer and 60 women cheered. She and a friend celebrated with pizza, food she had been denied during chemotherapy, food it was "suggested" I not eat because of Pain. With a bandana still covering her scalp, her lips flirted with a smile. The sweet joy found in eating whatever she wanted to eat and doing what she wanted to do. Being reunited with the good health she had never asked to be separated from.

Then her cancer came back, and she shared about God. She wrestled with how to not feel resentful, her edgy tone suggesting she was. Just that morning, I had screamed at (G)od. *Fuck this! I'm so tired of being in Pain!* Lexa was right! It wasn't fair. I wanted to run up and hug her. Someone was speaking my language.

One Saturday, she announced she had a monthly panel that needed speakers. Panels are made up of sober alcoholics who visit detox facilities or treatment centers or jail and share their stories with newly sober souls trying to stay that way. I tapped her shoulder.

"I'd like to join your panel,"

She nodded but didn't smile.

JANUARY 31ST, 2017: Day 691

Four sober women arrived in four separate cars at the corner of San Pedro and 6th in a guarded parking lot. The sidewalks bordering the lot were littered with dark, bloated bodies, and towels cluttered with anything that might fetch these anguished souls a dime. Skid row.

I stepped out of my car into the warm evening. The air was the exquisite magic that is Southern California in the winter. When most of the country is buried in white, SoCal revels in the magic of whimsical breezes. I inhaled, catching notes of urine and body odor. I spotted Lexa's car pulling in and walked to meet her.

She emerged from her car elegant and tall through her disappearing frame. Her bony shoulders sported a black bolero jacket embroidered with sparkles. They twinkled, catching the headlights passing by. I knew what she was doing. At least, I like to think so. She was showing up in style, honoring a way of life that had saved our lives.

"Can I give you a hug?"

"Yes." I reached up and put my arms around her. Then she coughed.

Four of us entered a rundown building. Lexa, Melanie, Margot and me, were ushered in by a guard, who told us the elevator was broken. The staircase looked like one robust sneeze would blow it over. Up nine floors we trudged. None of us spoke. The rooms were matchbox-sized, with barely a bed inside, paint peeling, one shared bathroom on each floor. Homeless, transient, and traumatized women slept here, alcoholics and drug addicts laying their heads sober for maybe the first time, maybe the last.

My in-laws and my best friend from theatre school paid for my 60-day rehab in West Hollywood where two gourmet meals a day were delivered to my door. Could I have gotten sober here? I went to bury my nose in my shirt but stopped. I wanted to breathe this. It smelled foul, like a kind of struggle I had never known. When we got to the top, Lexa was out of breath.

We gathered in a common room with a low ceiling and brutal fluorescent lights. No soft twinkle lights or sunken couches here. Lexa set out the 12-Step pamphlets on a coffee table without fuss: Choosing Your Sponsor, A Guide to the 12 Steps, To the Newcomer. The clients drifted in, seven of them, most of them crowded together on a couch that in most homes would be relegated to the basement or Goodwill. Lexa coughed again. She decided three of us would speak for 15 minutes and then the clients could share.

"You're not going to speak?" I asked.

"No."

"Oh." I was disappointed. I wanted to learn more about Lexa.

"It hurts to talk." Her cough continued. The force of it scratched my throat.

"Do you want one of these?" I offered her a lozenge.

"Yes. My mouth sores from chemo are painful."

My heart squeezed. Her mouth hurt! Lexa turned to the group to start the meeting. As everyone closed their eyes, I peeked at my new friend, watching her lead us in prayer even though it hurt her to speak.

God grant us the serenity to accept the things we cannot change,
courage to change the things we can,
and wisdom to know the difference.

Post-meeting, the four of us stood in the parking lot, saying our goodbyes. From the soft looks on their faces they were humbled, like me. None of us will ever know if those women got sober, but speaking to them changed me. One woman spoke about how much she wanted to be sober but couldn't go home because of the abuse that lived there. How would she stay sober living on the streets? All I could offer was what got me sober, starting with one alcoholic talking with another.

The breeze sighed over my shoulders. What is it about warm nights? They feel rife with...something. Nostalgia? Was that it? Being here reminded me of my time at Klean. I was so lost when I first got sober, untethered without pills in my purse or wine stashed in my Secret Cupboard. I had never been homeless, but ached to feel at home. A place where the darkness inside me was understood.

The blinking city circus rose up behind me. I didn't need to look back. Surrounded by my three friends, and beyond us a world of drugs and alcohol that had almost killed us all, I felt anchored to something I was daring to call (G)od.

As the others climbed into their cars, I offered Lexa another lozenge.

"Sure. They're really good."

I thanked her. My fellow in a bolero jacket of stars, stunning accessory to the light inside her. She had led us in the language of the heart, by barely saying a word.

May 10th, 2017: Day 790

She was every cliché of the Stage IV cancer patient: thin, gray and bald. Plastic worms wiggled from her arms and nose into machines that beeped and blinked. She was talking as I slipped into the group of sober women surrounding her bed.

"When I came into Alcoholics Anonymous, I signed up for the whole enchilada."

There is a section in the Big Book that talks about the moment of crisis that every alcoholic faces — To believe or not to believe in God.

When we became alcoholics, crushed by a self-imposed crisis we could not postpone or evade, we had to fearlessly face the proposition that either God is everything or else He is nothing. God either is, or He isn't. What was our choice to be? (pg. 53)

It was a tough proposition to get behind. How was I supposed to believe (G)od was here as I stood in front of a woman dying of cancer?

Lexa looked down, working her mouth to form words. "I still believe that God is."

I held a hand to my heart. I had been looking for Lexa my whole sobriety. Someone suffering, randomly and unfairly, choosing to believe in God. The strains of "It works if you work it..." faded into the stale air, and I approached her bed.

"Can I hug you?"

She looked at me through her thick-framed glasses and oxygen mask. Then blinked.

"Yes." I pressed my lips against the tuft of white hair sprouting from her skull. Warm. She was so warm.

Five of us joined her on a slow lap of the floor, like my reprieves from the hospital bed, dragging my IV, leaning on Kevin like a walker. I would blink away tears as he headed to the elevator. I could name the tears now. Anger. Self-pity. Fear. At night, when the hallway lights went low, my resentment rose on a stream of opiates. *Why do you get to leave?*

Back then, I had no other way to deal with Pain. I had no other medicine other than drugs and anger. And I certainly had no (G)od.

Lexa folded her tiny body into a painful-looking mathematical shape — all bones and angles. Hugging my burning arms to myself, I was very aware that I was the one who got to leave today, even if it was with Pain.

When she left Cedars-Sinai a week later, it would be in an ambulance home to hospice.

May 30th, 2017: Day 810

AA brought meetings to her bedside for a couple of weeks. Then the email came. "You may bring food for the family, but Lexa is mostly sleeping now."

My heart pounded as I left two bags of groceries on her kitchen table. The apartment was still in the way that I hate. An unquiet that no distraction can cover. TV. Radio. Not even Chopin plunking his petal-soft notes in the other room. Lexa's best friend tap-tap tapped away on his laptop in the corner. Her mother whispered hello. Lexa lay across the room in a hospital bed, curled into her disease.

"Can I say hello?" she nodded and went into the bedroom. Lexa's terrier, Isabel, wandered with her tail at half-mast, settling beside her. Just me now, my pulse running wild.

I perched on the edge of the bed. Her pale body vanished against the white sheet, oxygen tubes tucked behind her ears. I scanned her face, wrinkleless, soft, her lips a thin line of peace. I longed to run my hand down her cheek. Touching her arm, her eyes half-opened.

"I want to thank you. You changed my recovery."

It took a few seconds, to make her lips come together, bend and form the words, "I'm glad." Her mouth struggled again.

"You don't have to talk."

"Okay," she smiled.

Lexa would die four days later.

WHEN YOU ARE CHRONICALLY ILL, you get called an inspiration a lot. These words feel like a twisted insurance policy healthy people buy into to protect themselves against "catching" pain or illness themselves. *You're so strong. I don't know how you do it!* Like, if they say the right things, they won't get sick. Karma buffering, as it were.

What choice do we have? If your kidneys fail, your kidneys fail. If you get cancer, you get cancer. The sick don't choose illness so we can have a battle to conquer and win. If I had a choice, I would be healthy. I'm nobody's inspiration.

Lexa hated being called an inspiration, too, and meditation gave her relief from resentment and pain. After a chemo session she lay on her floor for hours, curled into a toxic ball, unmoving. She told me the only thing she could do was meditate. It got her through intolerable pain with a tiny measure of peace.

"That's terrible!" I cried. "Why didn't you call someone?"

She paused for a moment. "Sometimes that makes it worse."

My insides rippled with identification. She was right. Sometimes talking about Pain didn't help. On the phone, I could hear people clanking around, washing their dishes, waxing their car or whatever multi-tasking activity they thought would be a good idea while I poured my heart out. They were only half listening while I was wholly suffering.

Or if they did say something it might be, "Well, have you ever felt worse?" which happened to me when I was three months away from my second time on dialysis, to which I wanted to reply, "Yes, but I would feel a whole lot better if I could punch you in the face."

I avoided people who posted about having a cold on Facebook, or their positive Covid test like they'd won Olympic gold, gathering consolation comments like flowers tossed at their feet. The problem with talking with someone, too, was that it always ended. I always had to hang up. Who would never leave? Who could be in my Pain with me all the time?

"How do you feel about God now, Lexa?"

"I'm not resentful anymore."

I STILL HAVE a memento from her memorial service. It's an image of her on a business card, standing in front of a lake, smiling, the trees reflected in the water with a lovely Monet-like blur. She stands tall. To her right is the Serenity Prayer. On the back are her words.

Now excuse me while I go find a field of wildflowers to run through.

More than anything, Lexa taught me about choice. I can choose to believe that (G)od is not punishing. Life just happens. My choice is how I respond to it. I am not being singled out. We are all going to die, but it's our choice how we want to live.

26

FIRE

By June of 2017, I was finished with Gabapentin, but Gabapentin was not finished with me. In two months, I lost 10 pounds. One morning I looked in the mirror and thought something had happened to my face, a condition like Bell's palsy. My lower cheek had literally fallen, like a wax figure's face melted on one side. I looked haggard and unwell. Even my latent anorexic was displeased.

If Pain was a pilot light, coming off Gabapentin turned it into a bonfire. My skin raged in violent and unpredictable ways that scared me. I would stare at the wild patches of red beneath my skin with body horror fascination. Sometimes it felt like Gabapentin had ignited a kind of demon.

There was a name for this Hell — PAWS: Post-acute withdrawal syndrome. This condition is a persistence of withdrawal symptoms from alcohol or drugs that can last for years after cessation of use. Although a drug is no longer in someone's system, withdrawal can deepen from the physical to the emotional and psychological, including prolonged depression, psychosis or anxiety.

Gabapentin's effect on my Central Nervous System had been catastrophic. I could literally feel my brain working in overdrive. I suffered from brain zaps, rapid and tiny explosions between by ears. My "generalized hyper-emotional state" included crying jags, continued insomnia and heart palpitations. My hotwired brain screamed from my last breath before sleep through my first breath at dawn, *Why did you take that drug?* *

By the summer, I had settled into phototherapy. The light therapy machine resembles a stand-up tanning booth, where I stood wearing sunglasses and underwear as a robotic voice counted down: 5...4...3... 2...1...BOOM! With a loud click, bulbs exploded with light and heat and Hope, a light so bright it was like standing on the red carpet with paparazzi swarming me. I visualized the light beams on my forearms, the origin site, holding my breath for good luck, even though it wasn't required. Over 12 seconds, then 18, then 24, then 48, then one minute of light therapy, I would pray.

Please (God), take this Pain away.

Katie ran the phototherapy booth. She had pin-up blond hair and glasses and was patient with my questions. *Have you ever seen anything like this before? How long did it take? Can I come more often?* She told me one patient got results only after a year.

Then I would come here for a year.

Katie showed me pictures of herself dressed up for auditions and we'd laugh. We bonded over my favorite drink — coconut Bai. I chose to believe that was a sign. I was always looking for a sign, anything to suggest I should hold on. Without these mind games, what did I have? An empty space where Hope didn't know where to land.

It was hard to say if phototherapy was working. Pain danced to its own beat the way it always had. Some days were a 4, and some a 7. By LA standards, I looked amazing. I was a scrawny rotisserie-brown woman-child, but this scared me. To look at me, no one would have believed I was sick. Conversations about my condition included, but were not restricted to, eyes glazing over, ending with the shoulder-punching "Well, you look great!" as if me looking the way they apparently wanted to look made up for the suffering they just couldn't see.

Three times a week, I went to phototherapy. Once a week, I went to my support group, Chronic Compassion. I had weekly phone calls and a monthly visit with Dr. G.: taking her drops, popping her pills, swigging her powders. I respected my food intolerances. Eliminating certain foods helped me with brain fog, headaches and sleep, but not Pain. I went to the gym almost every day. Anytime I caught some endorphins, Pain went down a few notches. For about an hour and a half.

Treating Pain now had a schedule.

JULY 25TH, 2017: Day 866 (111 lbs.)

A Day in the Life

5:45 am: Drove to Pasadena and told Big G off the whole way.

6:15 am: Lead an AA meeting.

7:30 am: Had coffee with alcoholic.

8:30 am: Worked out.

10 am: Errands & groceries.

12 noon: Eat. Pray. Lost it.

2 pm: Phototherapy.

3:30 pm: Wrote for an hour with ice packs on my arms.

4:30 pm: Eat. Pray. Lost it.

6:30 pm: Chronic Compassion support group.

7:30 pm: Marked four years of sobriety at my regular Women's' meeting.

9:30 pm: Eat. Pray. Lost it.

THERE WERE NO LONGER any big ideas for solving my Pain. Months went by. My schedule remained the same, give or take a neurology appointment or another dip in the float tank. In August, I took Introduction to Judaism at the American Jewish University. I visited my mum and brother Nick in Saskatoon. I finished the first draft of *Pillness*. In September, the La Tuna Canyon Fire crested the canyon opposite us and our view became charred and black. In October, Kevin and

I went to rock concerts, a wedding, and saw *Hamilton*. By November, my tinnitus had increased to a point where I was looking for an ENT. (There is no cure for tinnitus no matter what the pop-ups tell you).

And through it all, I burned.

I cried in my car, driving or parked. Ducked into bathroom stalls and got on my knees. Prayed everywhere, all the time, trying to connect to the only (O)ne that could be with me all the time. But I often couldn't find (H)im, and I rarely knew peace.

Dec. 5th, 2017: Day 999

At 10:30 am, a 4000-acre wildfire called the Creek Fire burned in Sylmar.

Kevin was pulling his things together for an audition and the day's photo shoot.

"I'll come with you when you leave and walk back," I called out. "I want to see where the fire is. It'll make me feel better." This, my friends, is known as irony.

We left the driveway and drove the bend of the road. Coughs of black smoke rolled towards us. I froze like a mouse. Black smoke is never good news.

"This is not good," Kevin tone chafed on me. We turned onto Hillrose Ave.

The normally quiet hilltop view was chaos. Cars were double parked everywhere, hazards blinking. 30-40 neighbors from our tiny ranch community gathered, most of them on their phones. Three helicopters zoomed overhead, dropping water in multiple locations. Black smoke rolled across the sky. This was bad. My hands shook as I held my hoodie over my head against the wind.

The fire had jumped the 210 freeway towards Shadow Hills. How could it have not? The gusts were ferocious, nearly knocking me over several times. With winds this wild, an ember can travel a mile and start a new fire. To my right, Little Tujunga Canyon burned. To my left, flames devoured the dry brush of Hansen Dam. And oddly, the 210 freeway remained open, vehicles zooming through it all. Hansen Dam runs parallel with Wentworth Ave. If the fire jumped Wentworth, it would be at the bottom of our hill.

We looked at each other. Kevin was white.

"We have to go pack."

Living in the foothills, we knew this day might come. Still, we lived dissociated from the reality in the way we know "Flying is so much safer than driving." You can't actually imagine being in a plane crash. We watched wildfires on the evening news, never imagining we might sustain her trauma live: sand in your eyes, wind in your ears, and smoke as far as the eye could see.

Kevin tore to the top of our driveway. He ran ahead, shouting about collecting his computers. Head spinning, I spread a blanket for Wahlter in the back seat, grabbed a bunch of recyclable bags, and tossed them into the middle of the living room.

What do you take when you might lose everything, and have minutes to decide? My brain moved slickly from one decision to the next: Medications. Wahlter's medications and food. AA inventory and literature. Computer. Hard Drive. Zip drive of *Pillness*. Sentimental jewelry. A picture of Mum and Kevin and me marking my transplants. A box of negatives. Daddy's letters.

Kevin packed his camera, computers, bagpipes, and our menorah. Wahlter never took his eyes off me. I opened two suitcases on the living room floor.

"Should we take clothes?" Dark smoke filled our neighbor's backyard.

"Let's get out of here."

Kevin drove away first. As I placed the chain link loop around our gate, I looked back at our cabin disappearing into the darkening sky. Was this the last time I would see our home?

I turned right toward Sunland Blvd. Several police cars blocked entry into Shadow Hills, masked officers waving us out of the area. Fast. Everything was happening so fast. The streets leading out of

Shadow Hills were clogged by this exodus. Blackness rolling down Sunland Blvd., sunny southern California suddenly become night.

By 1:00 pm the Creek Fire had spread to 11,000 acres.

We headed into Burbank when I realized I hadn't packed anything to sleep in — for Pain. So while Kevin sat in the parking lot of the local Kmart booking us a hotel, I perused the ladies' sleepwear section. There I was, rubbing various fabrics against my skin, as Andy Williams belted out his questionable opinion "It's the most wonderful time of the year!" As I waited in line, holding Rankin-Bass "Rudolph the Red-Nosed Reindeer" fleece pajamas in my hands, I wondered why there were no PJs with menorahs on them. That would've put a smile on Kevin's face.

Suddenly, I wanted to cry. I didn't want any part of what was happening. I didn't want my life. I was waiting in line (for 15 minutes!) to pay full price for pajama pants I would never have purchased under any other circumstances. Skin burning, ears ringing, sick with a cold, trying to find love and tolerance for the woman quibbling over her expired coupon, wondering if the flames had jumped Wentworth and our house was still there.

As I exited the store, I looked north toward the ominous mushroom cloud over Shadow Hills. Here in Burbank, cars zipped down San Fernando Rd. like nothing was going on. Questions like "Regular or non-fat?" were being asked across the street at Starbucks, while I took in Armageddon of the sky. Our cabin was built in 1947. Surely it had survived wildfires before.

Please. I don't want to lose our home.

The three of us sat in my car for a few moments, trying to take stock. We called our parents. I begged for prayers on Facebook. In crisis situations, some people shine, others offer ill-timed jokes. No matter, how could anyone understand what we were feeling when it was our world that might be burning to the ground?

By 4:00 pm the Creek Fire had spread to 15,000 acres.

Inside our room at the Safari Inn, we hugged. Perfunctory. I could not feel love in my arms. I couldn't feel anything, just a heaviness on the verge of throw up. Just then Wahlter hurled all over the bed.

"We all feel the same way, Bud," I cooed, wiping his mouth. Kevin scrolled through community postings, and messaged with a fireman friend.

"Are you ready to see if our house is still there?"

I turned on ABC-7 Eyewitness news and perched on the bed. A camera, that must have been mounted inside a truck, crept up a smoke-filled street. An eerie gray light filled the sky. I knew exactly where they were.

"Kevin! It's Johanna Avenue!" Kevin made a strangled sound, his eyes wide.

We cried in unison, "That's the house we looked at!"

The camera turned right at Radwin Ave. where I'd headed for home on my jog last week. The neighborhood was getting darker. The truck crawled uphill, ash snowing across the lens. The camera stopped moving. Fire engines blocked the street, red lights flashing. If you turned left, you would take a short stretch of Radwin to the fork at Hillrose and Wayside Drive, and down to our house.

The camera panned up to a raging inferno on a hill. A structure was completely engulfed in flames.

"KEVIN! IS THAT OUR HOUSE?"

My husband's hands flew to his face. I fell to the floor. My head spun. I couldn't see. I couldn't see! I couldn't figure it out.

The newscaster reported it was a structure on Hillrose. I grabbed my chest. The burning house was at the end of Hillrose. Only 10 houses away from ours.

He explained the firefighters' primary concern was the brutal Santa Ana winds. The gusts were too wild to allow the 747 Super-tanker to fly by and dump 19,000 gallons of water or fire retardant in six seconds. (The plane can fly as low as 200 feet above ground level and climb away at 6,000 feet per minute.) But they had to get this burning structure under control, or the fire could spread into the whole neighborhood.

And then they cut to the Thomas Fire in Ventura.

All we could do was wait.

I left Kevin with his iPhone and a beer and drove to my regular women's meeting. Driving down the freeway, I couldn't shake the image of ash snowing across our neighborhood. Switching lanes, I was struck again by the randomness of Mother Nature. Here I was calmly navigating the merge from the 101 to the 170 into North Hollywood, knowing in Shadow Hills, the winds could have shifted, and unruly flames engulfing our cabin might be tonight's top story on the evening news.

In the meeting, I confessed I was terrified we would lose everything. All we had taken were the clothes on our backs and a few essentials. My friend, Kim, rubbed my back. Tara smiled at me across the room.

"But I see the miracle. When Kevin left the room to go the car, it didn't occur to me to take a sip of his beer." And it was a miracle that I was using the word miracle when all I could feel was fear.

After the meeting, Shannon and Margot gave me the extra clothes they had in their car. I checked my phone. Kevin's fire captain friend had messaged: *Based on the aspect and defensible space of your neighbors, it looks like you guys might just be in the clear.*

By the 10 pm evening news, the winds shifted in our favor. They blew the fire down Wentworth away from us. The blaze had reached the bottom of the hillside, charring it black and destroying a total of 30 structures in all. No people died, but wildlife did. 50 horses from one ranch. Fast. It all happened so fast.

And just like that, it was over.

DECEMBER 7TH, 2017: Day 1001

We stayed another night at the Safari Inn until the hot spots were out, then when the evacuation order was lifted, we went home.

To find peace in my home has always been a priority. As a patient, I've needed a restorative space where I can find release and renewal from the burden of chronic illness. If my bed becomes my prison, my bedroom can be my world, littered with flickering candles, stacks of inspiring prose and memories in brass frames, walls that offer the soothe of dark green, or the energy of a vibrant gold, essential oils that cleanse the stale air, and luscious green leaves growing in the corner as I lie sick in the dark. A safe place where I can cry or sleep or vomit or detox or flex a firm middle finger to the sky. Home has always met dual needs — a place of necessity and spirituality. My sanctuary.

"Let's go look." Kevin wanted to drive by the house on Radwin.

Our small neighborhood was plague quiet. The barricades put up to prevent looting had just been removed, and it seemed no one had returned but us. I rolled down the windows, taking in the smell of fresh burn. We drove to the end of Wayside then stopped, panning our faces up the hill the way the news camera had.

"Oh..." I breathed.

The house was gone, just remnants of a frame that someone had built a dream on and the scorched hillside below. The highest house on the block caught the ember. The luck of the draw. The luck of the draft.

"Would you rebuild?" I asked.

"No." Kevin answered. I studied his profile, noticing the circles under his eyes. I had known for some time that he felt trapped in LA. Kevin was our sole breadwinner, aside from my post-transplant disability, and the hustle was getting to him. He made a great living that barely paid the bills. The sheen of Hollywood had dulled for him a long time ago. I loved living in California, but today it felt like it had run its course.

I kissed him on the cheek. "What was that for?" he asked, shy.

"Thank you." He looked confused as I lay my head on his free arm. "Just thank you."

Kevin went into his office, and I unpacked the bags. I moved my father's letters to the top of my dresser. I'd thought if the cabin had burned down, I would've lost my safe space. The wood floors where I prayed, the bath where I calmed, the view of green and sand, and the nighttime moving picture show of headlights and horns. Coming home, something had changed.

I went outside and soaked up the California sun that would never grow old. I looked around at the cobblestones and honeysuckle hedge, the ugly green trim we hadn't repainted, the cracked kitchen window and felt the years of tears and laughter twist my heart. I loved it here, but it wasn't my home anymore.

I'd been home during the hours we thought our house was burning to the ground. Home was the three of us in the Safari Inn holding on to each other as the television played, sleeping through ash and flames blowing across our dreamscapes. It was a bag of my sober sisters' clothes beside the possessions my husband and I had grabbed in shock. It was Pain insisting "The Pain must go on!" next to an open can of cold beer and realizing I was going to be just fine.

If the house had burned down, the paperwork would have been really inconvenient, and I would have lost things I'd had for a very long time. But things don't hold memories, they trigger memories in my heart, the place where they are actually held. I would have been okay if we had lost everything because everything I needed was inside of me.

My sanctuary was within. That was (G)od's world. I had found (G)od's world. Suddenly, I felt so free.

That night I prayed for help.

Please (G)od, show me what you would have me do. Show me how I can better contribute to this marriage. I don't know how. But I will trust you.

I couldn't see the answer yet, but I knew I would, because I could see that there were miracles everywhere, always, even if you have to squint through the eerie light of a wildfire to see them.

27

LETTERS

In June of 2012, I was six months out of rehab, and living a lie. I had relapsed on eight Vicodin tablets but hadn't told anyone. This lie kept me from feeling connected to AA which only works if you are honest, which would seem obvious but wasn't to me at the time. I was not in touch with my mother or brother, and Kevin and I had separated. I was alone and lonely inside the self-imposed prison I built with lies.

Through this time, I had one champion, my father's sister, Teresa who lived in Jerusalem. While I was in rehab, she wrote loving notes that included information on the genetic and environmental predispositions to alcoholism. She encouraged me to keep writing and publish my blog to help medical students understand alcoholism. On my blog, I shared memories and scanned photos of my father, his alcoholic death awakened after my overdoses and struggle to stay sober. But my memories and photos were few. One day Teresa offered me a gift.

From what I have gleaned...you seemed to know little of Peter and his past. After all you were only 10. If you like I can send you his letters that I kept. I feel they are more yours than mine since I knew him well, longer than you...I wish you calm waters. Teresa.

The letters arrived from Jerusalem in an ink-smeared envelope, with a note that said it was opened at customs. Kevin and I stood together, impossibly comfortable as our newly separated selves, studying the thick bundle with fascination. A package from a faraway place called the Middle East, one we had only seen on television, rife with religious bickering and righteous slaughter. I studied the Hebrew on the stamps, reminding me of the stacks of letters Daddy would save in a pile on his desk, waiting to be added to his collection.

When I returned to my furnished apartment in Glendale, decorated with DBT (dialectical behavioral therapy) diary cards and stacks of AA literature, I placed them on the carpet. Letters written in Toronto, mailed to Jerusalem and landed in Los Angeles.

The A/C wall unit rumbled just like it had in Daddy's den when I was a girl. I took the top letter and opened the past. My breath caught. There it was. His dramatic calligraphy in dark blue ink on his physician's letterhead. I brought the sheet to my nose. There he was, 34 years later. His warmth, the den, the back seat of the Jag. The paper was stained with the core of him, his good soul and sick body. Does everyone mark this scent? Was it just the smell of time? Or two hearts meeting again, one that no longer beats, and the other figuring out how to once more.

I clutched the page, devouring his words. The letter dated September 1970 is an exquisite plea for Teresa to visit Toronto after Nicky's birth three months earlier. My father is gushy and descriptive, extolling the virtues of a trip to his new hometown — night-fishing, the theatre (*"Hair" is still playing here*) and the Toronto Maple Leafs (*ice-hockey*).

He gives her flight information for our arrival in England on my second birthday and suggests she join us in Coventry with my grandparents. Finally, he ends the letter with a request.

Incidentally (I know this sounds ridiculous) but could you find out what BEERS I can safely drink in England. — seriously, this only if you can spare the time to phone a few breweries.

I held the letter to my chest for a moment. *He knew.* As a recently diagnosed Type 1 diabetic, he shouldn't have been drinking beer at all. Diabetes patients stay away from alcohol once they understand how carbohydrates (such as found in beer) affect their blood sugar levels, precipitating diabetic consequences like nerve, eye, and kidney damage. Alcoholics will go to any length to continue their relationship with their drink no matter the consequence. Even death.

Maybe this was why he drank Molson Golden Ale. Maybe he researched and believed it to be "safe." I thought he drank it for sentimental reasons, the way we randomly pick a sports team to cheer for when we're kids and grow attached to that decision.

When I read this, my heart broke and soared. *I understand you. I did the same thing.* I drank beer on dialysis — half a tall can after every session. Some nights I couldn't even finish it. Maybe because I was zoned out on Xanax; mostly because I was dying of renal failure.

In that moment, I knew I understood him better than anyone in his life ever had.

I poured over the letters for hours. He typed some (which I didn't like as much!) before reverting back to his calligraphic scrawl. His words waltzed around the page, energy popping from an extra-long exclamation point or a sardonic observation underlined many times. I studied his words greedily, seeking proof of his love for me. And it was everywhere.

...Henriette, now so pretty and delightful...It is already a memory that is etched itself very deep in me. You cannot imagine the love that flows when your child says his prayer, and hugs you tight..."Good Night, Daddy"...and kisses you not once, but over and again...

But there was a trade-off to this information. I felt it in the tears that fell, in the inscrutable flutter in my gut. Joy bubble-wrapped in pain. These letters had painfully rebooted his death. I was alive, struggling with my second chance, but my father was not.

And so for a few years, I put the letters aside. I wasn't ready. Something was coming up for me, some truth I wasn't ready to see about him, me, alcoholism. I was in a relapse, not actively drinking or using, but lying. And when you're living a lie, the truth is impossible to see.

~

DECEMBER 13TH, 2017: Day 1007

39 years AD — After Daddy

Eight days after the Creek Fire, Daddy's letters were still on my dresser, not returned to my sentimental trunk. I kept pausing to inhale them, wanting to get lost inside his world, his arms, his pain. I wanted to know his pain because it was my pain, too.

I gathered the bundle in my lap and scanned them, one-by-one, smiling, touching the faded words that were occasionally followed by a burst of bold ink where he must have stopped writing to replace an ink cartridge. On TV, Tchaikovsky's *The Nutcracker* played, a ballet I've always associated with Christmas — and by unfortunate default, December 13th, the anniversary of my father's death.

As a child, I delighted in its frothy costumes, the fluttering snowflakes coating the stage, its graceful tribute to the innocence of Christmas, reminiscent of our own Christmases with presents and candles, and overflowing bowls of nuts (although we never did have a little wooden man to crack them open).

Eyes closed, I lost myself in the building wail of the violins, the thunderous bass drum, the cello's haunting moan. I'd never heard the music this way before. I held the letters to my heart, cheesy, but vital, needing to feel a thing he touched, a reminder he was once here.

That he is not just a picture in a frame.

OUR BEDROOM WAS extra dark that night, shadows crawling in from every corner. I was in the bottom bunk, which I preferred. Every time I went up the ladder, I made Nicky promise not to tickle my toes, but sometimes he couldn't help himself, laughing as I scrambled to the top, shrieking, "STOP IT!"

Daddy was wearing his teeth, which I liked best. I felt bad when he smiled without them, although it made my heart grow three sizes like the Grinch's. His open grin made me love him even more because it was too wide, awkwardly magnifying his love. He was only 36. Is that when he let go? Did he start to give up? I know what it's like to have a foreign object inside you at all times.

He sat on the edge of my bed and leaned in to give me a kiss goodnight, that soft brown hair falling into his eyes. As he sat up, he whacked his head on the bunk's roof.

"I'm sorry!" I cried, reaching for his head, but Daddy just laughed. He rubbed at the spot, his slight arm brushing the bottom of Nicky's bunk. My heart flipped and tripped, worried. Intellectually, I knew it wasn't my fault. But my reaction wasn't a reflex, the good-girl Canadian in me learning to apologize for everything. No, I wanted to protect him from any more pain.

Children know. I knew. *Daddy just needs to go on vacation.* I knew what was coming.

But that night he chuckled softly, mending my shredded heart.

"You're too sensitive for this world, Henriette."

It is one of my fondest memories of him. It might be my favorite. In the quiet of a dark night, with a drop in his voice and a brush of his hand across my forehead, he saw me. He told me something I had yet to understand about myself: my heart was special, and I would get eaten alive every time I gave it away.

It was our father-daughter moment. Not the kind the world suggests — my first car, career advice, or walking me down the aisle. We never had those. We had this sliver of light on an exceptionally dark night. I can still see him there wanting to protect me from what he knew life would do to my heart.

Did anyone see you like this? I see you now, Daddy.

I wish we'd had more quiet moments like this, like talking about books. He wanted to write a novel. Mum told me Daddy brought his typewriter to Barbados and typed on the beach. Fedora on his head, cigarette in hand, shades tilted just right, banging out the pages of a mystery novel. He was a beautiful writer. A born storyteller. His letters are ink explosions of his soul. Long-winded thoughts that never lose me, intelligence and wit and charm in every line, and poetic humility for the love in his heart.

Daddy, you wrote just like me. Or is it, I write just like you?

28

CHRISTMAS

After the school concert at 10 years old, Christmas vanished along with my father. December the 13th was too close to the 24th and the magic got tangled up in my heart like a string of decorative lights. The next Christmas was back in our High Park apartment, and I found a Barbie house in the closet that "Santa" would bring me on Christmas morning. It's hard to believe in a jolly man dressed in red when you've seen your father lose his teeth at the dinner table.

I didn't know what (G)od felt like anymore. I knew what having a father felt like. A love so ferocious that when he died, I let church and Bible stories and prayer slip through my fingers because his fingerprints were all over them. It was too painful to return to a place I only enjoyed when he was there explaining it to me. An agnostic, Mum enabled my disappearance from Catholicism which helped it evaporate from my heart space the way Daddy had from our lives — sip by sip, tooth by tooth, pound by pound. There was no (G)od in a place where one day your father sits next to you smiling, explaining why priests swing around a smoking box, and the next you're at his funeral.

Christmas music was the deepest cut. The carols I loved to sing became the soundtrack to his death. Not the jingly-jangly sleigh ride trash, though. That Muzak marked the consumerism in which I loathed to participate. Watch me spend money on this bar of artisan soap or scented candle for someone I barely know and wonder why I feel empty walking through the crowded mall incurring debt. Yes. I hear it. Grinch, much? I went through the Christmas motions for a while — decorating, shopping, overeating; but when watching Rankin Bass' *Rudolph the Red-Nosed Reindeer* made my heart splinter into thousands of pine needles beneath the tree, I took a step back and asked myself: Why was I "doing" Christmas when I didn't know what I believed?

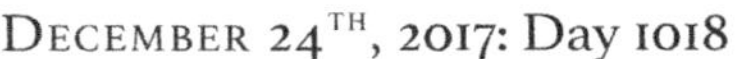

DECEMBER 24TH, 2017: Day 1018

Kevin was in NYC at a cantorial workshop focused on song in prayer. Before he left for the airport, I snapped a picture of him in a fedora and sharp gray suit, my heart cartwheeling at his mile-wide grin. Watching Kevin find Judaism felt like the sun coming out after a long and moody winter. I wasn't concerned about being alone over Christmas, but my sister-in-law, Kim, who loved Christmastime, was. I explained that Christmas was more of an inconvenience, and I would be fine, but maybe that's like trying to convince parents that children aren't necessary.

Pain was still doing its dictator thing, especially when I shopped for clothes, with a feel-first, try-on-later policy. Together, we purchased a couple of new shirts in the buttery smoothness of polyester. One was beige with stripes, the other a dark green with a chain-link print. I was leading an AA meeting this Christmas Eve at Tarzana Treatment Center. I chose the green one under a black jacket as my nod to the holiday season, taking a cue from Lexa, showing up in style for AA, no matter what.

My rehab bud, Steve came up from San Diego to join me and celebrate six years of recovery. When we walked into the dining hall, the energy was wild, pre-concert electric. It was a massive space with long benches and high ceilings, nothing like the cozy space under a pergola of white lights at Klean. There were a couple hundred clients, buzzing and talking and jostling in their seats. I suspect the noise had more to do with pheromones flying around like Frisbees than anyone anticipating my talk, but the vibe was thrilling.

Steve and I sat to the side waiting for the meeting to start. I took in his clean-shaven head and zippered athletic top. With a rush of gratitude, I reached for his hand. At Klean, we had been the "old ones" in our early 40's. We'd felt the magnetic pull of generation, and bonded. While the twenty-somethings hung out by the meds' room smoking, Steve and I, the only two non-smokers, sat on a patio outside my room and sipped tea. We called our moments "Tea for Two." Moments like that kept me sane in rehab, the normalcy of a cup of tea with a new friend while the world of drugs outside waited patiently for me to return.

"Do you remember our first conversation? I told you I drank rubbing alcohol?"

He looked puzzled, and then the light of remembrance played across his face. "Yes! And I chugged cough syrup!"

"Yes!" And we laughed. Joyously. Like bells.

I stood at the podium, unnervous. Pain gently revved beneath my skin, to which I gently insisted It take the night off. I had spirituality to attend to. To speak for 45 minutes about "what it was like, what happened and what it is like now." To share my story of addiction and recovery through Alcoholics Anonymous on Christmas Eve.

I began with my love affair with pills. How it blinded me to love, real and unconditional love not only from my husband, but a Higher Power. I shared how alcoholism hijacked my thoughts, convincing me Kevin would not want the opiates prescribed to him ahead of his nephrectomy (kidney donation) because he was allergic and would never use them all. How I snuck in and replaced his Tramadol (opiate) with my Xanaflex (a muscle relaxant), my alcoholism rationalizing this decision every insidious step of the way.

Suddenly from inside a sea of muscle shirts, I heard a roar without a face.

"That's terrible!"

I flinched at the judgment of my behavior. Are you kidding me? Probably half the addicts in this room had stolen drugs from other people. I took a breath. I knew his outburst meant I had connected with something inside of him. He was hearing alcoholism, and his reaction helped me remember what a bad case I had.

"Yes! It's a terrible disease!" I shouted back.

I told them about the Pain I'd lived with the last two and a half years, and the time spent on my knees with (G)od, reminding (H)im I do not approve. But no matter how angry I get, (H)e never fails to meet me there, which doesn't mean I am happy, but it does mean I stay sober.

I was okay with Tough Guy's reaction because I was okay with me. For four years, I had worked to relieve myself of the shame of my actions. It wasn't possible to shame me again. I understand alcoholism is a disease, which does not excuse my actions, but explains them. My responsibility going forward is to stay sober and carry the message.

Driving home, I rode the mild euphoria felt after a meeting. The nodding always gets me. The bodies rigid with identification, the way I sat when I first heard someone share about drugs and how bad it got for them. I didn't want to miss a word. I still don't. It's an inexplicable high, the immediate shorthand forged with another alky, from muscle T's to polyester shirts.

I turned onto Oxnard Blvd. and rolled down the car window. The night air was mild, but not cool enough to nip at my nose. I tingled all over. Alive. I drove down quiet Valley streets, taking in the decorations, especially the lights. They really were beautiful. I texted Steve and told him not to hurry back to my place. I was taking the side streets for a while. He said that was fine. He'd wait for me.

Through the early winter dark, glistening blue and white strands drooped from patios like icicles, silver displays glittered in windows, and multi-colored messes wound round and round and up and down anything with roots, which was, in its own way, quite beautiful. Rainbow explosions. I felt exquisite pain in seeing the lights again.

Then I was in Toronto, and Daddy was driving the Jag, instructed to take us for a ride while Mum finished the roast pork with caramel potatoes and red cabbage with rice pudding for Christmas Eve dinner. Nicky and I bubbled with anticipation. Christmas was coming!

I wiggled in the back seat, my face pressed to the glass as Daddy pointed out the displays, slowing to the perfect speed for us to take it all in. We oooh'ed and ahhh'ed each declaring our favorites. I loved all the colors, all the time, Technicolor tears falling on innocent snowy-white roofs.

Returning home, I spotted our building and counted up to the sixth floor. Mummy and Daddy chose this floor because it was the highest a fireman's ladder could reach. I squinted into the divine night. There they were! Two strands of giant bulbs. Red and green.

"Daddy! They're on!"

And he laughed. He always did when I was delighted. To my wide-eyed child they seemed the classiest of them all, elegant stand-outs from our neighbors whose lights were flung like spaghetti on the railings, landing any which way, and told no story. Our lights told the story of the simple beauty of light. Of Christmas.

Daddy and I went out onto the smaller balcony. The bare arms of High Park's trees reached upwards, gracefully, sacrificing themselves to a cold Winter's embrace.

It was an awesome night. The kind of winter night Canadians find beautiful. No wind, light snow, not cold. Snuggle weather. His arm was locked around me, holding me close, the other pointed towards the sky. I looked at his face, his forever smile and felt safe. Did he ever look at me and not smile? At the end. Just at the very end.

We were looking for Santa. He told me we might spot him if we tried our very best.

"Is that him?" I cried, pointing to the flickering light of a passing airplane.

"No," he explained. "Rudolph's light shines steady." And then he shouted, that joyous noise that told me how much he loved life.

"There he is! THERE'S SANTA!" I squirmed to see.

"WHERE?" Daddy pointed to a light moving eastward. There it was! I watched it for a moment, my heart pounding so so fast. Would it blink? NO! IT DID NOT BLINK! It moved steady, a rich rosy red floating across the sky. Rudolph! But where was he going?

"Why isn't Santa coming here?" I cried. I couldn't imagine Christmas without Santa!

"He's going to Montreal first." Oh, that made sense. The way Daddy explained everything always made sense. I leaned back into the warmth of him and gazed at the Christmas sky, full of possibility and light and magic.

And I believed.

I believed.

"Christmas is coming, the goose is getting fat...etc...It really is a feast for children. I had always heard the phrase, but never have I appreciated the truth of it until this year, when Henriette is now old enough to take delight in the decorations, lights, and trees springing up all over Toronto. Commercial as some and many of these displays may seem to be, and are, the delight in Henriette's eyes is so genuine—sparkling—smiling—lips—joyous squeals—that soppy as this may sound, just watching her reactions make my heart turn over, and make me feel as if that this...really this...was what I was born to experience, and if I never ever saw another, this would have been enough to have lived for."

December 25th, 2017: Day 1019

Christmas morning, Steve and I awoke in my home, six years after we lived in treatment together. All day we listened to choral music on Pandora and talked. No tree. No turkey. No lights. Just the warmth of our connection, and the music that gives people Hope around the world. What was wrong with celebrating that? The Christmas music was exquisite, stirring, and I loved it all over again. Only flinching, just a little, when "Once in Royal David's City" came on, evoking my broken 10-year-old heart.

He came down to earth from heaven / who is God and Lord of all

And I wondered.

Daddy, when Jesus came down from heaven did you guys cross paths along the way?

That Christmas, Steve and I celebrated the miracle of our birth. Our friendship and recovery. The one most people like us never realize. I hugged my friend, grateful for his light and joyous to feel Daddy's again.

It would be my last and best Christmas ever.

PART V

GOD IS EVERYTHING

29

ISRAEL (TERESA)

In early 2018, Dr. A., my neurologist, confirmed I had a nerve condition, which I knew a year earlier, but I don't have an MD behind my name. Thanks to phototherapy, my skin gleamed a golden-brown, but the electrical chaos beneath raved on. I was still in so much physical misery my latent anorexic began bargaining.

Please (G)od. I'll gain 30 lbs. I just don't want to be in Pain anymore.

At Chronic Compassion, I felt relief in the suffering of others. I needed the tremble in their voices, the fear dripping from their armpits, my armpits, to meld together in the terror the words "chronic illness" evoked in us all. To remember that *other people feel this.*

~

February 27th, 2018: Day 1083

After researching dry saunas for pain relief, I went on Craig's List and bought one from a couple in Long Beach. The kind owner drove it to Shadow Hills the next day and helped me put it together. The pieces lay on the floor around us like Lego. My new toy. *Maybe this time.*

"Why did you buy this?" he asked, his head down, hammering.

"I have chronic pain. It's like an electrical current going through me all the time." He was quiet for a moment.

"That sounds awful," continuing his hammering.

Why did I tell him that? Why didn't I say "I'm Scandinavian. I love a good sauna!" Had I become so desperate to be seen I would tell anyone who asked what Pain was doing to me? I watched his truck head to the freeway and back to his pain-free life, feeling oddly left behind, as I had when I was sick teenager, and Mum would leave for work. I'd turn over and sleep all day until she returned that night to take me to dialysis.

Maybe he was suffering, too. I knew nothing about him. No, I knew he was kind. But when I met new people, I did wonder if they also lived trapped inside a chamber of heat, as I went into the house to turn on mine.

Under a dim golden light, I wrapped my skinny arms around my legs, and lay my head on my knees. I let the tears fall, mixing with my sweat dripping onto the wooden floor. I pictured my nerves settling, soothed by the dry heat, the myelin (the sheath that forms around the nerves) growing plump and primed to absorb the relentless battering of Pain.

I posted a picture of my new intervention on Facebook and under someone's comment wrote:

Prayer is the only thing that's been keeping me sober for the last two-and a-half years.

March 15th, 2018: THREE YEARS

In 1974, Israel was all over the news. Every night, we saw the same story on TV. Gruesome footage of dead bodies covered in blankets, and dark-haired men pounding their fists into the air. Over Walter Cronkite's shoulder was the graphic "P.L.O."

"Daddy, why does it say please leave on?"

"It stands for Palestinian Liberation Organization," smiling at my error.

In my six-year-old world, P L.O. meant Please Leave On — an acronym understood between the teachers and custodians at school. Lessons the teachers wanted saved were circled and marked with P.L.O., and the custodians knew not to wipe the board. But to the rest of the world, mentioning the P.L.O. was to bring up the perennial strife between Israel and her neighbors, in this case Palestine. As Cronkite ended each broadcast with "And that's the way it is," Daddy tossed out a glib, "They're all crazy over there!" But he was worried. He wasn't watching religious freedoms clash; he was a brother witnessing his sister's newly adopted homeland live through a time of war. I am certain there were many nights in that pre-internet, pre-long distance phone plan era when he wished their letters could arrive sooner.

Born in Latvia, my father and his younger sister, Teresa, lived for four years in post-World War II German refugee camps (1944 to1948). They grew up in Coventry, England, and became doctors at Guy's Hospital in London. In 1968, Teresa was one of only two women to graduate from her class.

Sidebar: You might think in a family of Ivanans doctors — my father, aunt, and brother — I would've had a better shot at good health. But I guess that's like saying you can become an astronomer by looking at the stars.

When I was eight, Teresa came to visit us in Toronto. I have a picture from that day. My father wears a bathrobe with a striped pajama shirt underneath. His smile is small and tired, but his eyes read serene. My aunt looks radiant, her smile a bewitching blend of joy and relief. Her arms are around him as he holds his stomach, intestines, the source of his bleeding ulcers. In the click of their heads I feel their long-distance love undisrupted, a tender love that saw war as babies, and now as doctors, a war against illness that no one knew how to win.

Teresa has since told me that day she knew he was dying. When I look at the photo, I breathe in the heaviness, remembering how anguish pushed on my lungs like fists, the way diabetes and alcohol and the Klebsiella virus and pneumonias and lung drainage pushed down on his. She would go home to Israel, and he would never meet her there.

~

40 YEARS LATER, Kevin and I were going to Israel.

I was not up for Israel. The idea of leaving phototherapy, control of my diet, my special sheets, AA and gym routine felt untethering, never mind Pain and I buckling in together over a 15-hour flight. But this trip wasn't about me. Teresa wanted me to come, and Kevin needed to go.

Kevin's Jewish journey is not mine to share, but he has always been a Jew in his heart, if not from birth. His joy for the religion was obvious from the first time he baked challah and ate kosher. His commitment to learning and observing is pure, as is the love he holds for the word, prayers and song. I've never seen my husband smile and laugh and sing with such freedom since the Magen David came shining into our lives.

For me, Israel was not a religious destination. It was not a country of turbulence and war. After meeting only six times over our lifetimes, Israel was where I would know my Auntie at last. Israel was the country where Kevin's heart had always been, and where my blood had always been waiting.

~

APRIL 3RD, 2018: Day 1118

One of my first conversations with Teresa was about (G)od. She drove me to the gym through Jerusalem for some of those Pain-reducing endorphins. Kevin had gone to a Pesach (Passover) service with Miriam, a friend of Teresa's visiting from England. As they left, Miriam hugged me and said,

"Oh! All of Teresa's friends were in love with your father. He was so stylish and charming." Delight flooded me. *He's here.*

In the car, Teresa and I talked about the 12 Steps and (G)od, and how proud she was of my recovery. I looked out the window, smiling, thinking how similar the topography was to Los Angeles. Sandy hills, sunshine and bougainvilleas dripping from the trellises, those delicate paper-thin petals that didn't smell like anything at all.

I am sitting next to my father's sister.

"I am an atheist. I can't believe there is a God in this kind of world."

I understood that. I used to believe that because bad things happened there could be no God. I tried to explain what I was still trying to understand. That my (G)od was not a Santa Claus God who rewards good behavior with cars or jobs or even good health. My (G)od was a force and a Friend when I invited (H)im in.

"My (G)od is like a source of strength when I can't cope. I yell and cry and ask (H)im to guide my day." Teresa was quiet for a minute. I studied her profile, her white-blond hair pulled back.

"My mother had God."

She told me about my grandmother, Melania, and my grandfather Kazimirs. Catholics who fled Latvia when the country was caught between advancing Russians and retreating Germans in 1944. Melania had to leave her children in the German refugee camps while she and my grandfather went to find work. She once found two uncrushed cigarettes and traded them for milk and bread.

"I think her faith saved her."

Teresa was not judgmental. She was reflective, and smart. Tall and thin with an open wrinkled face, wearing jeans and a baggy floral blouse, just like me.

"All I know is that my life is better with (G)od, than without." With a lovely shiver, I realized I believed it.

How do you explain your God to an atheist on 12-minute car ride to the gym? Especially to a doctor. They're always looking for proof, but I had proof. I was sober almost five years, three of them through chronic pain. No pill had done that. And I sure as shit wasn't thanking myself every night as I drifted off to sleep.

April 9th, 2018: Day 1124

The Old City of Jerusalem is separated into three sections: the Muslim, Jewish and Christian quarters. The narrow streets of limestone are lined with vendors selling fabrics, foods, jewelry and religious items that lead, maze-like, into hidden hallways with tiny residences where Jews, Arabs and Christians live together year-round.

Giant Greek Orthodox crosses hung on black-sheathed priests as we stood behind a velvet rope waiting to see the Stone of Unction where Jesus is believed to have been prepared for burial. The entrance into the Jewish quarter was guarded by the IDF, young men and women strapped down with staggering machine guns. And an Arab man named Amir called me a "tough madam" for haggling over a table runner of beads and sequins.

Kevin bubbled, laughing. "This is like religious Disneyland!"

Checking the paper map, we moved through a tiny corridor, and then a metal detector with a sign in Hebrew, Arabic and English stating there would be absolutely no fuckery whatsoever at the Western Wall. The Western Wall is the last remaining outer wall of Temple Mount, the site of both ancient Jewish temples. It is the holiest site in Judaism and a place of pilgrimage and prayer. Traditionally, prayers are spoken, or written down and placed in the cracks of the wall. To pray here is the most meaningful experience a Jew can have. They have been praying here for over 2000 years.

The first thing I saw when I came through the metal detector was a wide-open plaza and, in the distance, people walking and praying at the Wall. The walls and ground were made of limestone, chalky-beige in color, and today, slippery, glistening with the morning rain.

"I'm going down." As I watched Kevin make his way down the stairs, a flash of raised voices, our voices, of fists on flesh, struck my heart. But the memory passed, and my smile grew witnessing him walk, prayer book in one hand and tallit in the other, toward the greatest moment for a Jew, eclipsing any moment from our marriage, made all the sweeter and stronger because we had chosen to stay and love on.

The stone sky overhead rolled with clouds as I headed towards the women's section. It was busy, but not packed the way I've seen religious sites like Mecca depicted. I stepped to the wall, noticing each woman lost in her reverie. Jammed into the cracks between the giant limestone blocks of were folded pieces of paper, thousands of them, many on the ground, soaked by the flash of morning rain.

Placing prayer notes in the Wall is associated with the belief that G-d (the divine presence) never leaves the wall, and prayers ascend to Heaven through the Temple Mount which borders this Wall. But the soaked prayers strewn around like garbage nauseated me. Litter didn't seem very spiritual.

Just then, the sky cracked. For a half a second I wondered if I'd heard a gunshot, but no sirens wailed, just rain sheeting down as people ran for cover. I looked over the barricade into the men's section, but couldn't find Kevin. There was shelter for the men in the back corner, but not for women.

The rain came down, hard and fast, but I didn't want to move. I had missed it so much living in LA. It felt glorious, like an outdoor shower, soaking my clothes right through. Most of the women ran from plaza, while some waited under nearby scaffolding. I was practically alone at the Western Wall.

The rain splattered my trench coat loudly as I placed my hands on the Wall. Lowering my head against a brick, I paused, drawing breath mindfully. Then I took my folded note and slid it into a crack on my right and whispered my prayer.

Please help me. Please take away my Pain.

The rain teemed down, but I didn't move. Maybe this moment would be my miracle, my burning bush in the pouring rain, where (G)od would finally reveal (H)imself to me. I wiped my face with my hands, wet on wet, and said the Third Step Prayer. (*Step Three: Made a decision to turn our will and our lives over to the care of God, as we understood Him.)*

"God I offer myself to Thee — to build with me and to do with me as Thou wilt. Relieve me of the bondage of self, that I may better do Thy will. Take away my difficulties, that victory over them may bear witness to those I would help of Thy Power, Thy Love, and Thy Way of life. May I do Thy will always!"

It didn't seem like the right prayer, but I didn't know any others by heart. I lingered there, leaning into the Wall, listening to the raindrops pelt the limestone plaza like gunfire. I didn't know what else to say. I waited for a miracle, knowing it wouldn't happen. I knew Pain wouldn't disappear when the rain stopped. There was no switch in the sky (Go)d would activate. That wasn't how it would work. But oh, how I wished (H)e would tell me how it would.

The rain stopped, but the sun stayed away, the sky unfurling bright and gray. I spotted Kevin across the plaza and waved, his smile radiating like I had never seen. Souls milled around again, returned to the Wall to pray or listen or maybe just be. I liked the Old City, a place where Jews and Muslims and Christians all lived and prayed out loud. It reminded me that miracles happen every day, and I should never give up on mine.

KEVIN and I burned though a packed trip with my family: My cousin's bat mitzvah, shopping in Jaffa, cutting through Palestine, swimming at Gordon Beach, floating in the Dead Sea, visiting Yad Vashem (the Holocaust museum), and attending two AA meetings (one in a Tel Aviv bomb shelter and one at a rabbi's house in Jerusalem). One day, my cousin organized a family archaeological dig for 12 of us in farmland not too far from the Gaza Strip. It was my worst Pain day. An 8. When we got back to Teresa's, I collapsed in our room, sobbing into Kevin's chest.

"I'm in Israel. I want to enjoy my life."

He held me, knowing there was nothing he could say to help.

How many times had I cried this cry? He placed his chin on my head and sighed.

"I am proud of you."

I burrowed my face into his chest and let my tears soak through another shirt. We both knew why he said this. Not one time over the last three years had I asked for drugs. I knew one pill was too many and a thousand was never enough. Maybe this was my Israeli miracle. Or maybe it was the biggest miracle of all.

DESPITE THE TIME we spent together, I struggled to connect with Teresa. She was respectful and educated and kind. They were generous with food and conversation and gave us space to come and go at will. She took us to a light show depicting the history of Judaism and a tour of the Old City archeological ducts. But I felt lost, overwhelmed by the chasm of time passed between us. I envied Kevin's ability to chat with anyone about anything. Where should I start? Should I sit next to her while she read the morning paper and ask, *What was it like being my dad's sister and watching him die from afar?*

In past emails, Teresa wrote eloquently about her relationship with my father, about trainspotting, cooking and following him to medical school.

As we grew older, bicycles gave us the freedom to fish in all the lakes and rivers of Warwickshire. We shared one glorious summer sunset at the bend of the Avon River as the sky was reflected, surreal, translucent colors in the still waters and time stood still, a moment of eternity.

Daddy and Nicky and I once went on a fishing trip north of Toronto. He showed us how to use bait on a switch fishing rod with real worms. When a fish hooked my bait, he whooped and stepped back, refusing to help me. They cheered me on as I grunted and sweated, so proud, so excited to see what I'd caught.

"Keep reeling, Darling! You've got a big one!" With a giant yank, the fish landed on the bank, except it wasn't a fish. I stared at it, panting. It was a shoe. A sneaker to be precise. A big stupid smelly sopping sneaker. The biggest dumbest fishing cliché, and I was the biggest and dumbest for catching it! Daddy howled. Nicky was probably too scared to laugh because I was MAD. How come Nicky caught a fish, and after all that work, all I had was a shoe!

Why didn't I tell Teresa this story? Why was it so hard? We could have shared a laugh. Maybe they once caught a sneaker, too.

I wandered into her room when no one was home. Just one or two steps past the open door. I didn't open any drawers or touch anything. The Catholic-informed sparseness, as was her upbringing, was classic. A beautiful blanket here. A solid bedframe there. Two photos hung by her bed, portraits of my father and my cousin, Jonathan, her son. Many suggested the resemblance between them was eerie, but I found it beautiful. My dad was living on in all of them: in Jonathan's face, Miriam's memory, and Teresa's home. What *was* eerie was Jonathan was now the age Daddy had been when he died. 38 years old.

The four of us sat at the table chatting as Kevin, fascinated by Israel, peppered Teresa and Yair with questions. Teresa's hands were knobby, gently arthritic, all thumbs since she confessed she'd accidentally bought 17 tickets for the light show on her phone, to which we all howled. Kevin flitted around making a second dinner for himself as Teresa brought out my grandmother's passport from 1941 when the Nazis occupied Latvia. I stared at the Swastika-watermarked pages of my blood's passport, stunned, drawing my finger across my grandmother's drawn face, her complicated expression looking so much older than her 33 years.

Teresa confessed to having no real memories of the war. Her first memory was of eating custard and prunes as a four-year-old, waiting for the ferry from Germany to England after four years in the refugee camps. She had missed the actual war. But what did the constant sound of bombing do to my baby father? What about playing parent to his sister as a five-year-old boy while his parents worked? His foundation had been bullet-riddled, rife with poverty, and rooted in religion. How had that shaped him? And how had it shaped Teresa, self-confessed side-kick to my dad, her protector and best friend.

Teresa smiled at something the ever-entertaining Kevin said. She was still stunning. I knew her to be a vivacious extrovert, all hips and angles. (How very me!) Her hands clasped a mug of tea. Hands I should have reached to hold for all she had lost, too.

Those hands held the hands of my father.

April 19th, 2018: Day 1134

On our last evening in Israel, I looked out a huge open window on the third floor. Teresa and Yair's neighborhood, Bait Va-Gan, was fascinating. It was not unlike being plunked into a scene from Yentl — sandy hills and payots and black hats walking in groups. One Friday night, Kevin and I strolled the neighborhood, Shabbat candles illuminating every window we passed, Jewish voices filling the rural-ish streets with gratitude for rest and G_d.

The sunset streaked the hills gold, as I felt Teresa join me at the window.

"I thought you would be more sick."

I flinched, wondering if she was judging me, like the doctor at Grand Rounds who thought Pain was all in my head.

"The dig was a tough day." I offered.

On paper, the archaeological dig had been a magical day. The family drove through Israeli vineyards in a minivan and sifted coins from the time of the Maccabees (134 BCE), but I wanted to run away. To where? To Gaza off in the distance? Back to LA? At this point in my relationship with Pain, I knew there was nowhere to run. So while everyone sang and chatted on the ride back, I curled into myself on the verge of screaming. That had been the worst day by far.

"You received news about your sponsor."

She was right. Although no longer my sponsor, Liz had relapsed again. It was devastating to learn how much she was suffering, but that wasn't why I was upset.

"Emotional trauma can cause pain," she added. I said nothing, unsure of where she was going with this.

Teresa had purchased polyester sheets for me to sleep on. She set up an air filter that sounded like a plane taking off to combat my tinnitus. She talked to an Israeli dermatologist to try and make phototherapy happen. She listed me as her daughter at the gym where she swam daily so I could work out. When we arrived there was a fruit bowl overflowing with apples and bananas and avocados — all foods I could eat — no oranges or grapes I couldn't. I'd been so moved I snapped a picture of the thoughtfulness. When Yair entered the kitchen on the first day and smirked *No cheese except mozzarella!* I realized he had memorized my food intolerances.

These people were on my side. She was not judging me. She caught the red patches flaring on my otherwise brown skin. She hugged my scrawny body. She saw the look of Pain in my eyes. It was always there. I could see it when I looked into the mirror and saw a body I didn't understand and had no choice but to claim.

We said nothing for a while. I loved standing here with her. The air around us was spacious and inviting, with no room for small talk.

"Your trauma over losing your father is as real as any I've seen. It's a kind of PTSD." I closed my eyes, the sunset's final rays landing on my face.

She was talking about Daddy.

For many years, Teresa worked as a physician with Israeli and Arab children who sustained the trauma of war. She witnessed how the psychological and physical effects of other people's battles ravaged the innocent. She knew Nicky and I watched our father rot over long and mysterious years, carried by a wisp of a mother, and a slip of a father before abandoning us with his death.

I remembered what Dr. C. shared with us at Klean. Addicts often emerge from childhoods of profound trauma and a rigid upbringing that manifest in OCD and control issues. When I was in rehab in 2011, this information helped me intellectualize potential causes and conditions for my addiction. I related to OCD with my lists, but Daddy's death didn't register as trauma. Trauma was reserved for war veterans. My childhood had been a lump of bad things in a row, but it wasn't trauma. Trauma was ongoing. My childhood was in the past.

Two years after Daddy died, I was up through the night crying, my 12-year-old heart aching with the impossible truth. Snot-dripping, breath-catching pain. Mum found me on the floor and said,

"If you're still crying this much, I'm taking you to a therapist."

Maybe if she said it in a different tone I would have accepted the help. The way I heard it suggested therapy was a punishment for having these feelings. Mum couldn't talk about him, so we didn't. I put my father in a frame, high on a shelf, a distant spectator to my life.

I invited him to my wedding as a candle, a faraway light that had once burned so bright in my life. The light of my life. After the candle was snuffed out, I went back to my intellectual love for him — *I once had a father* — unable to keep him alive in my heart because there just wasn't room to hold the pain.

I wrapped my arms around myself as the sun dipped below the hills. Teresa had just validated me through this diagnosis. I had never considered PTSD for myself. And by telling me it was normal because I couldn't, it was helping me open my heart to my father once more.

Teresa wanted me to be okay with not being okay.

I glanced at her shyly, wanting to throw my arms around her. The restlessness I had carried my entire life fell still. As if my heart was the ball in a pinball game, spinning up and down the flashing board, crashing through the world, powerless, lost, wondering why everything hurt so much, until this singular moment when the ball dropped into place, and the pain just stopped.

Because Teresa held my pain.

We stood for a few moments not talking. I looked at the apartments stacked on top of each other across the canyon, hundreds, thousands of souls nearby, so close together, all of us hurting, disconnected. All of us needing to be seen.

"Thank you." I whispered.

"I'm glad you came."

Suddenly, Kevin appeared in the garden below and snapped a

photo. It is a faraway image of our heads popping out of the window, two women smiling, happy they still can.

When she dropped us off at the airport in Tel Aviv, I did throw my arms around her.

"I love you! Thank you for everything. I'm so happy we came."

She smiled, avoiding eye contact, and told us to travel safe. Then she turned the car around and headed back to Jerusalem.

We sat for a while waiting for our flight home to LA. Yair had mentioned with his mischievous smirk that we shouldn't pass up the treats in the lounge. I sipped on my third iced grapefruit juice trying to drown the tightness in my chest.

Why was I upset? Because Teresa didn't say goodbye with tears in her eyes like me? Not everyone was a peacock with their emotions. Maybe I was upset because I didn't know what I'd been expecting from this trip, and now it was too late to figure it out. Maybe I was upset because she was literally the closest I'd been to my father in 40 years and I didn't want to leave. Maybe it was because we had one beautiful moment of connection and I wanted more.

I took a big drag on my straw and clicked open my email.

"I am not good at saying goodbye. I wanted to tell you too how much I love you too and how I admire your brave spirit standing up to all life has thrown at you. It was pure joy having you. For once the stars of fortune were aligned and in harmony. I love you my brother's daughter. The beautiful Henriette Ivanans."

My eyes filled with tears and I let them fall in the King David business class lounge watching planes land and take off, souls flying everywhere, rising to connect. Auntie T. and me. Maybe we did pretty well after all.

Maybe the death of a loved one is so embedded into the shredded fabric of our heart, that to peel it back and look, really look, would eviscerate what was left. Who would want to do that to their heart? Maybe it was enough to have one person with the same experience say, "I see you. Your pain is my pain."

Maybe it had to be enough.

The plane rose over the glittering lights of Tel Aviv, and I couldn't help but picture the horrors this country has known —the bombs, missiles and tanks. The warring factions, the peacemakers, the crucifix, Magen David, and the crescent moon and star. I pictured my beautiful Latvian aunt who fled the Russians and the Germans, was raised in the green gardens of England, became a young doctor in London, met an Israeli man in Jerusalem and would live the rest of her life there with him, in the most religious place in the world, and as an atheist, give me the greatest peace my heart had ever known.

The beautiful Teresa Ivanans.

30

EPIPHANY

April 23rd, 2018: Day 1138

Four days after returning from Israel, I waited in the Pain Management Clinic at USC. Dr A.+ knew I couldn't take anything mind-altering, but thought it would be worth it to "see what they can come up with." After year on phototherapy, she was phasing me out. Skin cancer was a concern with my immunosuppression. The truth was, for as many days when it seemed to bring relief, there were just as many it didn't.

Dr. H., my newest referral, was consulting with another physician. I slid down in the chair and sighed, unanxious to receive today's suggested intervention. There was no bubble of Hope in my chest. No *Maybe this time.* I just sat there, tired. So tired.

I rubbed my head, my Post-it of bullet points crumpled in my hand. I closed my eyes against the fluorescent glare and felt Pain raping my arms. When I opened them, all I could see was a thin arm stained a delicious brown.

It's your word against his.

A while ago, Kevin started doing this thing this where he circled his hand around my arm and pulled downward, "flicking" Pain off my skin like water droplets. "Go away. Leave my Hen alone." I had welled with tears then (and did now) remembering his sweetness. I flicked my arm a few times, but it didn't feel the same.

"We're going to treat this as small fiber neuropathy." Small fiber neuropathy is pain in the small sensory nerves, often starting in the feet and progressing upwards. Symptoms include burning pain, numbness, coldness and brief electric-shock like sensations. Once again, not quite right. My feet were fine. In fact, they were just about the only part of me that had been spared. And there was nothing brief about the electric shocks Pain administered all the livelong day.

"The options for treatment include Lidocaine ointment, Lidocaine IV, Mexiletine oral and Ketamine oral."

Dr. H. ordered blood work for a SCN9A and sodium channel blood test. There were pill options for these tests if they came back abnormal. He seemed very eager to please and handed me his card, which after 21 years of living in America, I still couldn't get over. *Pick me to be your doctor!*

As the vial filled with my blood, I thought about the miracle hiding in plain sight. I was at a pain clinic and had not asked for narcotics. I noticed the signs that said opioids were only prescribed in special circumstances, and wondered for a not-so-brief moment if my rosy cheeks and transcendent acting ability could still finagle me a prescription.

The phlebotomist placed the cotton ball on the exit poke and asked me to press. Seven years ago, I sat at Cedars' Pain Management Clinic and lied to Dr. Z.'s face, transmuting my post-surgical discomfort into crippling pain requiring Vicodin, Roxicodone, and a Lidoderm anesthetic patch I was warned could hurt The Kid. I was willing to lie and risk the health of my new kidney transplant. Anything to get my drugs.

I grabbed my purse and made my way through the lobby, clocking my body. My jeans scraped my thighs. My ears hissed and squealed. I was so tired of listening to Pain. I passed white coats and patients in wheelchairs, and pictured the prescriptions floating around this place, landing in sweaty hands and guilty pockets. My purse shifted and I remembered the lightness in my step knowing a script was zipped up inside or the rising taste of bile when the bottle rattled silent.

I had been a slave to pills. They hijacked my mind and dictated how to live each day. The places I needed to go and the things I needed to say. Pills really had been my God.

As I stepped outside, I felt dampness on my arm. Had I spilled something? I pulled up my sleeve and gasped. Red was everywhere. Blood soaked my sweatshirt and forearm, streaming from the crook of my elbow. In 36 years of blood draws I couldn't remember a single time this had happened. I bunched the shirt's fabric into the wound, and pressed down, realizing this was the origin site. Ground Zero was bleeding out.

I stood in the hospital's circular driveway for a moment, holding my arm, watching cars drop off patients, doctors and nurses and techs whizzing by. They all knew what they were doing here. I didn't anymore. I really didn't. Somehow, I knew if I kept going, I would circle this place forever, out one building and into the next, round and round and round.

I headed into the blood lab. Alcohol wipes and apologies removed the red mess and my arm emerged clean and brown. I listened to the tourniquets snapping off around me, the clinking of vials, the small talk as needles plunged through flesh tight with terror or resignation. There was a place for this. Of course there was. I was alive because of this world, but the solution to my Pain was not here.

I thought about the options to treat small fiber neuropathy. Lidocaine. The anesthesia in the lidocaine patch I wore to look the part of a transplant patient in pain was questionable. How could this be safe intravenously? And Ketamine? I already tried a Ketamine compound ointment that did nothing. Ketamine was a horse tranquilizer, used in veterinary clinics. Emerging research showed veterans experiencing relief from depression, anxiety and PTSD with LSD, psilocybin, MDMA, and ketamine. But ketamine was also abused to produce euphoric and dissociative effects, "out of body" experiences where the user feels detached from themselves and their surroundings. I pictured a young man's face in a documentary, gray skin and dead eyes, talking about how he couldn't stop using, even when he got to the point of pissing blood and screaming from the pain.

My body flooded with a thousand sighs. Maybe these options worked for some people but I knew this path was no longer for me. It felt lovely, this breeze of understanding, the way Bill W. in the Big Book describes his feeling of a great clean wind from a mountaintop blowing through and through his soul, lifting him to the realization that a spiritual life was his if he simply accepted it. I was accepting this. I knew I was done.

I flipped down my visor, and merged onto the 5. It had been three years. With every intervention, Pain had come back hotter, stronger, faster. Year one was a rash. Year two was a rash and Pain (Gabapentin). Year three, the rash became nerve pain and tinnitus and PAWS (post-acute withdrawal syndrome). Going to the Mayo or the NIH no longer made sense. The physiological damage had been done. First from a pumice stone, then steroid shots, steroid creams, Tacrolimus and Gabapentin. Drugs were not my path out of Pain. My beloved Medical Science was not my path out of Pain. It had not worked. It was not working. It was not going to work.

Or maybe, it wasn't supposed to work.

When I got home, I took out Dr. H.'s business card and stared at the words "pain management." What did managing pain mean anyway? Managing meant controlling or governing and certainly not listening to It. Maybe there was something I was meant to learn from Pain? To stop running and listen. As terrifying as that sounded, had I glimpsed a truth?

Pain was just life happening to me. *Life on life's terms* as we say in AA. It had nothing to do with God. He wasn't punishing me. What I kept coming back to was Pain was an opportunity to know God better. That's where my work was. Not running around the world seeking the magic pill, but building my relationship with the only thing that had given me peace in the last three years. And if God wasn't punishing, it meant He only wanted to help.

I ripped the card in half and tossed it, along with the blood-stained bandage from my pocket, into the trash.

Every day, I lived free of drugs by inviting God in. I could live free from Pain, with Pain, in Pain, but not by Pain.

Not alone, but with my God.

Was it really that simple? Yes, it was.

And really that hard.

On June 15th, I had my last phototherapy session, followed by a long conversation with Dr. A+. She took my suggestion and researched patient experience on Gabapentin withdrawal, thereby forever securing her + moniker. Some days the only thing that kept me sober was reading about other patients' random panic attacks and ear screeching and *burning burning burning* that was now three times worse than it had been before we started Gabapentin. Dr. A+ agreed with me. Gabapentin had done profound damage to my central nervous system and now my greatest tool was time. This would be echoed by Dr. J., coupled by another sad shake of his head.

List it as an allergy.

Could I list it as an asshole?

By September, I had been querying *Pillness* for nine months, unable to land an agent. I sponsored five women, and was secretary of three AA meetings a week. Kevin was studying Judaism, my mum came to visit, and Wahlter waddled along at 14.

Then Kevin was billed $1100 for a urology appointment he confirmed was covered. It wasn't. He was incensed, raging about greed and gouging happening in the name of health care. The American medical system had always been challenging to understand, but it was leaning criminal with this game of bait and switch. Dr. M. had been $135 a session and I paid for that out of pocket. Sometimes it felt like there was no point in having insurance at all.

The road was narrowing, and I couldn't see a way out. When I didn't know what to do, I prayed. But I'd been praying for nine months since the Creek Fire, asking for clarity on our future and guidance on how to contribute to our marriage. I understood the answers would come on God's time, but was it okay to ask Him to hurry up?

~

SEPTEMBER 20TH, 2018: Day 1288

On warm nights, I often prayed outside. I watched the city lights emerge, dazzling, like thousands of souls coming to life. If I was lucky, a slight breeze would play on my skin like God's fingers, my big Good soothing the embers beneath.

Closing my eyes, I took a few breaths, in and out. The roar of cars quieted but didn't disappear. LA never disappeared.

I was physically broken and we were broke. Kevin wanted to go back to school, but we didn't have the money. We lived with tarps and sandbags on the roof because our extra income went to medical expenses. He had a dream that he deserved to pursue, but I didn't know how to give that to him. I hadn't acted in years. I had no job. No real practical skills. The only money I pulled in was my post-transplant disability, which didn't even cover my medical bills. *Almost, but not quite.* I was willing to put my book on hold and do whatever it took to see him thrive. It was Kevin's time.

Please God. What would you have me do?

This night, an answer came. It wasn't a burning bush (which was a good thing considering we lived in a Very High fire zone); but it also wasn't what I expected like, "Go forth and become a dental hygienist!" It wasn't something I needed to do for Kevin, rather, it was a question I needed to ask myself.

What is most important to you going forward?

I closed my eyes. In a month, I would be 50. I had no interest in the mid-life crisis checklist: Botox. New car. A trip around the world. (Please. I could barely make it to the store.) But after two kidney transplants, five years of recovery and an acting career on hiatus, what was important to me moving forward?

I looked to the evening sky, glowing its periwinkle charms. Stunningly, four answers dropped into my heart with sparkling clarity: To be healthy and strong. To grow old with Kevin. To help alcoholics. To write books. A smile enveloped me, cocooning me in my truth. Relief like a fragrant breeze danced on my skin when I realized I could do those things anywhere, and LA was no longer the place to try. Yes. This was what I dreamed for myself moving forward.

I stood up, hands on hips, surveying the Hollywood view below. This meant moving back to Canada, probably Winnipeg. Moving countries was a formidable decision, but I could already feel its roots.

But what about Kevin? Less hustling, fewer money woes, and universal health care. All of it added up to more for my husband. For us. Kevin would catch fever of this decision. I knew it the way I know certain facts about my life: Kevin is my husband. I lived in Los Angeles. I love opiates.

It was divine. It was done.

I dropped to my knees.

"Thank you, God." I whispered.

My relationship with God had changed. One day, and I couldn't say when, it felt as real as any other relationship in my life. I missed God when we didn't talk. I looked forward to spending time with Him. He had become my anchor, my constant, the big relief I'd always been looking for. I looked to the brightest star in the sky, Polaris, the North Star, the one I could always count on to see. That was God for me.

Joy was mine tonight. I felt a strange widening inside as I realized I was sold on prayer. Sold on Something Out There wanting to guide me. My God.

My Big G.

31

DAWN

September 2015: Day 184

We sat on the curb of the church parking lot after our AA meeting. With my arms wrapped around my legs, I watched Dawn take a drag from her cigarette. She blew the smoke into the succulents beside her. Her eyes avoided mine.

"Would you sponsor me?"

Dawn had been let go by her sponsor after relapsing on weed, which seemed harsh to me, but I was new to sponsoring, so what did I know? I didn't know Dawn well. I had called her a couple times and sat with her in a few meetings, but I knew the look of relapse. Poof! Just like that, the spark of you is gone. *Why did I drink? I didn't even want to.* I could see it in her slump. She was wearing the mantle of shame we lay upon ourselves, the weight that bends our head, crooks it downward, Hellward. Plus, no one likes being broken up with. Please. I'm still getting over that guy from high school.

I rubbed her back and sighed. Look, I know I come across as a bit of an asshole in *Pillness*, but when I am sober I am basically a heart with legs. I cry at dog adoption videos, 80's movies, and makeover shows. My acupuncturist crowned me an empath and suggested I walk around with a purple crystal in my pocket to keep me "balanced" at meetings. Spoiler alert! It didn't work, or maybe I didn't want it to work. I don't really want to contain who I am.

We sat together for a moment as she took another drag, the smoke drifting into her long brown hair. Did she feel from me what I had felt from Liz? An instant connection. Safe. Seen. Did she really "want what I had" or was I just a rebound sponsor? It didn't matter to me. I couldn't say no when someone was hurting as much as she was. I reached for her hand. Her skin was rough.

"Of course I will, Dawn," and her eyes met mine in a tiny glimmer of light.

RIGHT OFF THE top we seemed a curious fit. There was something about Dawn, not so much that I didn't like, but didn't get. If my energy was spirited, hers was bawdy, dropping BJ jokes like we were in high school. She was a street-smart masseuse, older and shorter than me with two grown children. We didn't have much in common besides alcoholism.

I'd sponsored her for a month when she appeared at our Saturday morning women's meeting wearing a glittering mask of golden swirls, horns on her head and neon leggings.

"Hi!" she barked, grinning beneath the mask. I stared, unable to place the person exploding with sequins and feathers.

"It's Dawn!" Her body vibrated. Then she looked at my head. My hair had been chopped, pixie-style.

"You cut your hair," she paused. I nodded. I mean, obviously. It was all gone. "I don't like it, " she spat.

"Well, I don't like you," I wanted to spit back like a big ol' five-year-old, but didn't because I was supposed to be her spiritual guide. Before I could explain that my hair had fallen out after years of immunosuppression and drug abuse, she babbled on about how much she loved Halloween and her myriad plans for the day. I was already aware that Dawn was more interested in socializing than being sponsored.

As I watched her butt wiggle away in those crazy leggings, I remembered I didn't have to like her. It was just suggested I help her.

We started the Steps. *Step One: We admitted we were powerless over alcohol — that our lives had become unmanageable.*

Like me, Dawn was powerless over drugs and alcohol. Once she started drinking or using she couldn't stop, but drinking is just a symptom of alcoholism. Alcoholism is a disease centered in the mind. It is often called a disease of perception. When I believe life is against me, I become afraid of losing what I have or not getting what I want, and I behave badly. I punish. I bully. I am angered. I am in fear. I cut Kevin, my mother, my friends in verbal knife fights, leave them bleeding in the relationship gutter, and stand in the blood of their wounds with my arms crossed in defiance.

Dawn's behaviors were different from mine. She was a people-pleaser, which Liz told me is a nice way of saying you're lying. Dawn often ignored what she wanted in the name of helping others, but then cultivated resentments about how the help was received. Resentments are the number one reason why alcoholics drink again. As a sponsor, it was my job to point this out to her.

Step 2: Came to believe that a Power greater than ourselves could restore us to sanity. For Step Two, I asked Dawn to write about how she was restored. There was no wrong answer.

She sat crossed-legged on my couch, a coil notebook in her lap. She brought her hands together as she spoke, looking at them, touching them with reverence.

"I see sanity in my hands. The gift they are to others."

I cocked my head, surprised, seeing her through new eyes. She was reclaiming her talent as a masseuse. Not with ego, but humility for what made her special. I had been schooled.

"That's beautiful, Dawn."

When I held her hand that first day, her skin felt rough. It hadn't occurred to me that she had lost her sense of purpose. Now she had it back.

"I love being here with you, Hennybear," she bopped on the couch, grinning. My tummy flipped, made uncomfortable by her obvious affection. Why was she so happy to be here with me? Already calling me Hennybear because her nickname was Dawniebear. She even had a purple bear costume to back it up. *Sigh.* Was it ok for a sponsee to nickname a sponsor? I had never nicknamed Liz.

"I'm glad you're here," I offered, quick to put on the sponsor hat, hesitant to become the friend who wouldn't be able to call her on her shit. She grabbed from the blueberries and almonds I'd put out.

"OK," she chomped. In. Always in.

One day my sponsor suggested her sponsees and my sponsees meet for a monthly brunch and Big Book study. We started as seven, and as sponsees got sponsees, grew to 22. Fellows flaked, or relapsed, but Dawn was always there, showing up with a bag of hot bagels and her mile-wide smile, never still, bopping from conversation to conversation, her desire to belong so transparent it made my heart hurt. I crowned us "the Living Womb Women," but she wanted "the Gratitude Gang" after the gratitude train we emailed each other every day. Most of the time we referred to ourselves as The Sober Fam.

Dawn was an adrenaline junkie: a 12-hour Vegas round-trip for a Metallica concert; driving back at 6 am from a Joshua Tree retreat at 100 mph to make our brunch, or backing up our 40-degree angle driveway which neither Kevin or I dared try! Dawn wasn't for everyone. Her energy could be exhausting, much like a puppy's, but she didn't let lukewarm reactions raised eyebrows quell her zest for connection. She barrelled through life like a tank, inviting everyone along for the ride.

Sometimes I had to step in and act like a mom-adjacent sponsor. After Dawn and her brother sprayed some strangers with Silly String, she came to me confused when the victims turned aggressive and chased them.

"Dawn. Some people have medical conditions." She got really quiet. "Or maybe they saved for a year for the outfit they were wearing."

"I never thought of that."

"Know your audience."

Dawn was like misguided kid who came to me about her shoplifting, and how angry it made her feel.

"It's not yours. You don't get to take something unless you pay for it."

"But organic almond butter is $18!"

"I can't afford organic almond butter!" I knew my argument was weak, but wondered how she couldn't see that stealing was wrong. And yet, hadn't I justified stealing medication from Kevin? Friends? Strangers? Who was I to pass judgment? This realization felt awfully biblical. I knew I was no saint. I could only be an example and remind her she would have make amends by paying these companies back.

"But they are so rich!" she pouted.

"Yes, but you still don't get to steal."

Dawn was a Newcomer, and not ready to change her ways. Her alcoholism was popping up as stealing. She was riding the buzz of the steal and feeling the consequence of the bad behaviour. My job was not to fix her, it was to love her and call her on her shit no matter what.

July 19th, 2017: Day 860

A month after Dawn hit one year sober, we went to a 12-Step women's retreat at a Catholic monastery in the Sierra Madre hills. Driving through the gate, a gigantic crucifix dominated the property. 60 of us slept in sparse rooms with single beds, ate in a dining hall, and hiked up the back hillside where coyotes (and occasionally even a bear) were spotted.

At one of the meetings, it was Dawn's turn to share on a Step.

"Sorry you're going to find out this way," she whispered, head down. My heart stopped. What was going on? "I only have 34 days."

The room burbled with sighs, the energy shifting from passive to ignited, the way it always does when someone is brave enough to tell the truth. I ran up to her at the break and tried to squeeze the shame right out of her.

"Are you okay?"

"Yes." Her expression was soft, like the truth had been let out of her gently, and not with a disruptive pop.

"That was very brave." I rubbed her legs from my squat on the floor and promised we would talk. Women swarmed around her. Another woman whispered to me,

"Talk about the perfect sponsor..." It was true. I, too, took a cake for one year of sobriety knowing I had taken eight Vicodin a few months earlier. I knew the shame of relapse, and the freedom that came with finally telling the truth.

When the retreat ended, Dawn and I watched everyone carpool away, the chatter settling into the quiet of a hot summer day. We sat under an overhang, looking out to the landscaped area home to the Stations of the Cross: 14 events portraying the passion of Jesus Christ, from his condemnation from Pontius Pilate to his entombment. They were marked by marble monuments along a path shaded by gnarled trees.

Catholicism still felt icky to me decades after my father's death, but I had to admit, I found walking through the garden peaceful. Taking in the statues, I heard deer munching, or felt them nearby with the snap of a twig. As sunlight streamed through the trees and onto my shoulders, I felt the presence, not of a Catholic God I understood, but of others' belief in one. And it reminded me of my best moments with Daddy in church. That felt meaningful.

But this place also reminded me of all the dogma I never understood. How Catholics believe in denial and sin and confession and punishment. Had I sinned? Sin is defined as "an immoral act considered to be a transgression against divine law."

I had not asked for alcoholism. I wasn't a bad person. We weren't bad people. I had done bad things in my disease, but was that sinning? That didn't seem right. And it shouldn't be up to another man to decide if I had sinned. We were all flawed and no one had the right to point a finger at another. I believed only God could point a finger.

The God I chose in Alcoholics Anonymous wouldn't call me a sinner. I had chosen a patient and loving God; not so I could continue my bad behavior, my "sinning," but so I could be free from it.

I rubbed Dawn's back. She looked tired, but not unhappy.

"Do you want to work with another sponsor?"

She shook her head. "I don't want to work with anyone else."

"Okay. What happened?" She looked down the long driveway toward the priest's house where deer were often spotted.

"I wanted to be a cool mom." She had smoked pot with her son, but it had been miserable, disconnecting her from everyone, and especially herself. I felt her anguish in my bones. I had been there, too.

"It stops working." I said.

"And it feels like Hell."

I nodded and took her hand. She was done. I could see it in her eyes. It was not shame or defeat, but a gentle surrender like that of a child. *I didn't want that stupid toy anyway.* She wanted to be sober and free.

WE WERE READING Step One on the grass outside an AA meeting. She offered me a slice of her organic Fuji apple from the paring knife.

"Isn't this the best apple you've ever tasted?" It wasn't, but her joy was precious, so I swerved around the truth.

"It's delicious, Dawn."

She read me some ideas for a mobile dance party — a potential side hustle for her massage gigs. She reminded me of Bedstemor, with her bright eyes and frenetic gestures and motor mouth that Dawn must have been teased about as a child. I prayed to my Danish grandmother in the beginning of my recovery because of her gratitude for everything — from a bowl of ice cream to satellites in space. She was present for it all.

Dawn offered me another slice of her apple and I laughed. She had showed up at the Saturday morning meeting with a shit-eating grin wearing a "My sponsor can kick your sponsor's ass" T-shirt and we howled as she paraded around the room. Everywhere we went, she beamed introducing me as her sponsor, adding...*she lives in chronic pain...her skin is always burning...*Darn it if I wasn't falling in love with her a little. This wonderful and nutty tank of love, reminding me to be present for that apple slice, because the small things in life are the big things after all.

DURING A ROUTINE MAMMOGRAM in early 2018, a lump was found in Dawn's breast. It came back as Stage 1 triple negative breast cancer, the most aggressive type of breast cancer. Most patients die within five years. Her oncologist wanted her to have a lumpectomy, but Dawn wanted to wait and treat it holistically through diet. She stopped smoking. By April, the lump had grown.

"You would have the surgery?"

"Yes, Dawn. Yesterday."

I began reading about cancer. Watched documentaries. Cancer deserved respect. It was a fucking demon. I was convinced Dawn was making a mistake believing in diet as a cure. I knew she was afraid of the procedures and chemo and pain, of entering a medical world she knew nothing about and hadn't wanted to. She was telling herself diet would work so cancer wouldn't become real. And oh, how I related.

In 2007, I read an article on a woman who did not need immunosuppression for her kidney transplant. She was an anomaly, but I made that information my North Star. Immediately, I, too, wanted to be the transplant patient who no longer needed Medical Science. I stopped taking half of my immunosuppression and likely caused the rejection of my kidney transplant a year later. My transplant was 21 years old and possibly on its way out, so I will never know for sure, but I know I acted out of fear.

I was afraid of the colds and viruses that went on for days and weeks, in fear of the long-term side-effects of immunosuppression like osteoporosis and cancer. Fearful I would always be sick, and therefore left behind. I wanted to be in control of my health.

If I had run my decision by anyone, they would have said, "That sounds ill-informed." If I had gone to my transplant team they would have said, "You will reject." And I brushed Kevin off when he asked why I had extra boxes of immunosuppression. I didn't talk to anyone. I wanted to protect my right to believe in the most rare and random truth. And I rejected.

Do I regret it? Yes. Would I have done anything differently? I don't know. We only learn through consequences, right? But I understood Dawn. I understand how illness can swallow you whole and you'll believe anything to find your way out of the whale.

June 11th, 2018: Day 1187

Dawn had a lumpectomy six months after diagnosis. I was driving home when the call came through.

"He says I will die if I don't get chemotherapy."

I swallowed. My hands tightened around the steering wheel as I climbed northwest up the 2 Freeway. The sun melted, slithering behind the hills, leaving ribbons of tangerine and violet. Such beauty before the end of the day. Such glory before its goodbye.

I paused, aware that my next words should be profound, but I didn't know what to say to someone who was going to die of cancer.

"Well, this is fucking devastating."

"Yeah." We were quiet. Dawn was driving back from a friend who pushed supplements like they were narcotics and Dawn was buying. I felt my eyes roll when she told me, grateful she couldn't see me.

"I'm going to Texas to do a 10-day fast." My chest tightened.

"Are you sure you want to do that?" Dawn was no academic, but she wasn't dumb.

"I'll keep eating healthy..."

My body shook with a bizarre and unchecked rage. Why was she disregarding Medical Science? I didn't want her to listen to her 20-year-old daughter who wouldn't take a Tylenol for an infection. I didn't want her to take supplements. I wanted to go back to January and make her get the lumpectomy. I wanted my friend to be well.

"Juice doesn't fucking cure cancer!" I screamed.

The second it was out, I felt terrible. I wanted to dive into the atmosphere and take it back, take a straw and slurp up the words, loudly, comically, making funny faces to force us to laugh.

"I'm sorry, Dawn. That was wrong." My voice was shaking. The engine roared beneath me and realized I was speeding. I lifted my foot from the accelerator and took a few breaths.

"No," she insisted. "I want you to speak your truth." I said nothing, stunned by her generous heart.

My truth. What was my truth? I wanted Dawn to choose Medical Science. My friend Laurie had triple negative breast cancer and lived almost 10 years past her diagnosis, but her treatments were frequent and brutal. At her end, chemotherapy was injected straight into her brain through an Ommaya reservoir, tens of times. She had more time with her children, but at what cost to her quality of life?

The transplant team had pushed me on the immunosuppressant Tacrolimus as safer for my kidney, but the side effects (migraines, tremors, anorexia, nausea, back pain) were intolerable after one day, never mind a lifetime, and I declined. I take Cyclosporine instead, an immunosuppressant that is more toxic to my kidney, thereby decreasing the kidney's life, but increasing my quality of life.

Hadn't I told the dermatologists that if they could stop my Pain, if they could find the Off switch, I would give them three, four, five years of my life? Years. Yes. Happily. If I could live a better quality of life.

You decide if your life is worthwhile.

The last pop of orange vanished into the horizon. If Dawn wanted to spend the rest of her life fasting and drinking juice and swallowing supplements, it was her choice. Maybe extra time pumped full of toxic medications and shitty side effects wasn't worth it to her? There would be consequences, perhaps even death, but I understood her willingness to roll that die.

She had cancer, but it would not have her.

~

In September, Dawn went from Stage 1 to Stage IV. In October, she tried her first chemotherapy pill even as I thought, *It's much too late for this, my darling friend*. She immediately complained of burning feet and hands.

"I don't know how you do it," she cried.

"I don't either."

Didn't I? Any peace in my body came from connecting to Big G, but I didn't judge Dawn. If it had been a pill making my skin burn, I would have stopped, too.

She stopped taking chemotherapy as abruptly as she had started.

December was the last Sober Fam she would attend. In January, she was hospitalized and learned the cancer had spread to her liver. She declined another PET scan. She knew it was everywhere.

~

February 2nd, 2019: Day 1423

Our torsos pressed together as 60 women cackled around us, sipping coffees and grabbing seats. Dawn was warm, her clutch strong, but her breath came in slight shudders. I shivered, picturing the cancer clawing at her lungs, devouring her breasts, her liver, her. But she wouldn't let go. We hugged on, calm, smothering the glut of disease between us: alcoholism, cancer, transplants, Pain. Then she shifted. I flinched when she let go.

"Your skin hurts," she said. I gave her a small smile.

"Yes," I laughed, although none of this was funny.

Dawn loved hard. Once you bonded with her, she noticed everything, like she was captain of your ship and it was her mission to watch over and protect you. She held her side as she took a seat, and my heart twisted. It was the first time I realized I wanted to be seen without bringing Pain up. That seeing each other is the greatest gift we can offer.

But that this gift should come from her...

FEBRUARY 3RD, 2019: Day 1424

The summer before, Dawn had organized a prayer circle for my Pain. She wore tie dye and a look of peace that softened her fine lines. She researched a format and used a Tibetan singing bowl to guide 10 women around me in a circle. She was masterful, encouraging them to make eye contact and offer whatever words of healing sprang to heart. Tears streamed down my face as I accepted this gift in awe. She stood tall in love, full circle from the woman who sat on a curb smoking, head down, cigarette smoke unable to cloud her shame.

The next day, she was visibly surprised when I told her I still had Pain. It was adorable. I had not believed my Pain would be gone the next day, but that Dawn expected it to made me wonder why I hadn't.

A GO FUND Me was no prayer circle, but I wanted to do something for Dawn who struggled to make ends meet. Shannon, a sponsee, helped me set it up, and read it back to me.

"As most of you know, our precious friend Dawn Michelle Whitesell has been ill. Dawn has incurable, Stage IV, triple negative, metastatic breast cancer. She is no longer compatible with chemotherapy..."

Silence fell hard. It felt wrong. Like writing a eulogy for someone who was still alive. We sat a few minutes looking through the wall of windows into the dark. While we'd been working, night had swooped in with its blanket of shadows. Coyotes and cars were out there, but from where we sat it was all black. Was God out there? All I could feel was the finality of death. No light, no movement, no sound. Shannon spoke.

"I don't get it. She got sober. Had a year clean..."

"And then this?"

I got sober for this?

Yes. We get sober for this.

FEBRUARY 5TH, 2019: Day 1426

Dawn was admitted to the hospital with dyspnea — when cancer spreads from other organs to the lungs. This is also called "air hunger," the name of which makes me want to burst into tears. I stayed with her for hours. We talked, played cards, and lapped the floor together. If she could do it twice, she could go home. I went to get her a smoothie while she napped and then Lucy, her daughter, brought homemade soup. Not one time did she ask for pain relief. She wasn't on anything that day. I couldn't imagine she wasn't in any pain.

For months Dawn and I talked about the question of pain meds. How can we use them responsibly in recovery? But Dawn had become stone cold sober. She no longer wanted to be high or out of pain or out of cancer. I was watching someone fight to be in every last minute of her life no matter how uncomfortable that was. Dawn didn't want to lose the connection she had finally found — to us, to God, and most importantly, I think, to herself.

At one point she stopped talking and looked at me.

"I want to come to Canada to visit you." My breath caught and I tried not to look surprised. Didn't she know she was actively dying? I was moving in three months. She would never visit me in Canada. But she had never acknowledged death as a possibility, so who was I to invite it into the conversation?

She was losing her body to cancer, but maybe she was refusing to let it have the rest — her heart and soul. That's how she needed to live now, believing all dreams were still possible. Maybe that's denial.

Who fucking cares. I wanted her to visit me in Canada. I wanted her to have that. I pinched myself under the tray table, refusing to pop tears.

"I want you to come to Canada."

On the drive home from the hospital, Dawn texted me. *That's the most time we've ever spent together! I'm so happy!* I doubled over at the wheel, wailing. It was so unfair. The way Dawn lived in the moment was exquisite and deserving of a long life, not one she must have known was almost over.

Two years earlier, when we read Step Three, we talked about God. (*Step 3: Made a decision to turn our will and our lives over to the care of God, as we understood Him.*) She believed there was no good or bad in life. She believed God was in everything, and that sadness and joy were interwoven with meaning we will never understand. For Dawn, God was trusting that life would always balance itself out the way it was supposed to.

I wiped away the tears and texted her back.

It's a joy to spend time with you, Dawniebear. An absolute joy.

She would lap the floor again and go home for the last time.

February 11th, 2019: Day 1432

When I met her at the oncologist, she introduced me as her sister. (Weren't we, though?) Dawn sat in a wheelchair, wheezing, her skin the color of daffodils. With great sadness, and perhaps a bit of judgment darkening his face, her oncologist told her *it didn't have to be this way* and to *make some decisions;* she bluntly amended this to *put my affairs in order?* to which he nodded, and left.

She was curled on the exam table. I hovered near her face and whispered.

"Dawn..." Her eyes were closed. "We've raised $15,000 for your children."

She opened her eyes. They were yellow. It was happening.

"Hennybear..." she breathed, and closed them again.

I didn't mention the money was also for her memorial because we still weren't talking about death.

FEBRUARY 14TH, 2019: Day 1435

When I walked into Dawn's apartment I could hear her throwing up. A coldness gripped me. Up to 60% of cancer patients at the end of their lives throw up brown liquid.

"Do you need help?" I called out. The door opened and I nodded at her ex-husband, John. Dawn leaned against him, struggling to walk.

"Not feeling so good, Hennybear." My stomach lurched, as I set down a bag of snacks and books.

"I know, Sweetheart."

John tucked her into bed. She lived in a large one-bedroom apartment, but her son had the bedroom, so Dawn slept in the middle of her living room. To someone who didn't know her, this would seem disrespectful or wrong, but I knew it was where she was happiest. She lived to exist in the center of the world she had created — family and friends coming and going and sleeping and laughing and talking and crying as she lay dying.

I wiped my palms on my jeans. One by one, they arrived, bringing Dawn an AA meeting. My sponsor Danielle, beautiful and stoic, who held her cards close to the vest. My sponsee Justine, brilliant and independent. Danielle's sponsee and my soul sister Amy who worked in hospice. And sensitive Shannon who strutted in bearing a magnificent arrangement of orchids from all of us. Justine turned into me for a hug, crying. She was the closest to Dawn, my first two sponsees who loved each other like siblings.

We settled on the bed around her, hands over thighs over legs. Dawn was propped up against multiple pillows, her stomach distended, a mountain of malignancy. Her eyes fluttered shut for long seconds, even minutes at a time. She struggled to speak, pushing through words as if her tongue was frozen. Never had I wanted to hear the babbling brook of her voice more.

"I just want to say..." Her mouth contracted as if chewing through taffy, straining to form the next words. Justine squeezed my hand. There we sat, all of us, tears brimming, poised at the edge of our eyelids, ready to tumble down cheeks flushed with disbelief, watching our friend fight for every last word.

"I know you guys can't tell, but I'm actually jumping up and down." We laughed brokenly, stung by the irony. That the one person who never stood still for anything could now barely move.

Then Dawn hugged Sobear, the teddy bear that had her children's voices inside. With a flicker of a grin, she squeezed a leg and cried out, "Listen!"

I love you sooo much, Mom! It was her son's voice. A gasp erupted beside me. Danielle's face was scrunched and red, a burst of agony ripping her heart. Then tears. I had never seen Danielle cry.

I had never seen Dawn so happy. There we were, her chosen family, the pile of us, smothering and holding her up, woven into the shredding tapestry of her final moments. Squeezing hands and kissing foreheads, hearts ripping and smiles breaking. The good and the bad interwoven, love and disease, laughter and tears, heartbreak and pain, her life and death. Unmistakably, the presence of God.

On my way home, I pictured that tiny person who came racing up to me dripping sequins and joy. My cheeks stung with tears. She was leaving me.

Leaving. I thought leaving was the worst thing a person could do.

Dawn believed God was in everything. Embracing the bad with the good is where we find Him. In my life and Pain. In her life and cancer. Not playing God, deciding that cancer or Pain is wrong. Embracing all of it is where my peace lives. It is where I find my God at last. She left me with that.

Oh, Dawn. You aren't leaving me at all.

Written on February 16th, 2019: Day 1437

Dawniebear—

You left last night during a wild and nourishing rainstorm much like your spirit. A powerful force of nature roaring through life, showering love wherever you went.

You could not help yourself, Dawniebear. You lived with the most magical of all maladies: Tourette's of the heart. Always asking, helping, loving those around you.

It was your way. To squeeze every possible drop out of life. You found value in every overlooked moment and spun it into gold.

It is a bright and glorious morning as the rays lick the cold canyon awake. My heart is simultaneously breaking and rejoicing. Your body has stilled, Dawn, but your dazzling soul will shine on.

Your Hennybear.

~

February 12th, 2019: Day 1433

Two nights before she died, Dawn sent her last gratitude list. I like to read it on days when I forget Big G is in the house, and remember that all I have to do is open the door.

~

GRATEFUL:

That I'm sober and feeling stronger.

To see so many things that support a vision that God seems to have for me now.

So happy.

DID WELL:

Rested.

Connected deep.

Cried a lot.

MOOD:

Happy.
SAW GOD:
In everything.

32

GALLBLADDER

It's been said that God has a sense of humor, but I never had a spiritual funny bone until now. Those who read *Pillness* will recall my hate-on for Winnipeg the size of, well, Winnipeg...

*For long, long months, winter dominates. Brutal arctic temperatures pound the city with a gavel of unrelenting cold. I could never warm up, outside or in...*Dramatic, much?...*Outside the heavens revealed endless hues of gray. If the color were a paint chit, it would have been called "Suicidal Sludge."* Good God!

Winnipeg. It was the last thing I ever thought I would suggest to Kevin. And yet, there I was, on the eve of my 50th birthday, suggesting we move back to his hometown affectionately known as Winterpeg, Manisnowba, the place he left at 18, swore never to return to, and where I knew beyond a shadow of a doubt we would end up.

With a floppy smile and semi-sad eyes, I saw Kevin was on board. In Los Angeles, we had fallen into the middle-class gap — too poor to thrive and too rich to get breaks. Moving made sense for work, school, family, and health care. The light of our future flickered off the shimmering snowflakes sure to fall due north.

Needing a warm coat five (six? seven?) months out of the year and leaving our LA communities would be an adjustment. Who knew a pandemic would zoom in with technology to change how we communicated forever. As I watched Kevin step lighter, smile brighter, stand straighter in our final Californian months, I trusted the decision. It hadn't been made for me, us. We had made it. Big G and me. Funny, eh?

~

March 15th, 2019: FOUR YEARS

On January 7th, I became Miriam bat Sarah. Dawn died in February, and by March I had flown to Winnipeg to buy our new house.

By April, our magical cabin in the hills, the place where we had our transplant, loved three dogs, healed our marriage, I found recovery and wrote *Pillness*, the longest place I had ever lived, was sold. On May 3rd, 2019, a week after Dawn's memorial, we were U-Hauling it up to the Great White North.

Our return to Canada was invigorating. The familiar pull of a light jacket over my shoulders in the May crispness, the sassy waddle of the Canadian goose, and the stunning miracle of spring, glowing green blades emerging from frozen soil. It was right. This move felt good. Big G was tracking.

Kevin and I got all the things: a palace of a house, a yard, and we lived close to Kevin's family. In canine twist no one saw coming, Wahlter, now in his 15th year, took to the cooler weather with renewed waddle. Kevin settled into photography and acting, and returned seven times to LA to work and play pipes. I self-published *Pillness* in July. It would go on to sell 9000 copies, en par with most traditionally published books.

But here's the thing about moving. You take it with you. You, body and soul. Moving to Winnipeg meant Pain was here, too.

~

DECEMBER 15TH, 2019: DAY 1739

The first thing we set up in the house was my sauna. I joined a gym for those endorphins, got in with the transplant clinic, and a primary care physician, and referrals. My dermatologist, Dr. S. worked quickly, reading through my literal stacks of medical records and setting me up with Winnipeg's equivalent of a Grand Rounds with 11 dermatologists. I had met one of them, a Dr. Ihateu, a month earlier. She barely glanced at my skin or paperwork, and made no eye contact as she diagnosed me with dermographism (red welts!) and prescribed a minty lotion. I let myself cry in the car for five minutes before getting another referral for Dermatologist #2, Dr. S. Despite the word on the street, Canadians can be assholes, too.

Dr. S. reviewed the feedback from Grand Rounds and concluded that Pain was most likely a nerve issue, as Dr. A. in LA had suspected. Therefore, he would not approve phototherapy, despite my year at USC.

"Your immunosuppression is a concern. Skin cancer might be an issue in five to ten years."

I got very quiet and took a deep breath before speaking. *Do not cry.*

"I know the risks. I would give you years of my life to make this pain stop."

"I feel bad for you," his voice cracked. "I'm sorry."

You had to hand it to him for apologizing. I wanted to say, "If you're going to deny me the treatment, at least be a dick about it," but I didn't. I did wonder how it had come to be that I was the one in Pain, knew what would help me, was willing to absorb any risk, the head of transplantation at Cedars-Sinai didn't have a problem with phototherapy, but one doc dude in Winnipeg had the power to say no.

Along with his apology, he suggested an allergy pill that might get rid of the redness that rarely appeared anymore. Medical science, eh!

My Canadian medical adventures continued. The transplant clinic suggested I go on Septra, an antibiotic that can prevent a strain of pneumonia that recently killed a few immunosuppressed patients.

After one day on it, Pain flared at an 8 for three weeks. Panicked, I refused it. Could Septra really have done that after one day? Tacrolimus slayed me with side effects after a few short hours. I must have seemed crazy to the Canadians. An ooey-gooey hippie Californian declining medical protocol. All I knew was what Pain told me, and despite how far Big G and me had come, there were days when I couldn't hear anything but Pain.

I couldn't believe I was still holding my body Hangman-taut so clothes wouldn't touch it, still fondling thrift store finds for their potential to harm. *It's cute, but do I want to wear sandpaper?* With a sweet smile, Kevin suggested we travel. *Wouldn't that be fun?* and I thought *No. Traveling is no longer fun.* Away from my bedsheets, sauna, and white noise machines? The feel of the airplane seat, the quest to find uninflammatory foods, disruption from my predictable and middling existence? No. Unfun.

I had dark moments. Eclipse dark. I hated being called an inspiration for staying sober. I knew it was something to be proud of, but was tired of unimmediate gratification. I wanted one glass of wine to relax, or a pill to sleep. You get to kick off your shoes and have a beer. I wanted to kick off Pain and have a cold one, too. Cliches like "One day at a time," "Let go and let God," "Easy does it," felt tired and empty. Like me.

There were nights in my gigantic Canadian house when I felt like I'd lost my way. Wandering through rooms, turning on lights, trying to find the light within, Pain stalking every step. Some days, I couldn't feel Big G at all, never mind in everything, as Dawn believed.

Pain felt punishing again, and so I punished back, as I had in my past when relationships didn't go my way. I stopped talking to Him. I stopped trusting the big balancing act in the sky. I stopped choosing to believe there is no good or bad, just God. There was bad and it was Pain! Bad! Bad! Bad!

And I would be alone in the Pain again.

~

MARCH 12TH, 2021: SIX YEARS

JULY 2ND, 2021: Day 2304

Eat. Swim. Love. It's what you do on summer nights in Winnipeg. The nights are long and bright, reminding me of Danish summer evenings popping with birdsong and bloom. A time when sickness tap-tap-tapped its finger on my tiny shoulder from across an ocean. It followed us there, floated on the salty brine to stalk two small siblings, trying for a moment, if not a summer, to escape the inescapable. The same ocean my parents travelled as soul mates, newly married, best friends, to a new country, and as the cliché goes, grew oceans apart, and became, eventually, foam on the sea. My Danish summers were monstrous and poetic in their clarity of what can co-exist — heartbreak tethered to joy.

With summer in Winnipeg you must find water — the lake, a splash pad or a pool. For as cold as the winters are, the summers are hot and sopping, with long, romantic nights. One evening, I snapped a picture of Kevin and me on our way to swim — me in my bathing suit and pink shorts pulled over my bum, Kevin complaining about heartburn.

"Hang on! I just wanna post," as I wrote *My ride or die!*

When we got home, his complaints had increased. This was unusual for Kevin who basically bit down on a stick after giving me a kidney. He kept rubbing the upper right area of his abdomen. All evening I pointed to one fact.

"That's your liver, Sweetheart."

"Yeah. I think I should go."

At a quarter to midnight a cab came to take him to the ER, Covid-19 restrictions forbidding me from coming along for the wait.

"It's probably just heartburn." His voice was tight with discomfort.

"I hope so. Better safe than sorry."

There were no lingering kisses, just a quick hug. He'd be right back.

I waved from the doorstep until the tail lights vanished, and then waved still. Just because I could no longer see him, didn't mean he could no longer see me.

At the end of our Danish summers, Bedstemor and Bedstefar waved us up the escalator to international departures. We waved back, laughing, tripping at the top because we were so busy matching them wave for wave, smile for smile. Before we reached security, I looked back. Bedstemor was windshield wiping her arms, Bedstefar standing tall, Scandinavian and strong, waving arms that held our hands, hands that held us in the water, limbs rippling like the seaweed we dodged, like branches blowing in the winds of change, swaying from the shoulders I sat on as a girl. I took one step toward the gate, and whirled around again. They were gone! *No!* I cried. *Bedstefar!* Through tears, I spotted the tips of Bedstefar's fingers wiggling in the air — unable to see me, trusting I could see him, wanting me to know he was still waving, loving me still.

KEVIN'S GALLBLADDER CAME OUT. Although a routine procedure, it was worrisome since he had already sustained multiple laparoscopic procedures in his core — a double hernia, nephrectomy, and spinal fusion. When I picked him up two days later, he waddled out of the ER like an old man, clutching a rounded tummy. The ER nurse caught it, too.

"Are you okay?" she called out.

"It hurts," he managed, carefully folding himself into the car.

My tummy flopped. I hated knowing he was in pain with nothing I could do to help. The Canadian health care system is notoriously strict with pain meds, and he was prescribed T3s (Tylenol 3 with codeine), the dregs of pain relief. Quite constipating. Very unfun.

Kevin never relaxed, holding his side all evening. I left him alone by request, his generally good-natured mood punctured by pain. The situation confused me. I knew four people with gall-bladder removals, and they had experienced only minor discomfort.

~

July 7th, 2021: Day 2309

By morning, his pain was worse. Much worse.

"Sweetheart..." His breath escaped in puffs.

"Have you pooped yet?" I asked, but could see that wasn't the problem. His stomach was massive, ballooning out beneath clenched hands. He paced with a rigidity I recognized from holding my own body against Pain.

"What's your pain level?"

"Nine." The word sputtered out of him. I wanted to throw up.

On the phone, our family doctor said he didn't like that Kevin's stomach was distended.

"Go back to Emerg."

Kevin writhed as I swerved around potholes, crying out at the tiniest bump. He pushed at his abdomen, shoving the hot water bottle into his flesh, searing it red. I knew that move. Pitting pain against pain to make it all go away.

I walked with him as far as I could before security blocked my path into the ER.

"Tell them you were just here!" My stomach churned with upset, crazed I wasn't allowed to wait with him. I needed to fight for his right to be seen. One thing I knew how to do was fight.

Kevin saluted at half mast, then hobbled into the shadows of the waiting room. I waved until I could no longer see him, then stretched my arms up like Bedstefar, and waved on. *Can you see me, Sweetheart?* Arms that had pounded and caressed him, arms that wanted to pull him back into our world and never let him go.

That evening, I took Wahlter on one of his last walks. He was 17 now, snow white and bony. We plodded along together, the air sick with humidity. Unstirring. Heavy. All of me felt heavy, longing for

Kevin. Longing to have my world restored. How quickly it had turned upside down without him.

Wahlter sniffed at the sticky sidewalks. Aphids left their sugar water-like residue on everything. Harmless (but gross) infection-like gunk that contributed to the general dark mood of the summer. It was LA hot, stifling and dry. Drought conditions had seared the green lawns into patches of straw, yellow and fried. Wildfires plagued much of Canada, especially the northern prairies.

I coughed with the smoke. There was no one on the street. Everyone was inside with air conditioning or swimming in pools. Pulling the top of my sundress over my nose, I looked up, spotting that familiar neon orb popping through the haze, the burning sun, the one that had terrified me after our evacuation. With a global pandemic still vibrating around the globe, life felt End of Times-ish.

I checked my phone. No updates. I knew Kevin had been admitted and his gallbladder surgeon had revisited his wound. They'd given him something for pain, but it wasn't helping, which brought me to nausea. I couldn't shake the feeling of dread. Of feeling so very small in this world.

Finally, my husband called. It was a whisper.

"They're putting me back under." Kevin's breath sounded punctured, raspy and short. "It hurts to breathe."

"sweetheart," I whispered, all lower case.

"The surgeon is going to call you."

"Kevin is leaking bile into his abdomen." My heart rapped in my throat as I strained to hear her faraway voice. "This happens in 1% of gallbladder removals."

Because his gallbladder was remarkably diseased, the clamps used to close off his bile duct during surgery cut the withered tissue and created a leak. Leaking bile inflames our abdominal cavity and is extremely painful. If left untreated, a bile duct leak can be fatal. The surgery was an emergency re-laparoscopy to place a stent in the duct and stop the leakage. It would take about an hour.

How could this happen? I wanted to yell at the 28-year-old kid-surgeon Kevin had found on Facebook with three mutual friends. But this person was trying to save my husband's life, so with a bitter swallow, I thanked her instead.

"Take care of him. I'll be here."

I wandered through the house, stuffy and warm. We had no air conditioning. Why invest for the one month out of the year it was needed? Opening a window was pointless. There was no movement outside, no air I could create within. Breath hung out in my lungs, trapped. *Breathe, Henriette.* My world and the rest of the world on lockdown. My phone dinged.

I sent you an email.

I clicked on my mail. In the subject line was one word:

Passwords.

I fell on the bed and wailed.

Wahlter sat beside me, his withered old body curled into a hard-won ball. I stroked the nape of him, bending to kiss his still-soft fur. His eyes locked on me. I lay down beside him, sinking into the indent bodies had made over time, sick and excited and tired bodies, wanting to eviscerate this agony, this falling into dark. Kevin was being opened up and there was nothing I could do.

I pulled my legs in toward my torso, bending my limbs just fine. No flares of annoyance. Strange that my broken body should feel so calm. But my heart. What if he had been leaking for bile too long? What if...I wouldn't Google. She said it would be an hour. All I had to do was wait for an hour. I couldn't do it. Yes, I could. Did I want a drink? No. Did I want a drug? No. What did I want?

I wanted Kevin to be okay.

I moved to the open window and dropped to my knees. Tears rolled down my cheeks as I brought my hands under my chin and whispered into the thick air.

God / Grant me the serenity / to accept the things I cannot change / courage to change the things I can / and wisdom to know the difference.

The Serenity Prayer. It had been my first attempt at prayer after Daddy. On the floor, in rehab, I muddled through these strange words as my addicted life came back to me in sober flashes, arms up on my tiny bed, hands inaugurally, awkwardly clasped in prayer.

10 years ago. A time when I could not imagine life without pills and the relief they brought from the burden of my life. How had I landed in a treatment center, 10 minutes away from the Hollywood Walk of Fame, where I had always imagined myself shining from the ground, left there by my shattered husband, who I dragged through addiction for unforgiveable miles?

Somehow, we had survived.

The evening light was ashy and dim, with a flash of blue. Unconditional blue. I pictured Kevin's eyes closed, his stomach clamped open, swirling bile, liquid black, drowning him, taking him away from me.

Leaving. I thought leaving was the worst thing a person could do.

I sobbed against the sill. "Please, God. Take me instead."

I reached for our trees, their green leaves soft and melty from the heat. I needed to touch something, feel anything other than this. Through the branches, a wisp of air touched my face like a sigh. A moment of peace rippled through me. I closed my eyes and the sobs came harder.

"I can't live without him." I lay my forehead on my arms for a while.

When I opened my eyes, night had fallen. The air was smoky and stank, beautiful in its own way.

"Kevin..." I murmured.

A love that would break me in two if taken from me. A marriage that had not been easy or calm, but dense with love, thick with it, sometimes quicksand-thick, threatening to sink us both, sometimes Siamese-twins, thick-as-thieves thick, bonded like Crazy Glue in the crazy. How he saved me, and the ways I saved him that people never saw, that were just for us, *'cause they don't know about us.*

Good swirling in with bad.

Something was moving. Air rustled through the trees. The moon glowed, spotlighting ash floating on the breeze. I looked down our street. All quiet. No, it wasn't outside. It was inside me. I brought my hands to my chest and whispered.

"God..."

He had always met me here. Calm inside the chaos. I had forgotten.

I was not alone. Even if it felt like I was alone. Even when I was in so much Pain I couldn't feel Him. Even if things weren't going my way. Even if tears of gratitude weren't streaming down my face. Even if I didn't understand what was happening. Even if Kevin was in critical condition. Even if He wouldn't take me instead.

God was here.

Peace reigned in this horrible and beautiful moment. Peace co-existing with pain, small p.

I looked down at my phone. No texts. No call.

Nothing.

My heart was breaking.

I was going to be okay.

Everything was going to be okay.

33

DECEMBER 13 (GOD)

Daddy —

I can still picture the building. It's not there anymore. The College-Manning Medical Center in Toronto. We are here to clean out your office. How long is it after you died? A week? A month? I'm sure Mum doesn't want to pay the rent any longer than necessary.

When I walk through the front doors, I'm hit by the medicinal smell. It's stale, too, like the air in your bedroom when you have the flu. I picture the X-ray room in the basement with its sick green color on the walls — the color of vomit, phlegm and scrubs. I hate that green. So does Mum. It was the color of our house on Geoffrey Street, the house she bought with your life insurance a year after you died. She painted it soon after.

The vending machine is outside the door to your office. On days you brought us here after school, to take us along on house calls, you would let us get our favorite sodas — Crush cream soda for Nicky and grape for me. The pharmacy is across the hall, but I was too young to pick up anything from the pharmacy. You weren't.

It is a shared office space, one doctor on one side and you on the other. There are chairs in the waiting room and a coat rack dividing the space in half. There is a desk in the corner where your secretary Philomena, works. There is the cupboard of papers I sat in one summer and filed. What was I filing? It couldn't have been too complicated because I was only seven. In the morning, we walked to the Jag together through the underground garage. You were always nattering about something. Probably why I got "chatterbox" on my report card. I inherited the gab from you.

You told me investing in gold was always a good idea. (In your letters to Teresa you were clearly a bit of a gambler, playing the stocks. Even Mum did, too.) I was so proud you asked me to come to work, bouncing beside you, holding your hand. Just you and me. Mum made me the most beautiful summer dresses. Three dresses of a floral print with smocking across the chest, one in green, blue and gold. The green one felt a titch too short, and I kept pulling it down all day.

I glance into the exam room where you burned a wart off my foot without freezing. That HURT. I want to say you burned my flesh, but maybe that's too dramatic, which would be on point. Afterwards, you sent me to school with a note that said *I suggest also, you watch out for Henriette exaggerating the gravity and pain involved re her op.* to which my teacher responded, "*Henriette never mentions her "operation" unless prompted to.* I was no dummy. I knew how to work a room at seven. But you, Daddy. Did you have me pegged? Did you suspect this chatty drama queen would one day master the Pain Scale?

I enter your office. There is a wall of shelves full of books and papers. Mum says we can take whatever we want. I feel flash of delight. *Anything of Daddy's?!* Until the reason why hits me and I want to throw up.

I choose a canon. A small black canon I kept through my twenties, but got rid of because I never knew what meaning it held for you. I take two decorative wooden boxes, one is narrow with sections for stamps and the other stored all my ID, like my birth certificate. Why did I get rid of them? I wish I hadn't. Maybe I got caught up in the hoarding movement. Or the power of now. *Live in the present!* like Mum always says. Except, I think sometimes we use the present as an escape from the past, not freedom from.

Nicky looks around with huge eyes, balancing his big head with a big brain on top of a big heart that is broken like mine. He doesn't take much and gets rid of everything after high school. He didn't even want to keep his yearbooks. It was like he, too, wanted the past to disappear. We haven't talked about you much. It seems hard for him and that is hard for me because I love him very much.

I take your address book. I still have it. When I stick my nose inside, I smell you, and my heart goes wild. It's the leathery smell of you, still there after all this time. A scent thick with depth and weight. The pages are anarchy, full of asterisks and footnotes and emphatic underlines with a red Bic pen. ALCOHOLISM is capitalized next to a phone number in the "A" section. It's only seven numbers long, from the 1970's, a time before Toronto needed an area code. I wonder if you ever called it? I wonder why I never have?

I take 8 x 10 sheets with your letterhead on them. You have boxes of them which hurts my heart. You planned for a career to grow old with. On those sheets, I invited Nicky, now known as Nick, for sleep-overs in my room in our new house. We blew up an air mattress and slept on each other's floors for years, talking into the night. We got very close after you died. It's safe to say the three of us existed inside a group hug after you left, holding on tight, making sure our small family didn't get any smaller.

Because you did leave us.

Leaving. I thought leaving was the worst thing a person can do.

I wish Mum had kept your book. The thriller-in-progress you pounded out on your typewriter on the Barbados shore. Where you drank an entire bottle of port one night and your friends intervened. Did you pshaw them away? *I'm on vacation! You're overreacting!* I would have done the same thing. Did you not think about your diabetes the way I didn't think about my transplant until there was a consequence like acute rejection, or in your case, coma from a klebsiella aerogenes bacterial lung infection prevalent in diabetic and alcohol abusers? And then short-term memory loss and the pen and paper in your shirt pocket that helped you remember your day.

When I asked Mum about your drinking recently, she looked away and said, "I didn't know." She knew you drank, but didn't know what she was dealing with. I used to judge her, but then realized Kevin went through the same thing. And she lost her Kevin. She lost her Kevin. When I realized that, all my judgment melted away.

Alcoholism. They didn't ask for it to land in their lap. They just hoped Hell would disappear. The way the pills did. The way the alcohol did. The way you did. The way I nearly did.

You are sitting at your desk, a cup of Red Rose tea with milk steaming beside you. A cigarette burns in the ashtray, and the Globe and Mail is spread open on your desk. (No glasses. No problem with your eyesight.) You're talking into a cassette recorder, working on another tape to send to Denmark. I strain my ears, listen for slurring, clues to your alcoholism, but there are none. You grin and tell us to enjoy the time in Denmark....*don't you worry about not writing too many letters...you know that you'll always have your Mum and Dad around...*

In 2022, I had the cassette tapes transferred to digital. It had been over two decades since I heard them. You interviewed our neighbor, Jeff Sawchuk who was one year older than me. He had been to the inaugural game opener for the Toronto Blue Jays. I laughed remembering entering the contest to name Toronto's new baseball team. Nicky suggested the Toronto Bats and I suggested the Toronto Balls. You were so delicate in explaining why "The Balls" would never be chosen. Jeff talked about the Osmonds' concert he'd been to at the Ex and you cooed, *"Ohhh, Henriette would be so very jealous of you."* I felt a rush of love for you. That you knew what I loved. That you knew things about me, like my crush on Donny Osmond, and carried this knowledge in your heart.

Death is a trickster. When I play the cassette, it's like you're beside me chuckling and story-telling as if you are still here. Then I hit stop and you leave, just like that, and I am living in Winnipeg with my husband of 29 years and you're actually not here. I am a 55-year-old woman with tears rolling down her face because it is just like that. You left when I was a girl and you were my Daddy.

I see your doctor's bag. "Can I have it?" I ask Mum. She nods. My heart flips. Your long leather bag is full of syringes, medicine and an old Mars bar. The one you took on house calls into Little Italy, checking in on patients with sparkling eyes for you and couches covered in plastic. They adored you almost as much as I did.

I open the bag and pull out your stethoscope and blood pressure cuff. It looks grand and complicated. Kevin used it every day for two years when I went into rejection with Mum's kidney. We had it calibrated in Dr. D.'s office at Cedars-Sinai, but it was in perfect condition. Imagine. 30 years later, and it still worked like a charm. It's when you started coming back to me, into my heart and blogs. I like to think you were there with Kevin, in the wrap of the cuff, and the pump of the gauge, guiding him through your daughter's decline.

I look out the window, behind the patient chairs, and down to your parking spot. I was always so impressed that you had your own spot. Nick told me Marianna looked out the window and caught you drinking. She was visiting and you excused yourself and she saw you retrieve a bottle. Where did you keep it? In the trunk? Under the seat? I only saw them between your legs, or on the floor of the passenger seat. I never hid my drugs in the car. Too risky. Kevin drove too much.

Did she stare, horrified, as you brought the bottle to your lips? Or did she feel compassion, she a doctor too, knowing alcoholism is a disease? Or were you the man in the trench coat on the park bench, clutching a bottle of alcohol in a paper bag? Most people still think about us that way. Like we're some sub-species of human who can't get their shit together, when we try so hard and don't understand why we can't stop.

Had you been thinking about it all morning? Did you shudder with relief with that first sip? I always did. I once ran into the house ahead of Kevin and tore into a bottle of wine with a wrench I grabbed from the toolbox because the grooves on the wine cap were defective and the cap kept spinning round and round. I chugged one glass and then hid a second glass behind the water heater, away from Kevin, thinking, *I'm not an alcoholic. I just don't want to upset my husband.*

Marianna told Nick you were being investigated by the RCMP for falsifying prescriptions. You used Bedstefar's name, Gunnar Kristensen, on prescriptions you picked up. Did you get the idea when they visited for the Montreal Olympics in 1976, two years before you died? Because you felt sick from diabetes and drink? I understand that. I often wished I could have prescribed myself something. Not because I wanted to get high, but because I was tired of feeling sick from kidney failure.

The addict in me wonders what you were taking. Speed to wake you up after drinking too much? You could rationalize needing to be alert for your patients. I could always justify a pill's use. Benzodiazepines for tremors from the immunosuppressants. Barbiturates for my migraines. Opiates for a ruptured cyst. And what about nausea, fatigue and insomnia from renal failure? Or disappointment, judgment or anger? Or my nail broke, Maggie peed in the house or its Wednesday? Those ills deserved a pill, too. They worked well for hangovers, too, even if those were our fault.

But, Daddy, how many prescriptions were you prescribing for the RCMP to be involved? There was no computerized tracking system back then. Did the clinic's pharmacist bust you? When you picked them up across the hall, did they look at you suspicious, the way I always felt the pharmacist looked at me?

I take piles of your prescription pads and think about all the lists I will write. Lists were my first obsession at six. What-I-am-doing-What-I-would-like-to-do-What-I-have-done. Teresa noticed I made them when she came to visit us from Jerusalem. She saw my list-making as an intense form of OCD in someone so young. Now I see list-making as a drug. Getting relief by trying to control the uncontrollable.

I never thought about them as prescription pads, tools for getting drugs, which I suppose is ironic, but I was only 10. They were just pads of paper I used because I liked seeing your name every day.

Having you close. Still somehow a part of my world. I have 197 lists on my iNotes. I make lists all the time, but leave them for months. Don't look at them or update them. Like Kevin's bottles of scotch in the house that I don't want to drink. This feels like freedom.

I leave your office and walk through the waiting area. For decades this was where I thought you fell, unconscious. Last summer, Mum told me you collapsed in your endocrinologist's office. You were rushed to hospital, and then transferred to St. Joseph's Hospital where you would die a few days later. Every time I ask a question, she tries, answering one or two, before flickering like an old lightbulb and going dark. Then she changes the subject.

I love her so much.

I wish I'd been older when you died. I would have kept all your papers. Studied them. Learned about you. But maybe I would have thrown them out, like the canon and the wooden boxes. And what would I have learned? What can we really know about another person when we don't have them here? I have Teresa's letters and the cassettes, and don't know you the way I want to. I still don't know why you had to leave.

I walk outside to College Avenue and hop onto the 506 Carlton streetcar. The route ends in a loop in the east side of High Park where we moved after you died. Mum told me you guys drove down Parkside Drive screaming "I love Onions" by Susan Christie when you first moved to Canada. I love picturing that. I can't visit the park without thinking about you. About soccer games and tobogganing and leisurely drives spotting the most colorful autumn leaves.

For a long time, I compartmentalized you. You were a picture in a frame on a shelf. Over the years, I looked at you and dusted the frame, but couldn't let you live in my heart. I'm sorry, Daddy. I feel like I need to say sorry for that. But I couldn't breathe without you, and I needed to breathe. We all did. The sickness and darkness had lifted and we needed to breathe again.

When I was a child I told people you died from pneumonia, which was officially the truth. But I always knew diabetes and the brown bottles were involved. You were a doctor. You knew your wild blood sugars caused by drinking beer, at a time when it was very difficult to control insulin levels, made it impossible for the doctors to control your infections. But I knew drinking rubbing alcohol on one kidney was a bad idea, and I did it anyway. I didn't know what I was dealing with, and suspect neither did you.

In high school, I told people you died from alcoholism, not without emotion, but without understanding. I certainly thought you chose beer over us, which is almost true. I didn't realize you had <u>no</u> choice, until it became true for me.

You became something I talked about in the same breath as all my other "bad." "My father died when I was 10, I was diagnosed with chronic kidney disease at 13 and had a kidney transplant at 19." You weren't on my heart during my first kidney transplant. It was still too soon to take you down from the shelf. And then I found Codeine, and everything became about me.

I pass the allotment gardens where we had a patch. I see the snap dragons, their funny puffy blooms in pops of fuchsia and neon yellow. They became my favorite because they were yours. We grew carrots and tomatoes. How did you do it all? You must have felt terrible with your diabetes. Or just sad. Were you happy? I used to walk through the park for hours in my teens and twenties, through the snow and the leaves and the blossoms, and wonder why I felt off. Never quite happy.

As a girl, I once passed our bathroom and saw you strain over the toilet, a piece of poo hitting the floor. I scurried away thinking I should help, but not knowing how. The mat was washed and left a small brown stain in the powder blue faux fur. We used this bathmat for years after you died. I guess Mum never noticed. Every time I saw it, I thought, *I should tell Mum that's Daddy's poo,* but it was a piece of you and I didn't want her to take it away.

When I knew I was going to binge Her, I lined my underwear with maxi pads or stuffed them with Kevin's underwear, knowing I would soil my pants overnight from the amount I took. I could not stop once She was in my hands. And I remembered you and the bathmat.

When I was dopesick and out of narcotics, I would pop six

Excedrin at a time. The stomach pain was agony and I chugged Pepto-Bismol like water, despite antacids being off limits for transplant patients. I would think about you swigging that thick, pink medicine for your bleeding ulcers and coffee-ground stools, and in the most curious of ways, these memories made me feel good. The horrors we endured in the name of disease. Sick daughter to sick father. Because you had been through it, I didn't feel so alone.

I stand in front of the tree Mum planted for you many years after you died. 18 years later. We had just had our transplant, me and Mum. Maybe that's why. The gift of life was very much on our hearts. There was a plaque that read "Life is precious. Peteris Ivanans 1940-1978" but a few years later someone stole it. Well, fuck them, because the tree is still there.

It is a linden tree. As a sapling, it was thin and elegant, new gray bark with no leaves. Today it is a magnificent beast of nature. A thick trunk with arms reaching for the sky, plucking stars at night, and brushing the bird's wing by day. Nick has one planted for you in his backyard. Sweet Nicky. They are both healthy and glorious and strong.

In your last letter to Teresa you sounded off. Your charming spark gone out. *I find it demeaning that even my children have to put up with the sight of Spiderman. I need time, peace, peace, and time,...*You did not get time. When you collapsed on the floor of your endocrinologist's office did you have peace in your heart? This is my agony.

I picture you in your hospital bed, tubes coming out of you, the way they would one day come out of me. Where was your peace? Was God with you? After 291 pages, what can I say about God? I know He always shows up when I ask, which I think means He is always with me, us, rooting for us to join Him, ready at the drop of a hat to be our Friend.

I know he was your Friend, too.

God doesn't mean there will be no Pain. God means we don't have to be in It alone.

I believe with my whole broken little girl sober woman heart that if someone is loved, they are never alone. So you were not alone,

ABOUT THE AUTHOR

Big G and Me: In Pillness and in Health 2 is Ms. Ivanans' second book. It is the sequel to *In Pillness and in Health: A Memoir. Pillness* is available in Spain as *Hasta Que Las Pastillas Nos Separen (O No)*.

Ms. Ivanans is a two-time kidney-transplanted, sober woman and occasional actor. She lives with her living donor and mensch, Kevin, and their dog Jack, in Winnipeg. She is writing her next book entitled *Are You There Judy Blume? It's Me, Henriette*. She will interrupt you mid-sentence if she sees a dog.

If you enjoyed Ms. Ivanans' books, please consider leaving a review on Amazon and Goodreads.

Made in the USA
Monee, IL
19 November 2024

70582688R00173